T0216605

Practical Maintenance Plans in SQL Server

Automation for the DBA

Bradley Beard

Apress®

Practical Maintenance Plans in SQL Server

Bradley Beard
Palm Bay
Florida, USA

ISBN-13 (pbk): 978-1-4842-1894-5   ISBN-13 (electronic): 978-1-4842-1895-2
DOI 10.1007/978-1-4842-1895-2

Library of Congress Control Number: 2016938532

Managing Director: Welmoed Spahr
Lead Editor: Jonathan Gennick
Development Editor: Douglas Pundick
Technical Reviewer: Mike McQuillan
Editorial Board: Steve Anglin, Pramila Balen, Louise Corrigan, Jim DeWolf, Jonathan Gennick, Robert Hutchinson, Celestin Suresh John, Michelle Lowman, James Markham, Susan McDermott, Matthew Moodie, Jeffrey Pepper, Douglas Pundick, Ben Renow-Clarke, Gwenan Spearing
Coordinating Editor: Jill Balzano
Copy Editor: Kim Burton-Weisman
Compositor: SPi Global
Indexer: SPi Global
Artist: SPi Global
Cover Designer: Anna Ishchenko

Distributed to the book trade worldwide by Springer Science+Business Media New York, 233 Spring Street, 6th Floor, New York, NY 10013. Phone 1-800-SPRINGER, fax (201) 348-4505, e-mail orders-ny@springer-sbm.com, or visit www.springer.com. Apress Media, LLC is a California LLC and the sole member (owner) is Springer Science + Business Media Finance Inc (SSBM Finance Inc). SSBM Finance Inc is a Delaware corporation.

For information on translations, please e-mail rights@apress.com, or visit www.apress.com.

Apress and friends of ED books may be purchased in bulk for academic, corporate, or promotional use. eBook versions and licenses are also available for most titles. For more information, reference our Special Bulk Sales–eBook Licensing web page at www.apress.com/bulk-sales.

Any source code or other supplementary material referenced by the author in this text is available to readers at www.apress.com. For detailed information about how to locate your book's source code, go to www.apress.com/source-code/.

Printed on acid-free paper

For you, my dearest Jessica

Contents at a Glance

About the Author xiii

About the Technical Reviewer xv

Acknowledgments xvii

Introduction xix

■Chapter 1: Introduction to Maintenance Plans 1

■Chapter 2: Backing Up a Database 7

■Chapter 3: Checking Database Integrity 33

■Chapter 4: Executing SQL Server Agent Jobs 45

■Chapter 5: Cleaning Up SQL Server Agent History 93

■Chapter 6: Cleaning Up Maintenance Files 107

■Chapter 7: Rebuilding Indexes 131

■Chapter 8: Reorganizing Indexes 147

■Chapter 9: Shrinking the Database and Files 155

■Chapter 10: Updating Object Statistics 165

■Chapter 11: Executing T-SQL Statements 175

■Chapter 12: Notifying Database Operators 189

■Chapter 13: Tying It All Together 205

Index 269

Contents

About the Author xiii

About the Technical Reviewer xv

Acknowledgments xvii

Introduction xix

■Chapter 1: Introduction to Maintenance Plans 1

Before We Start 1

What Is a Maintenance Plan? 2

Maintenance Plan Wizard Task Options 3

Maintenance Plan Design Surface Options 4

Summary 6

■Chapter 2: Backing Up a Database 7

Recovery Models 7

Full 9

Bulk Logged 9

Simple 9

Backup Types 9

Full Backups 10

Differential Backups 10

Transaction Log Backups 10

Setting Up the Maintenance Plan 12

Full Backup Configuration 12

Differential Backup Configuration 18

Transaction Log Backup Configuration 21

Configuring the Jobs 25

Summary 31

■Chapter 3: Checking Database Integrity 33

What Is Database Integrity? 33

Practical Application of Database Integrity Principles 34

Setting Up the Maintenance Plan 36

Summary 43

■Chapter 4: Executing SQL Server Agent Jobs 45

E-mail from the Database 45

Configuring E-mail 46

Sending a Test E-mail 56

Enabling the Mail Profile 57

SQL Agent Job Creation 59

Creating an Example Table 60

Writing a Query for the Job 60

Creating a SQL Agent Job 61

SQL Server Agent Options 62

Steps Tab 63

Schedules Tab 68

Alerts Tab 70

Notifications 76

Targets 79

Gmail's SMTP 80

Setting Up a Profile 80

Testing E-mail Configuration 88

Allowing Access to Google's SMTP Server 89

Enabling POP E-mail 90

Summary 91

■**Chapter 5: Cleaning Up SQL Server Agent History** **93**

Setting Up the Maintenance Plan 93

Choosing Tasks 96

Define What to Clean 100

Review 102

Summary 105

■**Chapter 6: Cleaning Up Maintenance Files** **107**

Separation of History from Maintenance 107

Setting Up the Maintenance Plan 108

Backups Cleanup 108

    Deleting Backup Files 113

    Deleting a Specific File 113

    Searching and Deleting Based on Extension 113

Logs Cleanup 117

Text Files Cleanup 124

Summary 130

■**Chapter 7: Rebuilding Indexes** **131**

Indexes Explained 131

    Beginning Indexes 132

    B-Tree Structures 136

Rebuilding vs. Reorganizing 137

Setting Up the Maintenance Plan 137

Summary 146

■**Chapter 8: Reorganizing Indexes** **147**

Reorganizing vs. Rebuilding 147

Setting Up the Maintenance Plan 148

Summary 154

■Chapter 9: Shrinking the Database and Files 155

Disk Usage Reporting 155

Disk Space Considerations.. 156

The Transaction Log 157

Setting Up the Maintenance Plan 157

Summary.. 164

■Chapter 10: Updating Object Statistics.. 165

Distribution Statistics Explained 165

Setting Up the Maintenance Task.. 166

Summary.. 174

■Chapter 11: Executing T-SQL Statements 175

Setting Up the Maintenance Plan 175

Implementing the Maintenance Plan.. 180

Executing the Maintenance Plan 183

Summary.. 187

■Chapter 12: Notifying Database Operators 189

Setting Up the Maintenance Plan 189

Creating an Operator Profile.. 199

Summary.. 203

■Chapter 13: Tying It All Together 205

Checking Your Environment 205

Ordering of the Maintenance Tasks... 206

Determining Complexity of the Maintenance Plan 207

Planning the Maintenance Plan... 209

Scenario 1 209

Scenario 2 210

Creating the Maintenance Plan 213

Editing the Jobs.. 213

Finalizing the Jobs... 214

Saving the Changes 219

Reviewing Your Schedule Needs 220

Adding the Tasks to the Plan 220

Full Backup Maintenance Activities 222

Adding the Check Integrity Task 222

Adding the Rebuild Index Task 224

Adding the Shrink Database Task 225

Adding the Update Statistics Task 226

Adding the Cleanup History Task 228

Adding the bak Files Task 229

Adding the txt Files Task 231

Adding the trn Files Task 233

Differential Backup Maintenance Activities 235

Adding the Check Integrity Task 236

Adding the Reorganize Index Task 238

Adding the Shrink Database Task 239

Adding the Update Statistics Task 240

Transaction Log Backup Maintenance Activities 242

Adding the Check Integrity Task 242

Adding the Reorganize Index Task 244

Adding the Shrink Database Task 245

Adding the Update Statistics Task 247

Precedence Constraints 248

Constraint Options 250

Multiple Constraints 251

Testing the Maintenance Plan 255

Starting a Job from a T-SQL Script 256

Summary 267

Index 269

About the Author

Bradley Beard is a software engineer with more than 15 years' experience writing dynamic, interactive web sites using ColdFusion and SQL Server. He graduated from Florida Institute of Technology in 2007 with a master of science in computer information systems, and studied for his undergraduate degrees in CIS and technology management at Herzing University. In 2013, he earned the MCSA: SQL Server 2012 certification from Microsoft, and in 2016, he earned the MCSE: Business Intelligence certification as well. His continual quest for learning has earned him shelves full of books at home and at work, most of which are about SQL Server, ColdFusion, or general web architectures or frameworks.

Bradley lives in Palm Bay, Florida, with his wife, Jessica, and children, Josh, Kaylee, Matthew, and Emma. He also apparently runs an animal shelter made up of his dogs, Lady and Bella, and cats, Spice, Simba, Mercury, and Dobby. In his free time, he enjoys fishing and spending time with his wife and kids.

Bradley is available for consultation and third-shift remote employment on ColdFusion and SQL Server by contacting bradley.beard@gmail.com.

About the Technical Reviewer

Mike McQuillan is a software and database specialist who lives with his wife and daughter in the United Kingdom. Mike is a polyglot programmer who began messing around with computers in the 1980s, first with an Atari 800XL and then a Sinclair Spectrum. He took up databases in the 1990s, and quickly fell in love with SQL. He's been working with SQL Server since version 7 and he is an SQL Server MCSA.

When he's not tinkering with computers, Mike and his family enjoy lengthy walks around Cheshire with the family pups, Dolly and Bertie (who keep his feet warm when he's writing).

Acknowledgments

First of all, a huge thanks to Jonathan Gennick for all the guidance and tips along the way.

A big thanks to my wife and kids for understanding.

Big, huge, gigantic thanks to my good friend and mentor John Wysocki, without whom I would not know half as much as I do about anything related to databases (or chemistry, or plumbing, or nuclear physics... seriously, he knows everything).

Thanks to my other database nerd friends, including Cam, Eric (phpfreak), Leisha, Kyle, Isabelle, and everyone else in the MCSA class, and the guru herself, Suzy Moore. You guys are awesome.

To my friends, brothers, and sisters. I told you I was writing a book and none of y'all believed me.

To my brother Brian and my niece Holly, thanks for being you... even when I was too dumb to appreciate it.

And finally, thank you, Lord, for second chances. I could never deserve your mercy and love.

Introduction

Have you ever wondered about what keeps your database running smoothly? We all hope the database keeps running as well as it did as when it was first installed, but what really is happening under the covers? More importantly, can we control what is happening? As it turns out, we certainly can control these events, and they are extremely powerful tools that we can use to make sure that our databases stay in good shape.

This book will introduce you to the core concepts of creating a maintenance plan that will handle all of the tasks necessary to keep your database functioning at 100%. There are exercises that you can run in your own installation of SQL Server to ensure heightened data security and integrity by harnessing the power of SQL Server Agent. With the proper amount of foresight and planning, database administrators of any experience level will be confidently using the tools available in SQL Server to create extremely versatile maintenance plans in a short amount of time.

What Is the Scope of this Book?

In the scope of this book, I am going to concentrate on using the SQL Server 2012 Management Studio interface as much as possible. I am not going to get into a lot of scripting by hand; it will be point-and-click as much as possible. There will be some areas where we will venture into the void, but I'll keep that to a minimum. To be clear, I will be working with the Maintenance Plan Wizard, and not from the Maintenance Plan Design Surface. There will be times when I will focus directly on the design surface, but for the most part, we will work with the wizard. Most of what I detail and outline here is transferable between the two interfaces anyway, as you will soon see.

We are going to make a single maintenance plan that will automatically execute every day on a set schedule. I am going to show you how we can manipulate the database engine into performing the maintenance activities we choose on the schedule we choose. I am also going to show you how to expand on the concept of reporting and logging, from the database point of view, to keep us aware of any possible issues. In the end, we are going to have a maintenance plan that does everything we need it to do, period. This will give us an assistant, so to speak, that runs these menial although important tasks without our supervision. When I think of maintenance plans, I immediately think of the old Ron Popeil commercials with "set it… aaaaaaand forget it!" That's exactly what we do here. We are going to take the time to set it up correctly, and examine the why and not just the how. We are then going to ensure that our reporting and logging is set up correctly, so that we are aware of any issues. After that, it will be smooth sailing and you can enjoy your newly augmented rock star DBA status.

Who Is this Book Written For?

This book was written for you, of course! It should be a refresher course for the majority of readers. My hope is that this book will augment what you already know, and perhaps shed some light on some concepts that you didn't know. At a minimum, you should come away from this book with a clear understanding of what a maintenance plan is, how it benefits a database, how to structure it correctly, how it runs, and how to possibly make it run more efficiently. I would like to think that this isn't the first you have read about maintenance plans, as there is a certain level of assumed knowledge about the interface and mechanics of SQL Server. If it is the first you've heard of it, that's fine; I keep everything as simple as possible so that anyone can read along and understand... even my 12-year-old daughter! I try to keep things "light", meaning that I tend to try and put some element of humor into my writing to keep things interesting, but I will cover some pretty heavy topics also, so sometimes it gets serious.

Chapter 1 provides introduction into the separate components of the maintenance plans, and concise examples of what you can do to make the maintenance plan work for you. Chapters 2 through 12 will detail each of the tasks available within the maintenance plan, and Chapter 13 will tie everything together so that you can create a complete maintenance plan based on your specific needs. Along the way, I will examine the multitude of rabbit holes that pop up, because there are actually quite a few little bits of interesting things that need to be discussed. In the end, you will have a complete set of tools and the knowledge to use those tools to achieve great things for your database.

Having said all that, let's dive into this adventure! You can use any installation of SQL Server you would like, provided that you have SSIS installed. That implies any version after and including SQL Server 2005, and it must be Standard, Enterprise, or Business Intelligence versions. Although this book was specifically written with SQL Server 2012 in mind, I also ran everything through SQL Server 2014 and had absolutely no issues beyond slight interface differences.

CHAPTER 1

Introduction to Maintenance Plans

Ever heard of the faster/cheaper/better paradox? It says that anything can be broken down into three groups: get it faster, get it cheaper, or get it better... but you can only pick two. So something must always be sacrificed: faster and cheaper means it won't be better, and cheaper and better means it won't be faster. Does this strike anyone as a bit unrealistic? Why can't something be all three?

Proper planning can isolate almost any failure. Correctly aligning resources can diminish nearly any risk. At the heart of database administration is the ever-present challenge to provide these three principles: *faster* performance, *cheaper* overhead, and *better* quality data. The failure to provide these for the organization employing you will definitely result in your lack of employment. Most of the time, it's not really as serious as this, but the point can be made that you are the person responsible for the safe handling of the company's most important asset—its data. Whether proprietary or trade data, or government classifications, or even just a simple database holding names and phone numbers, the data that you are responsible for is important to the people that need to access it. For that reason, we as DBAs are the last line of defense to make sure that we are maintaining our databases correctly in order to provide a higher level of database integrity for our end users, whether they are our grandmothers, or stockbrokers, or any other level of user.

The most important part to database administration, beyond installation and actual development, is the maintenance of the database. This ongoing practice should be a part of the daily life of any seasoned database administrator (DBA). Since the DBA is the primary focal point for the database, if it goes poof in the dark, you had better hope it's not your fault. Luckily, SQL Server provides a wealth of tools specifically geared toward giving a lot of power to the DBA in as small a package as possible, with the hope that the DBA uses these tools to mitigate any possible risk to the data they are responsible for.

After all, the primary responsibility of the DBA is to ensure protection, integrity, consistency, and availability of their data. Following the instructions in this book and implementing a complete maintenance plan will get you started accomplishing those goals.

Before We Start

I have a very specific way that I have my files structured. You might or might not, but I wanted to explain it because I frequently reference it throughout this book.

I have a logical E:\ drive that I use for all of my SQL Server files. Not the installation files, just the database files. The root of this drive is E:\ and there is exactly one folder named SQL Server. So, the main directory for all of my database files is E:\SQL Server. Inside of this folder, I have the following directories.

- **Backups**: The .bak files for each backup, stored in folders per database

- **Data**: The .mdf and .ldf files for each database, stored in folders per database

- **Logs**: The .trn files for each database, stored in folders per database

© Bradley Beard 2016

B. Beard, *Practical Maintenance Plans in SQL Server,* DOI 10.1007/978-1-4842-1895-2_1

Everything that I need for SQL Server development is found in these folders. This might not work for your setup, but I hope it does. If it doesn't, just adjust your own particular folder structure to the examples in the chapters. I am going to be adding folders to this structure in later chapters, so read on to find out what they will contain.

You will also need a Windows login with sysadmin rights to the database engine, and a SQL Server login with sysadmin rights as well (usually, your sa account works just fine). These accounts are very common in newer SQL Server installations, so it shouldn't be an issue. The large majority of the book will use the Windows login, as that login typically either owns the database, or has sysadmin permission to modify the database as needed. If you don't have an account that has these permissions, you may not be able to create and execute the plans against the database you need to maintain. In this case, you are really not a DBA and are more like a "data facilitator." As a DBA, you should have one account that gives you complete and total control of the database. Use that account to set up the things in this book.

What Is a Maintenance Plan?

When you create a maintenance plan, SQL Server creates an Integration Services package that is executed by the SQL Server Agent. A maintenance plan exists for one reason: to make the life of a DBA easier by automating administrative tasks. That's it! With a well-thought-out maintenance plan, you can do all sorts of things automatically on a set schedule.

So, exactly what things can be done in a maintenance plan, you ask? First of all, fire up SQL Server Management Studio and expand the Management section. Expand the Maintenance Plans section next. On a clean install, there won't be anything in here, which is fine. That's why you're reading this, hopefully. You might see what is in Figure 1-1.

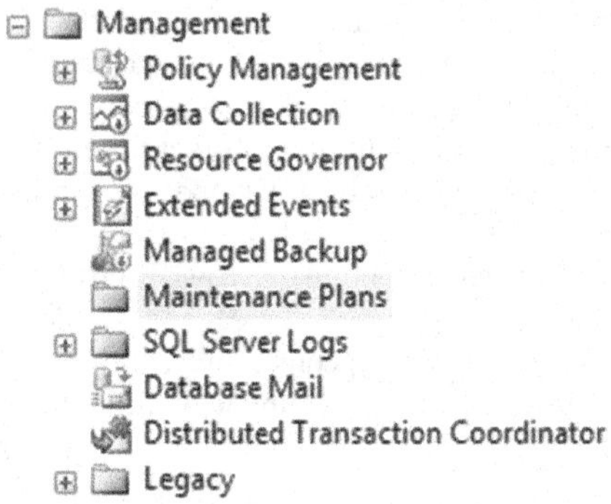

Figure 1-1. *Nothing in the Maintenance Plans folder!*

There are two ways to set up a maintenance plan from here. You can either go with the wizard or create it from scratch yourself by using what is referred to as the Maintenance Plan Design Surface. The differences between the two choices are slight, but there is no real power difference. Let's examine the differences.

Right-click Maintenance Plans and choose Maintenance Plan Wizard. An introduction screen pops up with general information about the wizard, so just click Next to continue.

You are then presented with the first "real" screen of the wizard. Just click Next here, because we're going to cancel it after the next step. This is just to get us familiar with the maintenance plan task choices.

Maintenance Plan Wizard Task Options

After you hit Next, you are presented with the following options, which can be set up from the wizard interface.

- **Check Database Integrity**: The Check Database Integrity task performs internal consistency checks of the data and index pages within the database.

- **Shrink Database**: The Shrink Database task reduces the disk space consumed by the database and log files by removing empty data and log pages.

- **Reorganize Index**: The Reorganize Index task defragments and compacts clustered and nonclustered indexes on tables and views. This improves index-scanning performance.

- **Rebuild Index**: The Rebuild Index task reorganizes data on the data and index pages by rebuilding indexes. This improves performance of index scans and seeks. This task also optimizes the distribution of data and free space on the index pages, allowing faster future growth.

- **Update Statistics**: The Update Statistics task ensures the query optimizer has up-to-date information about the distribution of data values in the tables. This allows the optimizer to make better judgments about data access strategies.

- **Clean Up History**: The History Cleanup task deletes historical data about Backup and Restore, SQL Server Agent, and Maintenance Plan operations. This wizard allows you to specify the type and age of the data to be deleted.

- **Execute SQL Server Agent Job**: The Execute SQL Server Agent Job task allows you to select SQL Server Agent jobs to run as part of the maintenance plan.

- **Back Up Database (Full)**: The Back Up Database (Full) task allows you to specify the source databases, destination files or tapes, and overwrite options for a Full backup of a database or transaction log.

- **Back Up Database (Differential)**: The Back Up Database task allows you to specify the source databases, destination files or tapes, and overwrite options for a Differential backup of a database or transaction log.

- **Back Up Database (Transaction Log)**: The Back Up Database task allows you to specify the source databases, destination files or tapes, and overwrite options for a Transaction Log backup of a database or transaction log.

- **Maintenance Cleanup Task**: The Maintenance Cleanup task removes files left over from executing a maintenance plan.

Go ahead and cancel that screen now. Go back and right-click Maintenance Plans again, but this time, choose New Maintenance Plan....

The first thing you need to do is give it a name, but you can just click OK here. Again, we're just looking at the options for now. A whole new interface opens with a toolbox on the left Subplan information across the top. This is the Maintenance Plan Design Surface. Figure 1-2 should be what you see now.

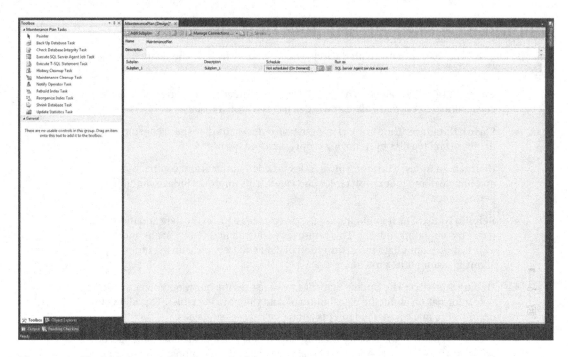

Figure 1-2. *The Maintenance Plan Design Surface*

■ **Tip** If you don't see the Toolbox, just press Ctrl+Alt+X and it will show.

Maintenance Plan Design Surface Options

If you look in the toolbox on the left, you have some different choices here. I wonder why that is? I will explain why in just a second. Let's look at the options first.

- **Back Up Database**: The Back Up Database task allows you to specify the source databases, destination files or tapes, and overwrite options for a full backup of a database or transaction log.

- **Check Database Integrity**: The Check Database Integrity task performs internal consistency checks of the data and index pages within the database.

- **Execute SQL Server Agent Job**: The Execute SQL Server Agent Job task allows you to select SQL Server Agent jobs to run as part of the maintenance plan.

- **Execute T-SQL Statement**: The Execute T-SQL task allows you to run SQL queries as part of the maintenance plan.

- **History Cleanup**: The History Cleanup task deletes historical data about Backup and Restore, SQL Server Agent, and Maintenance Plan operations. This wizard allows you to specify the type and age of the data to be deleted.

- **Maintenance Cleanup**: The Maintenance Cleanup task removes files left over from executing a maintenance plan.

- **Notify Operator**: The Notify Operator task allows for email to be sent from SQL Server after the execution of a maintenance plan. This is for both success and failure.

- **Rebuild Index**: The Rebuild Index task reorganizes data on the data and index pages by rebuilding indexes. This improves performance of index scans and seeks. This task also optimizes the distribution of data and free space on the index pages, allowing faster future growth.

- **Reorganize Index**: The Reorganize Index task defragments and compacts clustered and non-clustered indexes on tables and views. This improves index-scanning performance.

- **Shrink Database**: The Shrink Database task reduces the disk space consumed by the database and log files by removing empty data and log pages.

- **Update Statistics:** The Update Statistics task ensures the query optimizer has up-to-date information about the distribution of data values in the tables. This allows the optimizer to make better judgments about data access strategies.

Most of those look familiar, because they are mostly shared between the interfaces. What are the differences, you ask? Let's take a look and see. Figure 1-3 compares the two types of tasks.

Maintenance Plan Wizard Tasks	Maintenance Plan Design Surface Tasks
• Check Database Integrity	• Back Up Database
• Shrink Database	• Check Database Integrity
• Reorganize Index	• Execute SQL Server Agent Job
• Rebuild Index	• Execute T -SQL Statement
• Update Statistics	• History Cleanup
• Clean Up History	• Maintenance Cleanup
• Execute SQL Server Agent Job	• Notify Operator
• Back Up Database (Full)	• Rebuild Index
• Back Up Database (Differential)	• Reorganize Index
• Back Up Database (Transaction Log)	• Shrink Database
• Maintenance Cleanup Task	• Update Statistics

Figure 1-3. *Differences between the wizard and Design Surface Task*

There are 11 tasks in each area… but they are not the same. The difference is, basically, how you want to define the requirements for the workflow that you are creating as part of the maintenance plan. There really isn't a major difference between the two sections, as you can see in Figure 1-3. Or is there?

The first difference is the lack of the Execute T-SQL Statement task in the wizard, but if there is SQL that needs to be executed, it can easily be worked into the Execute SQL Server Agent Job task. Other than that, they are pretty much the same.

The second difference is the lack of the Notify Operator task in the wizard. You can always set the notifications in the tasks themselves though, so this really isn't an issue either.

The 11 tasks shown in Figure 1-3 (in either iteration, really) are at the very core of database administration. Please note that all of these tasks individually can be done manually within the SQL Server Management Studio interface. It's not like this is the only place you can find this functionality. Quite the opposite; true to Microsoft standard operating procedure, there are always at least two ways to do any one task.

It is also worth pointing out that any number of these tasks can be joined in the same maintenance plan, so you really are free to completely customize the maintenance plan to your exact need and purpose. The process of joining the tasks together to make a cohesive maintenance plan is what I call the "workflow" of the plan. Without this, the first thing would just run and then stop. Nothing else would execute unless explicitly told. So, to get around this, what we do is define constraints on the success or failure of a task; that way, we can at least track the error if something goes wrong.

Summary

Let's dive into this adventure! You can use any installation of SQL Server you would like, provided that you have SSIS installed. That implies any version after and including SQL Server 2005, and it must be Standard, Enterprise, or Business Intelligence versions. Although this book was specifically written with SQL Server 2012 in mind, I also ran everything through SQL Server 2014 and had absolutely no issues beyond slight interface differences.

CHAPTER 2

■ ■ ■

Backing Up a Database

Backing up a database is arguably the most important aspect to database administration. Without backups, you cannot recover in cases of data loss or corruption. You cannot rebuild quickly without the data that you, ultimately, are responsible for. Have you ever met a DBA that is sort of *mehhhh* about backups? I guarantee you that is because they are either lazy or have never had to recover from a catastrophic failure. The worst part about either of those reasons is that one is by choice and one is by circumstance, but both can be remediated with a little foresight and planning.

Don't get me wrong; sometimes, a failure is going to happen. It just will; Murphy's law says so. But that doesn't mean that we can't recover from it successfully, does it? The purpose of this chapter is to explain not only the importance of regular backups, but also the proper way to structure these into a cohesive and complete maintenance plan.

The one thing I want you to take from this chapter is one simple sentence: it makes absolutely no sense at all to NOT have database backups.

As you can guess, there are multiple different facets to database backups though. Let's look at those before I explain the actual task itself.

> **Recovery models**: This is how your database is set up to recover lost data. This is typically set during the installation of the database engine, but can be changed at any time.

> **Backup types**: Certain types of recovery models allow for certain types of backups. This can also be changed at any time, depending on the settings of the recovery model of the database needing to be backed up.

Recovery Models

An important note before starting this is that the recovery model for a specific database comes into play here. What is a recovery model? Simply put, it tells the database how to recover and in what way. The recovery model is set in the initial setup and configuration of the database, but can also be accessed by right-clicking the database name and choosing Properties. Choose Options from the menu choices, shown on the left in Figure 2-1, and the second option down will show the Recovery Mode.

© Bradley Beard 2016
B. Beard, *Practical Maintenance Plans in SQL Server,* DOI 10.1007/978-1-4842-1895-2_2

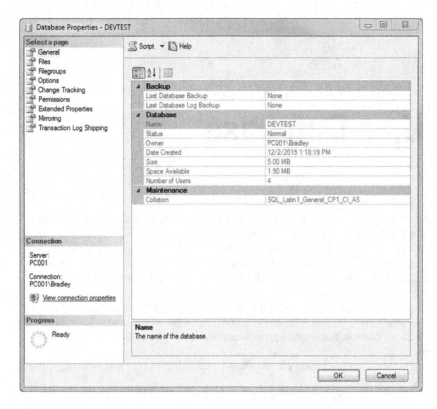

Figure 2-1. *Database Properties window*

Let's look at the differences in recovery models. Figure 2-2 shows the basic differences between the models available, so it's really up to the database administrator to determine the actual need or requirement to properly meet the need of the customer or application.

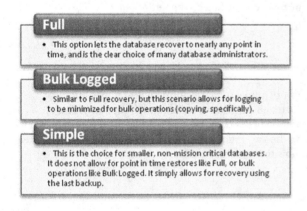

Figure 2-2. *Recovery models*

Full

Using the Full Recovery model, data loss is minimal because all of the data can be restored unless there is damage to the tail of the transaction log. The Full Recovery model can be thought of as the fail-safe model solution, since everything is included in the backup. The only caveat to this is that the transaction log plays an important role because, if it's damaged or incomplete, the full backup will fail.

Bulk Logged

The Bulk Logged Recovery model is a quick way to recover, but data can only be recovered from the last backup. This may not be a problem if the time between backups is low. For example, when using the Bulk Logged Recovery model, the last backup is the only really viable one because that is the only one that can be recovered. This means that if the backup period is set to every 6 hours, then 6 hours is the maximum amount of data that will be lost.

Simple

All data is lost from the time of the last backup until the data loss event. This option is not recommended because the likelihood of data loss is much higher with this model than the other two.

How do the recovery models work toward the Back Up Database task, though? Think about it like this: if you had a database with a Simple recovery model, but tried to enforce transaction log backups, it would fail. Why? Because the Simple recovery model doesn't do transaction log backups. It's sort of a sneaky way to get you to think about doing things a little bit differently; if you want transaction logs to *be* backed up, then you should probably *have* transaction logs to backup. Makes sense, right? So, what's the difference between the backup types?

Backup Types

Figure 2-3 shows that there are three backup types in SQL Server, each of which is unique, but all sort of related. When used correctly, all three can work together to give a heightened level of data security to the users.

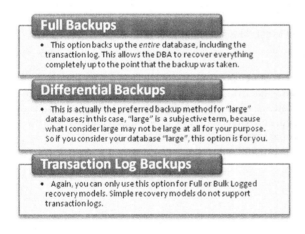

Figure 2-3. *Backup types*

Full Backups

Full backups back up everything in the *database*. That is the important part to remember; it will not backup the individual settings or components of SQL Server, in other words.

Differential Backups

Differential backups are related to full backups in that differential backups only have data since the last full backup. This can be a hard concept to understand. Think of full backups being the major yard lines on a football field (10, 20, 30, 40, etc.) and differential backups being the individual yard lines (11, 12, 13, 14, etc.). Can you get from the 10 yard line straight to the 30? Sure. But you can also get there going yard by yard. This is what differential backups give you— a "yard by yard" capture of the data. The beauty of differential backups is that data loss is minimized because the only loss is to the last differential backup. It is also much faster because the only data that is backed up is the data added or changed since the last full backup. The downside to differential backups is that the full backup must be restored; the differential backups are then applied to the base data. A differential backup without its parent full backup, for all intents and purposes, is useless since it cannot be used to restore anything.

Transaction Log Backups

Transaction logs are at the core of the concept of data recovery. They can be run as often as required up until the limit of a physical disk. The interval for backup is entirely up to the database administrator and can be set to backup down to the minute, although this is probably a little ridiculous because you would obviously generate 1,440 logs *per day*. If this is the requirement, it can certainly be achieved; however, as noted earlier, storage will be a major consideration in this case.

Keep in mind that the transaction log backup interval is basically the amount of time that has been agreed upon for maximum data loss. For some companies, this is absolute zero. For some, it may be 5 minutes, or 10, or 20. Whatever the interval agreed upon, that is what you are tasked to set up. If you get the company that says absolute zero, then the cost of additional fault tolerant storage needs to be added to the server configuration. More than likely, they will consider that they could go maybe 30 minutes with data loss, but that it should be mitigated as much as possible.

▪ **Tip** The minimum amount of time that you can have a scheduled task in SQL Server is 10 seconds. If you need tasks run more frequently than this, you may need to consider switching to decaf.

So that covers those concepts. Again, I *cannot stress enough* how important backups are for databases. It could be argued that it is the single most important thing that a database administrator is responsible for. To make this easier on you, your company, and your customers, always try to think two steps ahead of what is happening. A good way to help do this is to be prepared, and what better way to be prepared than to have a fresh, clean copy of the data always available for restoring in case of a catastrophic failure.

Figure 2-4 shows a closer look at how these recovery models affect the backup types.

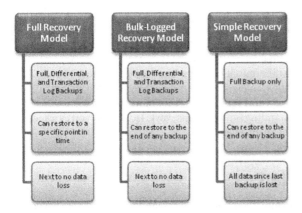

Figure 2-4. *Recovery models vs. Backup types*

Following the logic described in Figure 2-4, I would recommend a full backup with differential backups and transaction log backups. That way, the transaction logs would feed the differential backups, which rely on the full backups to restore correctly.

Figure 2-5 shows the ideal setting for backups, using the three types described earlier.

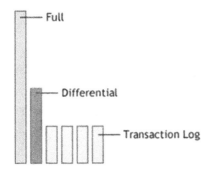

Figure 2-5. *Ideal backup settings*

Consider the backup schedule shown in Figure 2-6 using the colors and references from Figure 2-5. This is what I would call "absolutely ideal."

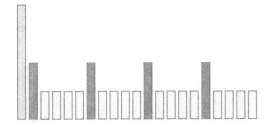

Figure 2-6. *Absolutely ideal backup settings*

The full backup starts the backup set, with the first differential being supported by the transaction log backups. Those backups would in turn feed the differential backups, which are placed on top of the full backups. The important thing to notice in Figure 2-6 is that there are no time constraints on it. It's totally up to you to determine what the amount of time is for all three types of backups. For example, say you wanted to have 10-minute transaction log backups supporting differential backups taken at 30-minute intervals, leading from a full backup taken nightly. The image shown in Figure 2-6 is a great way to quantify that, because all you need to do, graphically, is add more green and yellow bars (a lot more, honestly).

That sets us up with a good foundation on understanding how backups work. Hopefully, you can see the benefit to having data properly backed up in case of an emergency.

Setting Up the Maintenance Plan

I'm basically going to go screen by screen and explain this in sometimes excruciating detail, so here we go!

Full Backup Configuration

Right-click Maintenance Plans and select Maintenance Plan Wizard to get going. The first interface you see is Select Plan Properties. Enter **Backup Maintenance Plan** in the Name box. Next, enter a brief description. Click the "Separate schedules for each task" radio button. Leave the rest defaulted for now. Figure 2-7 should be what you see now.

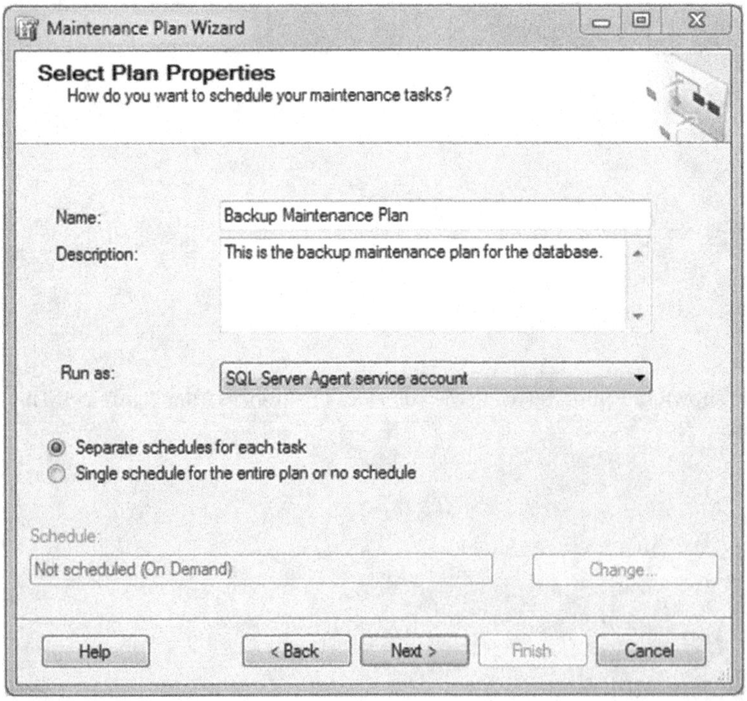

Figure 2-7. *Select Plan Properties*

Remember when we looked at the database's recovery model? Yours is hopefully set to Full. There are instances when you don't need this, and that's understandable; however, I would strongly recommend using Full.

Why did I bring this up? This information leads to the selection of backup tasks. If your database is in Full recovery model, then we can create a more stringent maintenance plan, and that is the goal of this book.

When you click Next on this screen, you will see the options we discussed earlier. Select all three backup options, as shown in Figure 2-8.

Figure 2-8. *Select Maintenance Tasks*

Now, click Next to set up the three parts of the backup. This is sort of a moot point, because the three parts will execute at different times and for different reasons. Recall earlier in this chapter when I said that the full backup is fed from the differential backups, which is fed from the transaction log backups. When you see the screen shown in Figure 2-9, just click Next.

Figure 2-9. *Select Maintenance Task*

This is where it starts to get interesting. The first interface that comes up is the Define Back Up Database (Full) Task screen. Your completed screen (except for the Schedule) should look like Figure 2-10.

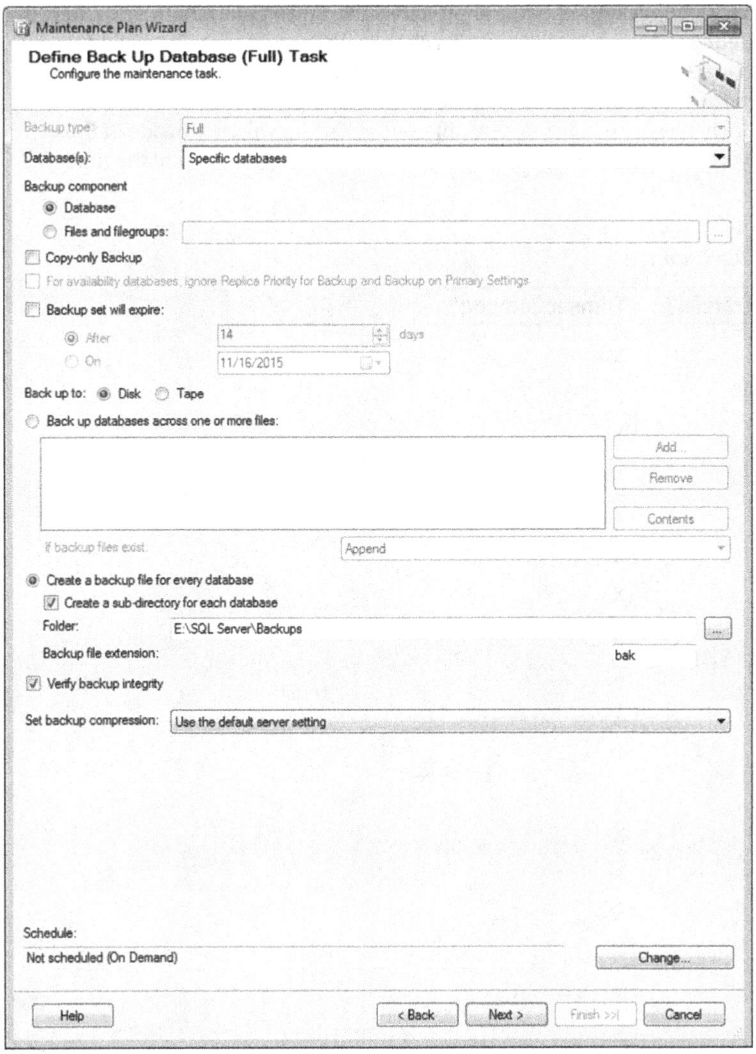

Figure 2-10. *Define Back Up Database (Full) Task*

■ **Tip** This interface is slightly different in SQL Server 2014 and SQL Server 2016, but the essence of the task is the same.

Pull down the Database(s) menu and select the databases that you would like to backup. It can be any single database or group of databases that you would like to backup. My database for this book is called DEVTEST, so you can use that name if you like, or you can choose another name. Notice that the "Create a backup file for every database" radio button is selected. Since we are using this specifically for configuring the setting for a full backup of the database, click the "Create a sub-directory for each database" check box under that option. What this means is that, for every database that you choose to back up, those backups are going to be kept in a directory with the name of the database as the name of the directory. At the bottom of the screen, click the Change... button to set up the schedule for this task.

While we're at it, let's define what our backup schedule should look like and when it should run. Recall when we went over the backup scheduling schemes earlier in this chapter. We can use that for a good starting point. Let's configure this for a 24-hour window, so there is minimal interruption of data. If the full backup is set for midnight, then the first differential should be set for midnight also, followed by the first transaction log backup as well. Then every 6 hours, a new differential backup will run. Inside of those, transaction log backups will run every hour. Table 2-1 shows a fairly accurate representation of the time block that I am describing.

Table 2-1. *24-Hour Backup Schedule Example*

Time	Full?	Differential?	Transaction Log?
12:00 AM	X	X	X
1:00 AM			X
2:00 AM			X
3:00 AM			X
4:00 AM			X
5:00 AM			X
6:00 AM		X	X
7:00 AM			X
8:00 AM			X
9:00 AM			X
10:00 AM			X
11:00 AM			X
12:00 PM		X	X
1:00 PM			X
2:00 PM			X
3:00 PM			X
4:00 PM			X
5:00 PM			X
6:00 PM		X	X
7:00 PM			X
8:00 PM			X
9:00 PM			X
10:00 PM			X
11:00 PM			X

Using this model, we can restore to any hour in a given day, meaning that the most data we will lose is 1 hour. If this is acceptable, we can move on. If not, then we can adjust the time between backups. We will stay with this schedule for now though. Figure 2-11 shows what you should see on the screen now.

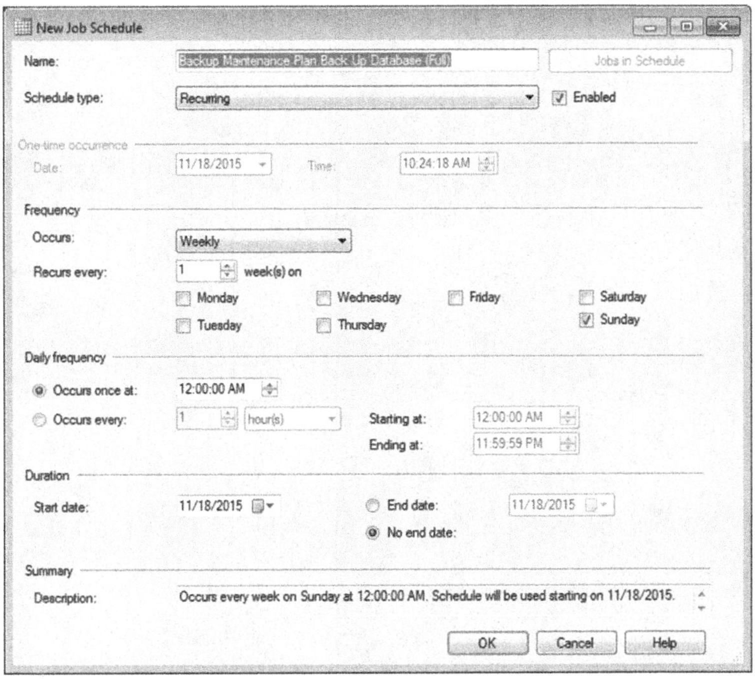

Figure 2-11. *New Job Schedule*

Notice that the defaults are not what we want for a full backup. All you need to do to make this available for our schedule is to pull down the Occurs menu and choose Daily. That's it. Notice the text in the Summary field now reads Occurs every day at 12:00:00 AM. Schedule will be used starting on [DATE]. This is perfect! Click OK here to save this schedule. Notice that the same Summary we just read has been transferred to the Schedule block on the interface. This completed screen is shown in Figure 2-12.

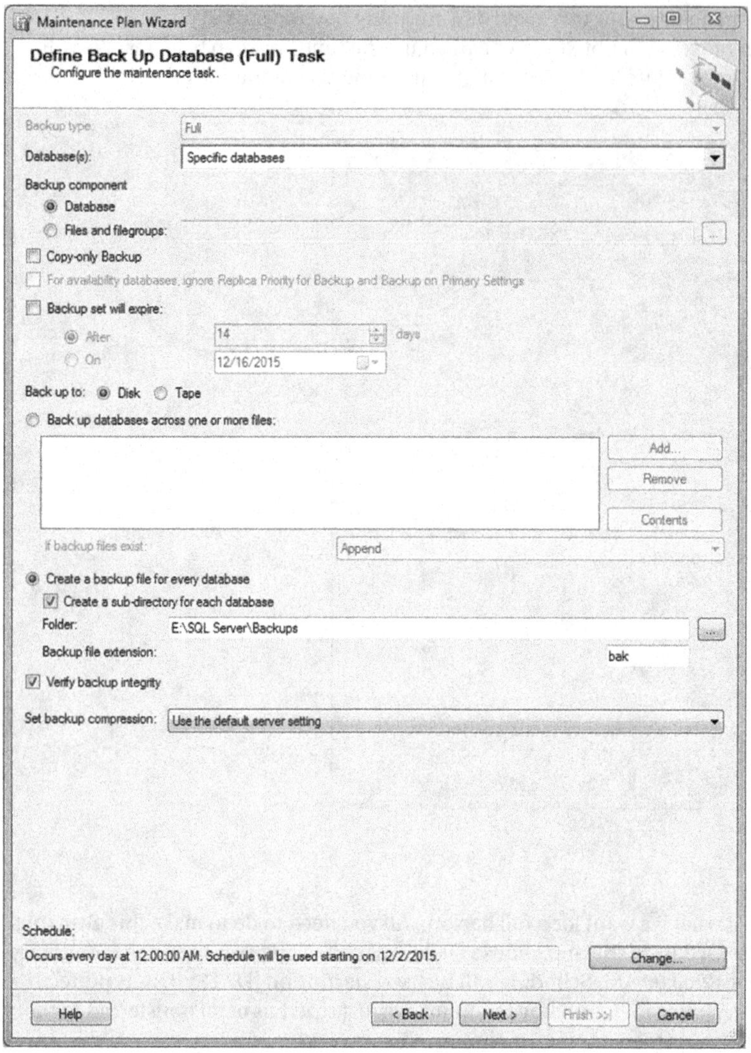

Figure 2-12. *Define Back Up Database (Full) Task, completed*

Click Next to continue setting up the plan.

Differential Backup Configuration

Next, the Define Back Up Database (Differential) Task interface is displayed. Same as before, choose the database from the Database(s) drop-down menu, update the folder location, and click the "Create a sub-directory for each database" check box. You can also check "Verify database integrity", but that's actually done in a later task as well, so it's up to you. Again, click Change… at the bottom of the screen to set up the schedule for the task.

The defaults in this area are not correct either! Oh well, that's why we're here. Change the Occurs selection to Daily. Under the "Daily frequency" area, click the "Occurs every" radio button and enter **6** in the first box. Your screen should look like Figure 2-13 when you are done.

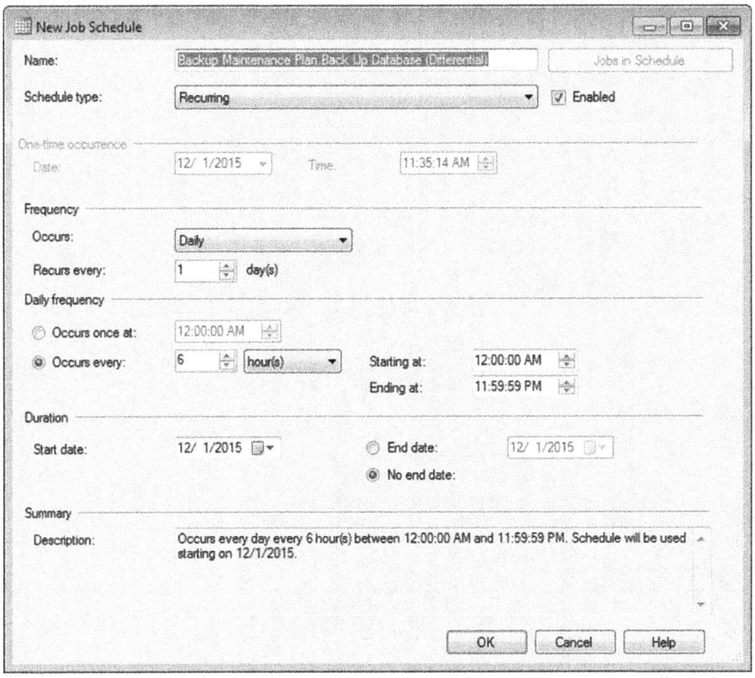

Figure 2-13. *New Job Schedule*

So this means that our differential backup will now run every 6 hours every day. Your completed interface for the differential backup section should look like Figure 2-14.

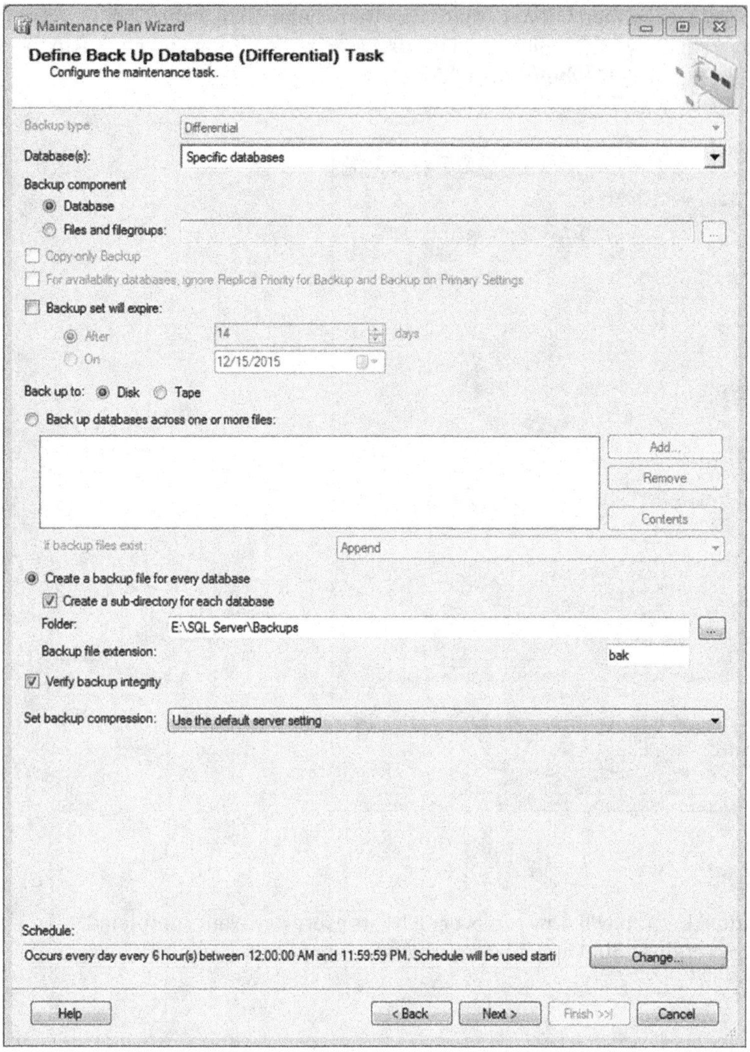

Figure 2-14. *Define Back Up Database (Differential) Task, completed*

It is interesting to note that this screen is the same as the full-backup screen, except for the Schedule portion.

Transaction Log Backup Configuration

Click OK and then click Next to continue. The next screen that opens is the Define Back Up Database (Transaction Log) Task screen. The same general settings as the two previous screens: select the database from the Database(s) menu, select the folder for the backup, which should be your E:\SQL Server\Logs folder, and check the "Create a sub-directory for each database" check box. When you're done, click the Change... button at the bottom of the interface to define this schedule. Change the Occurs value to Daily, and make sure that the "Occurs every" value is set to 1 hour(s). That's it for this area. Your screen should now resemble Figure 2-15.

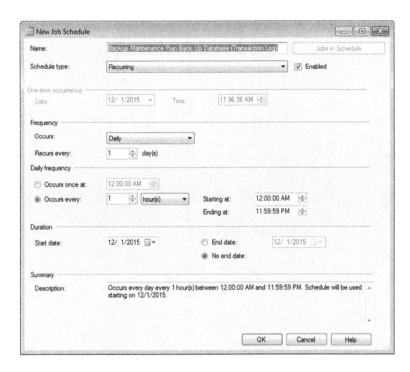

Figure 2-15. *New Job Schedule*

Click OK when you are done with the scheduling. You should then see what is shown in Figure 2-16.

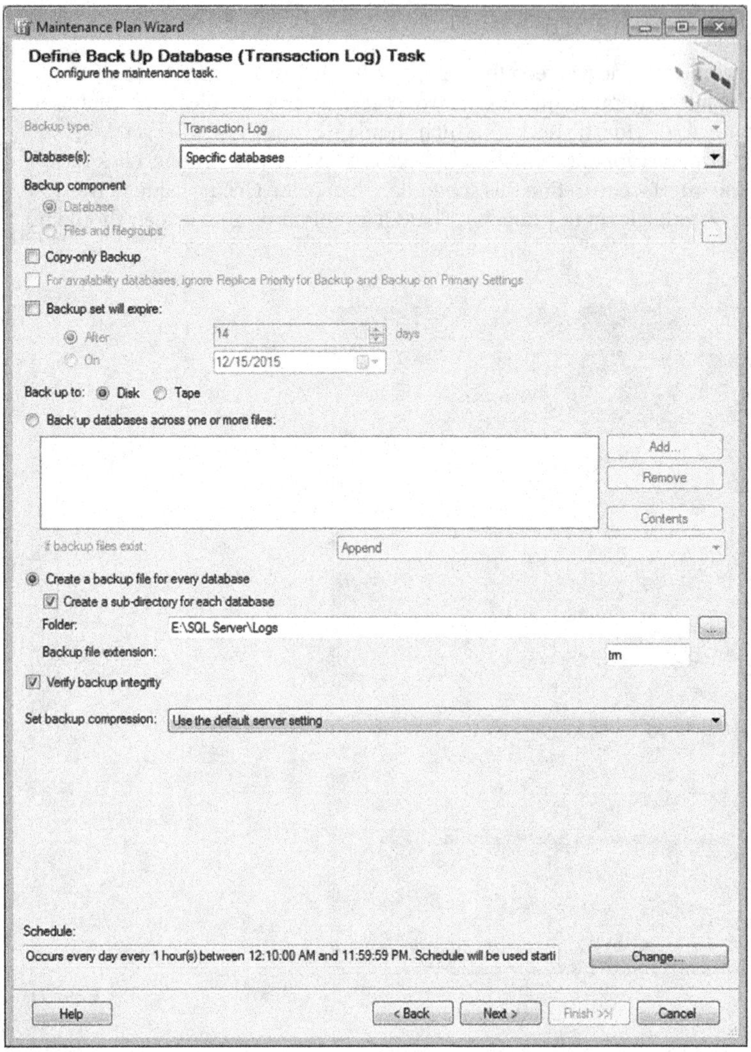

Figure 2-16. *Define Back Up Database (Transaction Log) Task, completed*

When you are ready, click Next.

The screen that opens is titled Select Report Options. You should now see what is shown in Figure 2-17.

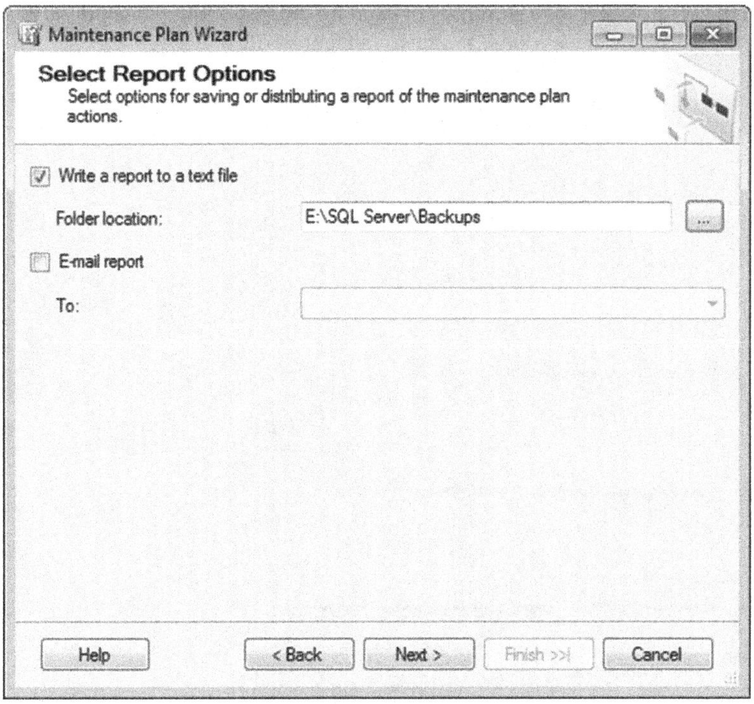

Figure 2-17. *Select Report Options*

Now, this is fairly self-explanatory. If you want a report written to a text file and popped into the file system, click the box. Notice that I have chosen the Backups directory, not the Logs directory. This is because I want to keep the Logs directory for my transaction logs. The Backups directory can be used to store the maintenance text files, whereas the individual folders inside of Backups store the actual .bak files in case you ever need to restore the database.

You can also get the report emailed to you, but you have to have an Operator defined (more on that later). If you have an Operator defined, select it here to receive the email. What this does is let you know, by email, when the maintenance plan runs and what the result was. For now, we will leave only the report option selected. Click Next to move on.

On the next screen, Complete the Wizard, you see a summary of what we did. Expanding the options in the interface will show the complete detail of what was done, as shown in Figure 2-18.

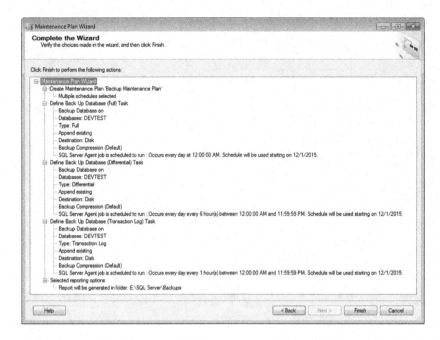

Figure 2-18. *Complete the Wizard*

Note that these options have not been saved yet. You could click Cancel right here and destroy all of the work that we've done thus far, but let's not do that. Instead, review what we did, and when you're ready, click Finish. Hopefully, you see what is shown in Figure 2-19.

Figure 2-19. *Maintenance Plan Wizard Progress*

Always a good sign! Click Close when you are ready. Notice that Backup Maintenance Plan now appears in the Maintenance Plans area of SSMS. It is now enabled and it will run on the schedule that we defined.

Configuring the Jobs

Notice that there are now jobs in the Jobs folder inside of SQL Server Agent. These aren't very descriptive, are they? Which is which? Let's fix this right now. Double-click Subplan_1. You should see what is shown in Figure 2-20.

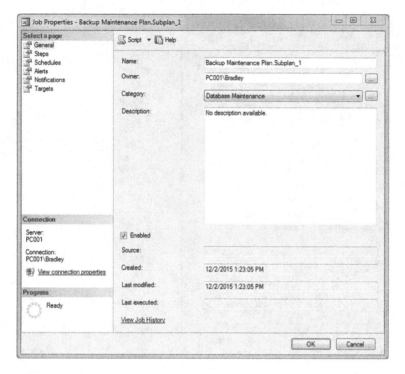

Figure 2-20. *Job Properties, General tab*

See that first box up there labeled Name? Just change the tail end of it to say **Full Backup** instead of Backup Maintenance Plan.Subplan_1. Notice that it is also set to Database Maintenance in the Category option. This is great, because this is what we are doing. Ensure that the Enabled check box is checked—and this screen is all set.

One thing I skipped over is the Owner selection. This typically should be set to the owner of the database.

Also notice that on the left of the screen, there are menu options. You are currently on the General option. If you click the Steps option, you will see what is shown in Figure 2-21.

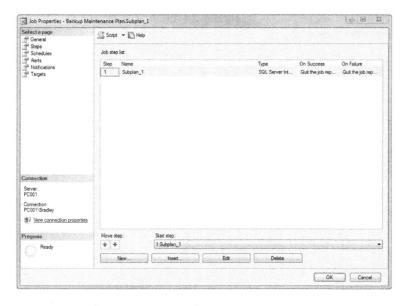

Figure 2-21. *Job Properties, Steps tab*

Notice that the menu bar does not show our new name yet. The Name in the Job step list isn't updated either. How frustrating. Let's fix that now.

Double-click the text Subplan_1. The Job Step Properties window opens, so change the "Step name" box to **Full Backup**, as shown in Figure 2-22.

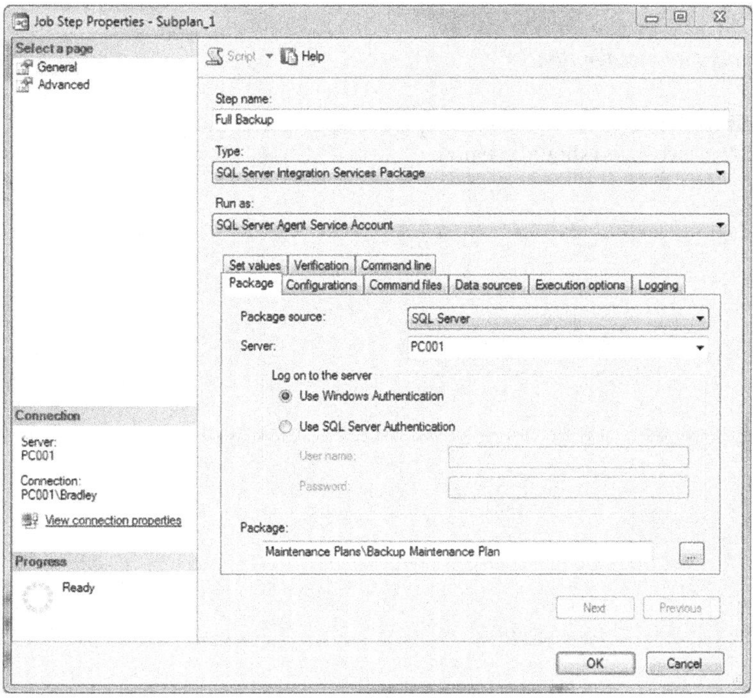

Figure 2-22. *Job Properties, Steps tab, General option*

Don't touch anything else on this screen just yet, except for clicking the Advanced option on the left. Adjust this screen to the settings shown in Figure 2-23.

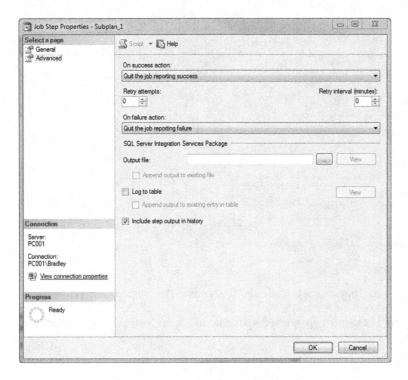

Figure 2-23. *Job Properties, Steps tab, Advanced option*

Click OK when this is done and you will go back to the Job Properties screen, with the text Full Backup now replacing Subplan_1. Figure 2-24 is what you should see now.

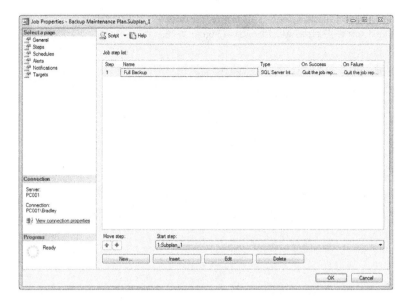

Figure 2-24. *Job Properties, Steps tab*

Click the Schedules option on the left and notice that our schedule is in there, and that it is enabled, as shown in Figure 2-25.

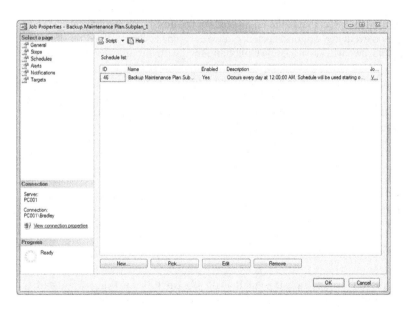

Figure 2-25. *Job Properties, Schedules tab*

Click the Alerts option and you will see a blank screen. This is fine, for now. Click the Notifications option and you will see what is shown in Figure 2-26.

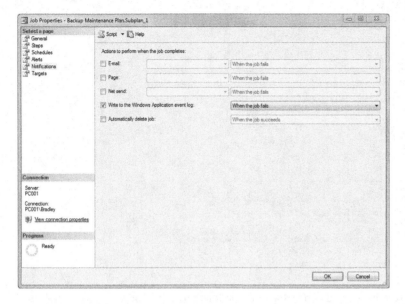

Figure 2-26. *Job Properties, Notifications tab*

If you have an Operator set up already, select that in the Email box. For the time being, we are going to keep the "Write to the Windows Application event log" option selected, but we are going to change the drop-down to "When the job completes"; that way, we will always know what happened with our job. More on this a bit later.

Clicking the Targets option will show a blank screen as well. This is fine, since we haven't defined any targets.

Click OK when you are through with the Targets option and have followed the directions for this area. You will then see that the Jobs folder has changed to what you see in Figure 2-27.

Figure 2-27. *Updated SQL Server Agent Jobs*

Now you can clearly see that this job is specifically the Full Backup job. Do the same things listed earlier for the other two and label them accordingly. Remember that we defined the full backup as the first task, the differential backup as the second task, and the transaction log as the third task. Those line up with the Subplan designations here. You should end up with what you see in Figure 2-28.

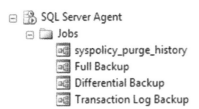

Figure 2-28. *Completed SQL Server Agent Jobs*

It's okay that syspolicy_purge_history is in there too. That's a job that SQL Server does on its own.

And that, my friend, is how you set up a database backup maintenance plan.

It's worth noting that you can also update the Job names from the Maintenance Plan itself by double-clicking and editing the Subplan names from the Design Surface, and then saving the plan. You may find this quicker, once you get experienced in setting up the maintenance plans.

Summary

This was a big chapter, but I wanted to be sure to cover all of the important bits needed to really get into the specifics of the tasks.

To review, you learned about the following:

- Full, Bulk Logged, and Simple recovery models

- Full, differential, and transaction log backups

- Configuration options for the backup tasks

Recall that I mentioned that database backups were arguably the most important part to database administration. I sincerely hope that you have learned exactly why this is in this chapter. Data integrity is an important topic, as is data protection, loss mitigation, and a host of other database concepts. At the core of each of these concepts is one very important piece of the puzzle that absolutely must be present: *data*. Protecting that data is our job as database administrators. And, properly maintained backups are integral in providing that puzzle piece.

CHAPTER 3

Checking Database Integrity

Being a database administrator means that you wear many different hats. For those unfamiliar with this phrase, it means that you may do different things throughout the day that aren't necessarily related. One thing will never change for a database administrator: the data is your life. Without it, you have no job. So for those of us working for a living, this is sort of important. Not only are we tasked with making sure that data coming in is sanitary, we also have to make sure that the data stays sanitary. This can be quite a daunting task, if not for *database integrity*.

What Is Database Integrity?

Database integrity is a concept that should be applied in the design phase of the database. The tables themselves determine whether there are rules to apply for inserting data into a table. These rules are going to cascade down to either a well-built database with integrity, or a poorly built database with little or no integrity.

Database integrity is an easy topic to understand. You want to be able to guarantee, as much as humanly possible, that this data is what it says it is. I have told my kids since they were little that the definition of integrity is "doing the right thing, even when no one is looking." In this context, we, as database administrators, have to guarantee that the data entrusted to us is going to be protected and maintained as best as we know how. There is no better way to guarantee the integrity of data than to adopt a proactive approach to daily maintenance that includes the guidelines found in this book.

How does this apply to data? Well, think about the implications if a record were entered into a table with the same UID (unique identifier) as another record, and then querying the database for that record. You would not return the data you thought you would get. This is clearly poor database design. How could this happen? If the UID field weren't defined as a unique key, that's how. Again, poor design leads to poor integrity.

An interesting point about database integrity is that even poorly designed databases can guarantee the integrity of the data. Ever heard the saying that "even a broken clock is right twice a day"? Same thing here. Basically, the database will guarantee that it will return the wrong data, every time, as requested. Is this ideal? Obviously not.

Another aspect to database integrity is the structural integrity of the tables and the indexes. Over time, they can become corrupted. Having a disaster recovery plan is the best way around this, and an important part of that recovery plan is ensuring that the data in the recovery is complete and correct. This can only be accomplished with database integrity.

There seems to always be time, money, and resources to do the job over again later, but there is never enough time, money, or resources to do the job correctly the first time. Any job you do is worth doing well, so if you're going to put your name on a project, make sure that you under-promise and over-deliver. In other words, your personal integrity (doing the right thing when no one is looking) leads to higher data integrity (quality/availability of data).

© Bradley Beard 2016

B. Beard, *Practical Maintenance Plans in SQL Server*, DOI 10.1007/978-1-4842-1895-2_3

■ **Tip** Take the time to do it right the first time instead of having to either do it over again or be forced to work with a poorly designed database.

Practical Application of Database Integrity Principles

Do you need to add this task to your maintenance plan? The short answer is yes. Let's take a look and find out though. In SQL Server Management Studio, right-click your database name, go to Reports ➤ Standard Reports ➤ Database Consistency History. This starts a report that shows you the number of errors found and the number of errors repaired, as shown in Figure 3-1.

Database Consistency History
[DEVTEST]
on PC001 at 12/2/2015 1:30:44 PM

This report provides a history of executions of DBCC CHECKDB as captured by the Default Trace.

Execution history of CHECKDB

No entry found for DBCC CHECKDB in the trace log.

Figure 3-1. *Database Consistency History Report with no data*

If you don't see any data in the report, open a new Query window and type the following:

```
DBCC CHECKDB([database_name]) WITH no_infomsgs
```

Obviously, replace [database_name] with the name of your database. Press F5 to run the query. It will take a few seconds. Switch back to the report and click the Refresh icon. Bingo! You've got a record. Figure 3-2 shows what the interface looks like once a record has been added.

■ **Tip** If you *get a failure at this point, the most common cause is going to be because the physical database files (the MDF and LDF files) are located on a partition that is formatted with FAT and not NTFS.* The database engine will fail trying to create a snapshot at this point, which is what it runs the DBCC commands against (instead of the actual database).

Database Consistency History
[DEVTEST]
on PC001 at 12/2/2015 1:32:30 PM

This report provides a history of executions of DBCC CHECKDB as captured by the Default Trace.

Execution history of CHECKDB

Command Text	Login Name	Start Time	# Errors	# Errors Repaired	Duration (hh:mm:ss)
DBCC CHECKDB (DEVTEST) WITH no_infomsgs	PC001\Bradley	12/2/2015 1:32:25 PM	0	0	0 :0 :1

Figure 3-2. *Database Consistency History Report with data*

So... what does the record in Figure 3-2 mean? Let's break it down and see. Figure 3-2 shows the data as recorded by the DBCC transaction. The following columns are returned:

Command Text: This column simply shows the SQL that was parsed and executed by the database engine. This should be exactly as written earlier.

Login Name: This is the name of the account that the Command Text was executed under. Different accounts have different permissions, so if the command failed, it could possibly be due to not having an account with permissions to run the DBCC command. In this event, you need to log in with an admin level account; otherwise, none of this will work.

Start Time: I wonder what this means...? Oh! This is the time that the query started execution. What's curious is that there isn't an End Time column. There is, however a Duration column, so it's up to the DBA to do the time parsing.

 # Errors: If you see a value here, you are in trouble. That means that something has started to go wrong; without further analysis, it will be impossible to determine what it is.

 # Errors Repaired: If you see a value in the # Errors column, and you don't see the same value in this column, you are about to have serious issues. This means that there are unresolved errors in the consistency of the data; this will definitely not be the last you see of the error.

Duration (hh:mm:ss): This is simply how long the query took to run. The database I ran this on is a brand-new database, so it was only around 8MB and it took 0 seconds for it to run.

As you can tell, this report is extremely useful in determining whether your database is "healthy." Keeping a close eye on this report helps mitigate future issues through early detection. Even though this record returned 0 errors, that doesn't mean that it doesn't need to be added to the maintenance plan. On the contrary, the fact that we see 0 here means that database integrity has been achieved to the point that there are no reportable errors with the consistency of the data, which is a very good thing. Having database integrity as a part of any maintenance plan is an absolute necessity.

Let's create a maintenance plan to cover database integrity now.

Setting Up the Maintenance Plan

Right-click Maintenance Plans and select Maintenance Plan Wizard, and then name it **Database Integrity Plan**. You can leave the radio button for the scheduling alone since there is only one task, but click the Change button to define the overall schedule, which is shown in Figure 3-3.

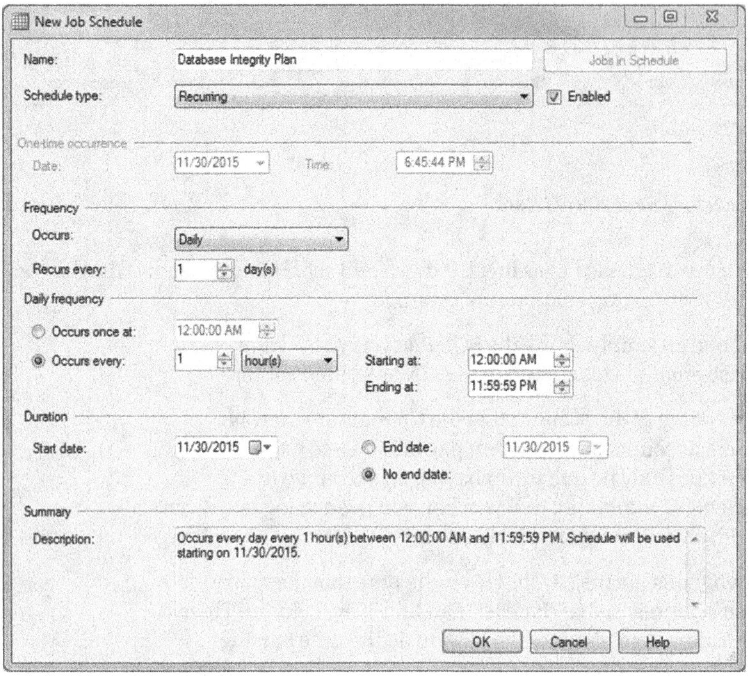

Figure 3-3. *New Job Schedule*

The schedule should reflect that we want the task to run once every hour, basically mirroring the schedule for the transaction log backups. Why is this? Because we're running a backup, we don't want to have to worry about coming up with data integrity issues hours after the issue comes up. We want to be aware as soon as possible; so to implement that, we run it after the transaction log backups. That way, any integrity issues get reported immediately.

Click OK on the New Job Schedule screen. You are returned to the Select Plan Properties screen, as shown in Figure 3-4.

Figure 3-4. *Select Plan Properties*

Click Next to continue. You should see the Select Maintenance Tasks screen, as shown in Figure 3-5. Choose the Check Database Integrity check box and then click Next.

Figure 3-5. *Select Maintenance Tasks*

You should see a screen titled Select Maintenance Task Order, as shown in Figure 3-6. Just click Next here since there is only one task.

Figure 3-6. *Select Maintenance Task Order*

Next, the Define Database Check Integrity Task interface appears, as shown in Figure 3-7. Choose your database from the drop-down menu, leave "Include indexes" selected, click OK, and then click Next.

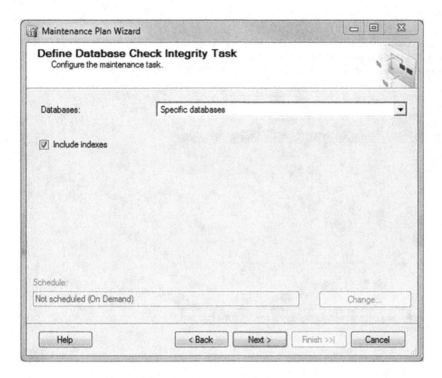

Figure 3-7. *Define Database Check Integrity Task*

The next screen, shown in Figure 3-8, is Select Report Options. Leave the report option checked and enter the backups location again. Remember that we are writing our maintenance logs to this location. Click Next when you are ready to move on.

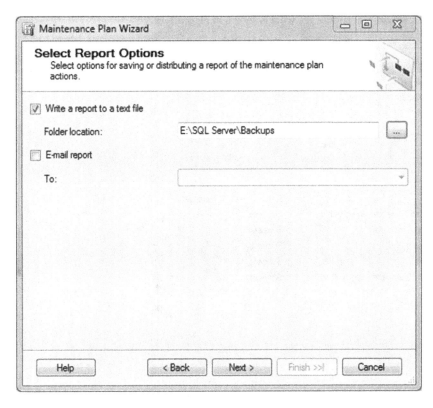

Figure 3-8. *Select Report Options*

That leads to the Summary section of this area, as shown in Figure 3-9.

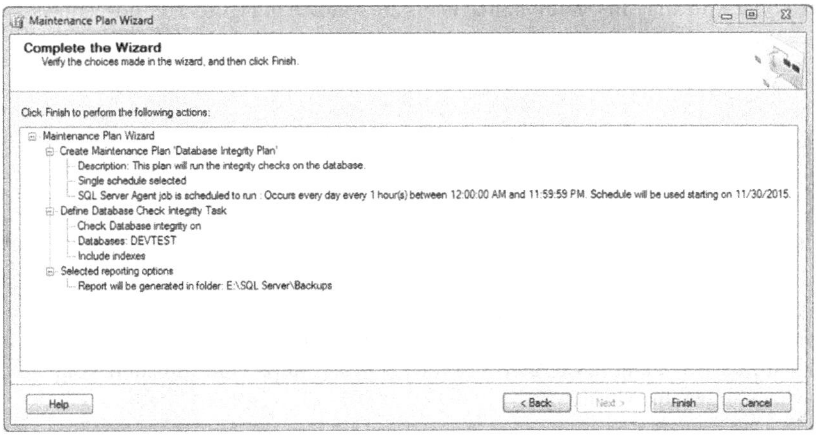

Figure 3-9. *Complete the Wizard*

When you're ready, click Finish. You should see what is shown in Figure 3-10.

Figure 3-10. *Maintenance Plan Wizard Progress*

Click Close when you're done. Note that the Maintenance Plans area shown in Figure 3-11 now shows the Database Integrity Plan.

Maintenance Plans
    Backup Maintenance Plan
    Database Integrity Plan

Figure 3-11. *Maintenance Plans*

You're going to want to update the job, as defined in Chapter 1. Double-click the job name in the Jobs folder inside SQL Server Agent. Change the Name of the Job from Database Integrity Plan.Subplan_1 to **Check Integrity** and continue from there. Refer to Chapter 1 for the necessary steps. Once finished, your Jobs folder should look like what's shown in Figure 3-12.

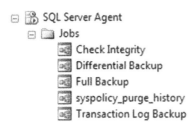

Figure 3-12. *SQL Server Agent Jobs*

Summary

Let's sum up what we've learned in this chapter.

- We learned about data integrity and the importance it carries.

- We learned how to check our database for consistency using DBCC CHECKDB.

- We learned how to set up the maintenance plan and update a job when the plan was completed.

In the coming chapters, we are going to get much more involved. Better get more coffee...

CHAPTER 4

■ ■ ■

Executing SQL Server Agent Jobs

Ah, good old SQL Server Agent. What would we do without you? Well, that's easy; nothing. Not in this book, anyway. The purpose of SQL Server Agent is to execute scheduled administrative tasks, so without it, we couldn't do anything automatically and we would have to do all of this manually. Now, don't get me wrong; all of this can be done in T-SQL... but why would you want to do that, when you can have trusty SQL Server Agent do it's one and only job?

Now, before we go any further, let me stop right here and state the obvious. You cannot use this task to run a job that doesn't exist. And I'm not bringing this up because I doubt the mental faculties of my readers; quite the contrary. I am embarrassed to admit that I have spent a considerable amount of time trying to track down why a task was failing, only to find that the job assigned to the task... didn't... actually... exist. Talk about a rookie error, right? It happens. Slap your forehead and move on.

Okay. So here we are, wanting to run a SQL Server Agent job. Do we have any jobs available to run? Let's check and find out. Expand SQL Server Agent and then expand the Jobs folder to show any jobs you may have in there. You should see something similar to Figure 4-1.

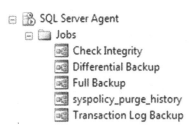

Figure 4-1. *SQL Server Agent Jobs*

We have our jobs that we've been creating and the default SQL Server job. I don't really want to use these though, since they are running on their own. That means we need to create one from scratch. Fun!

E-mail from the Database

Before we get into creating agent jobs, let's take the time to configure SQL Server to send e-mail. That way, you can create jobs that notify you when they are done. After all, what good is automation if you must manually check at the end?

B. Beard, *Practical Maintenance Plans in SQL Server*, DOI 10.1007/978-1-4842-1895-2_4

Here are a couple things to know about sending e-mail from SQL Server:

- SQL Server can only send e-mail over SMTP. It cannot receive e-mail in any way.

- The server must be set up with SMTP already. Work with your system administrator to be certain that SMTP is in place.

Your tasks now are to configure your database for e-mail, send a test e-mail to be sure of your configuration, and finally, to enable the mail profile in SQL Server Agent.

Configuring E-mail

First things first. Expand the Management node of your SQL Server installation, as shown in Figure 4-2. You should see Database Mail.

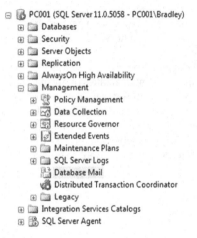

Figure 4-2. *Location of Database Mail in SSMS*

Right-click and select Configure Database Mail. You should see the information that is displayed in Figure 4-3.

Figure 4-3. *Database Main Configuration Wizard*

This is a great little wizard that walks you through how to step up your database mail. Once this is set up, I guarantee that you will start looking for reasons to employ database mail in your daily workflow. What purpose could this possibly lend to you? Think about how convenient it would be if you were to receive an e-mail after a task has run, or after the database has been backed up or restored successfully. What about when you are expecting an e-mail to say that your primary database was backed up, but you never receive that e-mail? That could be a trigger for bad things afoot. At least you will have sort of a heads up that something is wrong, as opposed to being blindsided by angry users or managers. This is a great tool for managing messaging as a database administrator, and has a role to play in nearly every application.

You can click the check box to not show this in the future, if you would like. I usually do. When you're ready, click Next to continue.

The next screen that comes up, as shown in Figure 4-4, allows you to select what you want to do: set up a new account, manage accounts, or change parameters.

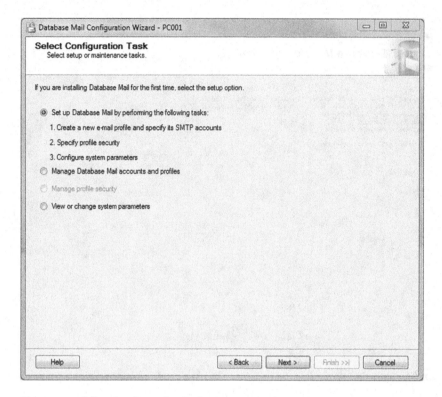

Figure 4-4. *Select Configuration Task*

Since we are setting up a new user, keep the default value of "Set up Database Mail..." selected and choose Next.

If you get an alert saying that the Database Mail feature is not available, select Yes to enable it. You shouldn't have to install anything, considering that a full SQL Server install was done.

You now are taken to the New Profile screen, which looks like Figure 4-5.

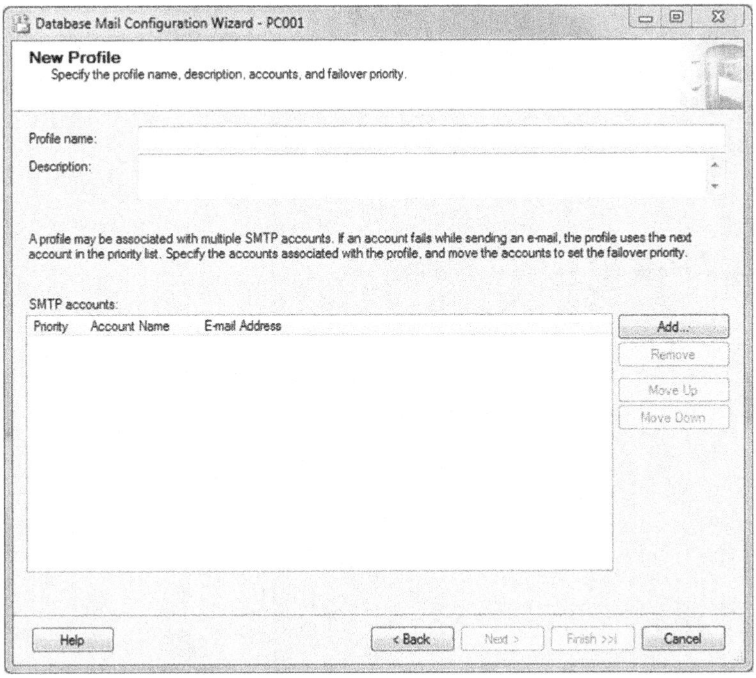

Figure 4-5. *New Profile (initial interface)*

This is where most of the work is done. Enter a profile name and description in the boxes. These help you to differentiate your accounts. I entered the values shown in Figure 4-6, but you can enter whatever you want.

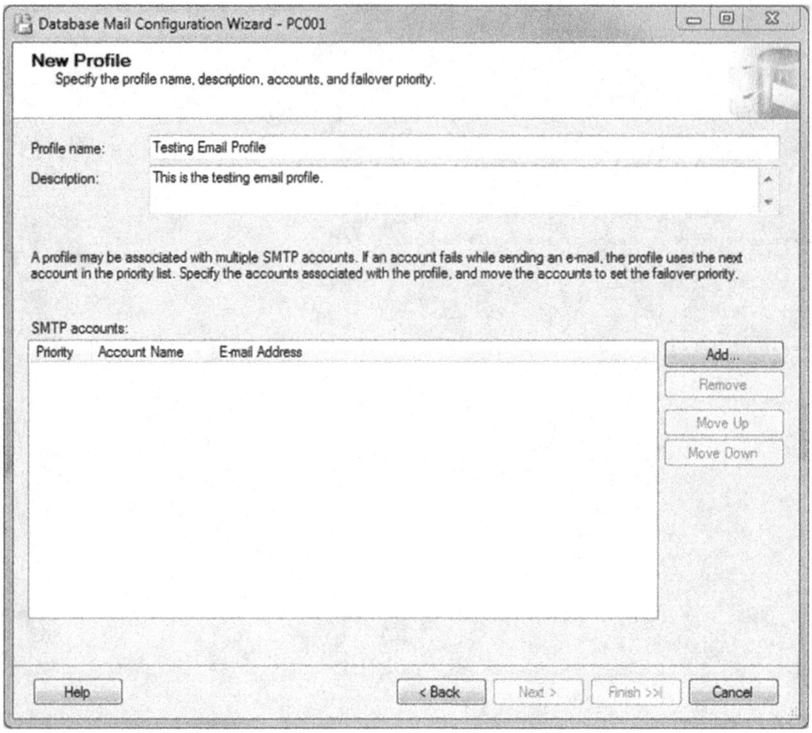

Figure 4-6. *New Profile, nearly complete*

When you're satisfied with the values you've entered, press the Add button on the right side of the interface. This allows you to add a new profile for database mail.

Yet another interface magically appears with the information shown in Figure 4-7. I filled it in so you can get an idea of what you need to enter. You may need to get some of this information from your system administrator.

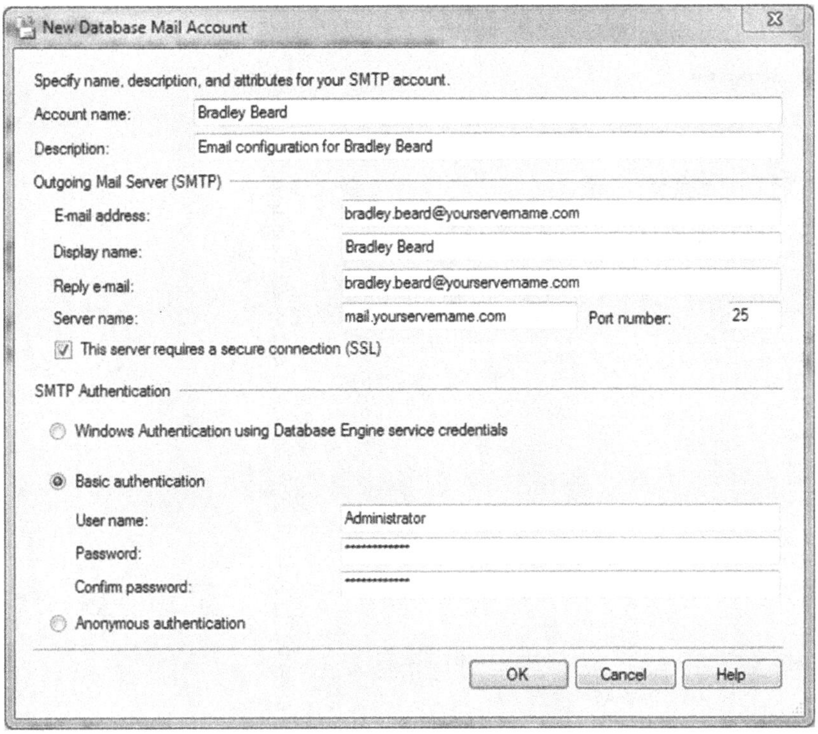

Figure 4-7. New Database Mail Account settings

The fields Account Name and Description are just placeholders, like in the previous screen. The outgoing mail information obviously has to be 100% correct or it will fail. The rest should be fairly obvious. Once you get everything filled in, click OK to be taken back to the previous interface, where you should now see the Account Name and E-mail Address in the grid area, as shown in Figure 4-8.

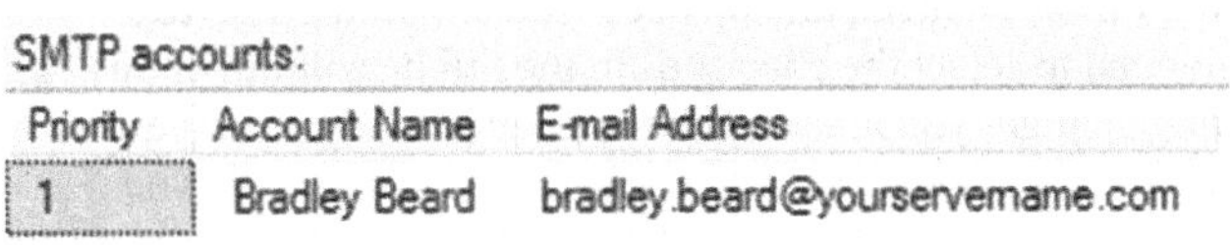

Figure 4-8. SMTP Accounts

When you're ready to move on, choose Next.

You are shown a screen titled Manage Profile Security that has two tabs: Public Profiles and Private Profiles. We are going to deal specifically with the Public Profile for this exercise, as shown in Figure 4-9.

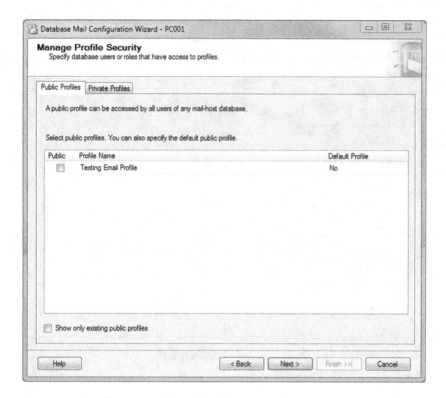

Figure 4-9. *New Database Mail Account settings*

What this means is that the database mail service is looking for the security of the object entered. You may recognize Profile Name because that's what was entered on the previous screen. I originally thought that this may have been pulling off of Active Directory or something, but in a distributed database system, you may not have an account on Active Directory, but this would still work. Therefore, it had to be a value that was previously entered into the interface by the user... in this case, you. You can see how it appears in Figure 4-10. If you like, press Back and change the Profile Name at the top of the screen, then press Next to see that the name is changed. Pretty cool! You need to select the check box in the Public column of this interface to enable it; otherwise, any future setting changes you make will be applied globally. Also, pull down the Default Profile menu and select Yes. In this case, you just want to edit this particular user. The completed interface is shown in Figure 4-10.

Figure 4-10. *Manage Profile Security*

Click Next when you're ready.

Oh look, Figure 4-11 shows another interface. Just for clarification, I use the term *interface* a lot. If that seems confusing, then you can always substitute "interface" for whatever term you have deemed to be what you call a change in on-screen appearance presented to the user in which a prompt or decision is displayed. I remember going through beginner Visual Basic 6 courses way back in the Stone Age, and my professor called them "interfaces." It just kind of stuck.

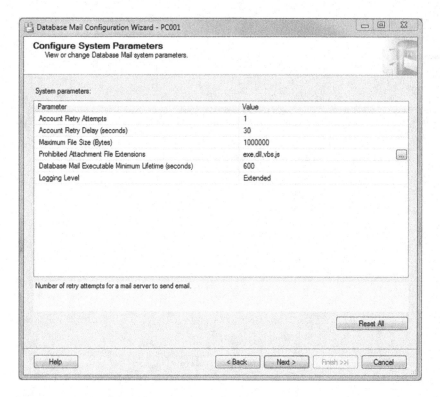

Figure 4-11. *Configure System Parameters*

This interface is what you see now. All of these fields are editable, so proceed at your own risk. You are free to make whatever choice you want here, or keep the defaults. Whatever your environment or security principles call for is what should be enforced here. For example, I would not recommend changing the Prohibited Attachment File Extensions. Those extensions listed are basically all of the current file extensions that can be accessed by SQL Server and can also be executed by the operating system. They can't necessarily be produced by SQL Server, but they can be added as attachments.

The following are the available options on this screen:

- **Account Retry Attempts**: Number of retry attempts for a mail server to send e-mail.

- **Account Retry Delay (seconds)**: Delay between attempts for a mail server to send e-mail in seconds.

- **Maximum File Size (Bytes)**: Maximum file size in bytes for an attachment for a mail server to send e-mail.

- **Prohibited Attachment File Extensions**: Prohibited file extensions for a mail server to send e-mail.

- **Database Mail Executable Minimum Lifetime (seconds)**: Minimum lifetime for Database Mail executable in seconds.

- **Logging Level**: Determines which events are written to the Database Mail event log.

The definitions for those options are straight from the interface shown in Figure 4-11. An interesting thing to note here: if you were to click the Reset All button, you will see that the value for Account Retry Delay changes to 5000 instead of 60. So instead of waiting 1 minute, the *default* is to wait for over an hour just to retry sending mail. Think about what happens in the event of using e-mail to report a catastrophic failure. Would you rather know right away, or over an hour after the event?

I'm going to select the default options for this interface and choose Next to proceed. You will see next an interface in Figure 4-12 that is titled Complete the Wizard, with a brief summary of the settings chosen. Let's look at those next.

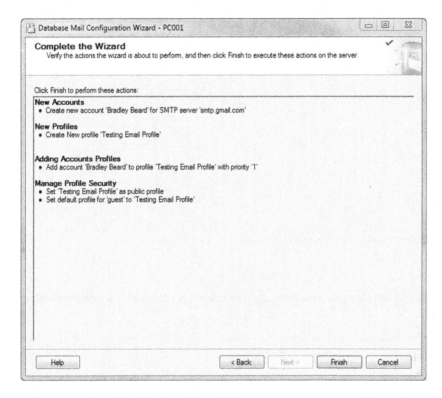

Figure 4-12. *Complete the Wizard*

From top to bottom, we see all the information that we previously entered.

It tells us we created a new account and profile. It tells us we added that new account to that new profile. Think of the profile like a security container of sorts; to edit the account, you have to edit the profile. Finally, it tells us that we set the profile as public.

Looks like we're ready to implement this, right? Click Finish to find out. Figure 4-13 shows the result you should get.

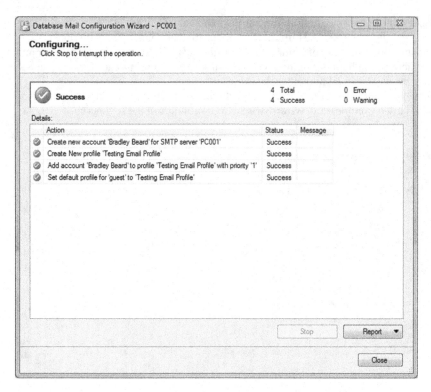

Figure 4-13. *Configuring...*

Woohoo! I always love seeing all those green check boxes! If you didn't get that, go back to the beginning of this chapter and start again.

Sending a Test E-mail

If you did get those green check boxes, congratulations! Let's move on to implementing database mail as a part of the database maintenance plan. Remember, the purpose of using e-mail is to ...? That's right, to keep us database administrators informed of any potential issues with the database. In this case, specifically, we will utilize database mail to send us a status report when a query runs successfully.

Right-click Database Mail again and select Send Test E-Mail. You will get a screen pop-up with information in it, as shown in Figure 4-14.

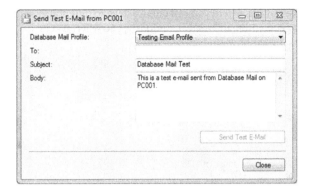

Figure 4-14. Send Test E-Mail

Fill out the To box with a valid e-mail address, and click Send Test E-Mail. It takes a second to get there, but it should show up. If it doesn't, then something was set up incorrectly and you probably need to go back to the beginning and figure out what you may have missed.

Enabling the Mail Profile

So now our database can send mail, right? You're going to hate me, but... yes and no. You see, SQL Server has this thing about *security principles*, and just because one user or login has permission to do something does not mean that all users and logins have permission to do that same thing. For this reason, it is important to bring up that, without an extra step, database mail will likely never run on its own.

Yes, the database has just sent the test mail. But remember this: *whatever you do when you're logged in to SQL Server is done under the context of your login.* If you have been granted permission to do something, guess what: you can do it. Consequently, if you haven't been granted that permission, you are not allowed to do it. For the most part, regular SQL Server logins (especially those that log in with the sa account) have permission to send mail by default. Interestingly enough, the SQL Server Agent does not, by default, have permission to send mail. Isn't that odd?

There are probably good reasons why sending mail isn't enabled by default, but I honestly can't think of any good ones, so I will punt to Microsoft on this one.

A key point that I can't stress enough is to make sure that you enable the mail profile in SQL Server Agent. Begin by right-clicking SQL Server Agent and choosing Properties, as shown in Figure 4-15.

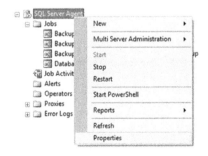

Figure 4-15. SQL Server Agent properties

Once that opens, on the left, you see that you have options where you can choose to go to different areas of the configuration of SQL Server Agent. Do not change anything in here yet. Seriously, you will regret it.

Click the Alert System option. An interface comes up, as shown in Figure 4-16.

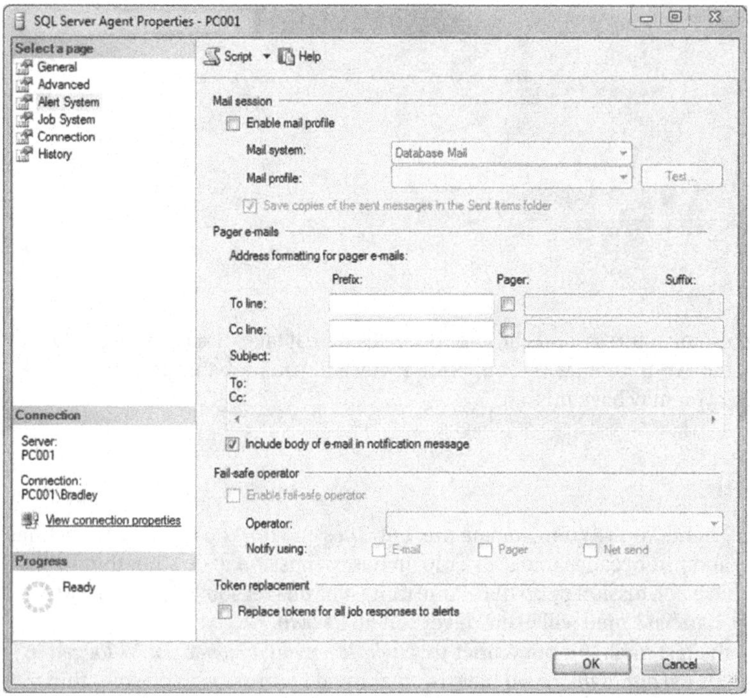

Figure 4-16. *SQL Server Agent Properties (initial interface)*

Those sneaky little Microsoft developers! Note that top check box next to "Enable mail profile" is unchecked. That is literally the only thing stopping you from sending automated e-mail from SQL Server. Select that check box, make sure that Database Mail is selected, and choose the mail profile we set up earlier. If you have previously defined an operator, you can set them up here as the fail-safe operator; so check the check box near the bottom next to Enable fail-safe operator and choose your operator. If you don't have an operator defined yet, we will do that shortly, and then you can skip back here and add it to these properties. Be sure to select the E-mail option also, so that the person is notified by e-mail. The completed interface should resemble Figure 4-17.

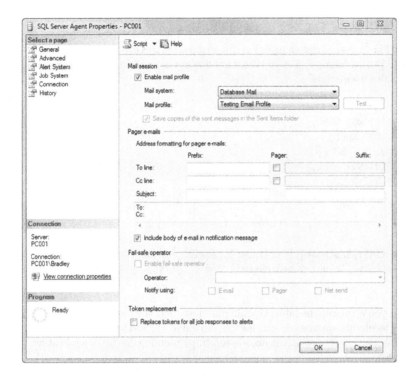

Figure 4-17. *SQL Server Agent Properties (completed interface)*

When that's all done, click OK, right-click SQL Server Agent, and select Restart. A prompt will pop up asking if you want to restart, so say Yes. That bounces the service and enables the database mail subsystem within SQL Server Agent.

Trust me. This is what will stop you later. When you get done with this chapter, go back and disable the mail profile and watch what happens. No e-mail!

Let's take a second and review what we've done for this exercise so far.

What did we want to do? We wanted to create a SQL Server Agent job that sends e-mail when a SQL query is run, and returns the status of that query in the e-mail.

Did we accomplish that successfully? Why or why not? Not yet. We haven't written the query or completed the SQL Server Agent job.

What is the next step? The next step is to write a simple query, and then integrate the query and the database mail into the SQL Server Agent job for testing.

Now we have a roadmap. First, write the query. Second, move the query and the mail into the steps of the job and begin testing.

SQL Agent Job Creation

Now that e-mail is configured, you can create SQL Agent jobs to execute, for example, queries. These may be simple SQL queries or they may represent T-SQL blocks.

Creating an Example Table

If you have a query that you would like to use, go right ahead. For the purposes of this exercise, if you don't have any tables yet and you want to run an example, just execute the following two queries. The first query creates the table; the second populates it with data.

```
CREATE TABLE [dbo].[Users](
        [uid] [int] IDENTITY(1,1) NOT NULL,
        [userid] [varchar](10) NOT NULL,
        [lastname] [varchar](20) NOT NULL,
        [firstname] [varchar](20) NOT NULL,
        [email] [varchar](100) NOT NULL,
        [phone] [varchar](25) NOT NULL,
        [admin] [bit] NOT NULL
) ON [PRIMARY]

INSERT INTO [dbo].[Users]([userid],[lastname],[firstname],[email],[phone],[admin])
VALUES ('beardbr1','Beard','Bradley','bradley.beard@gmail.com','555-555-5555',1);
GO
```

You can enter as much data as you want into the table. I would put more than one row in the table though. This information is just a placeholder so that you can see what to enter. The last field, admin, is to determine whether a user is an admin level user or not. 0 is no, 1 is yes. Implementing this in an application is up to you or the software developer.

Keep in mind that the preceding queries are not what we are going to use in the example SQL Server Agent job. They are just to set up a table with data for us to query.

Next, let's write the actual query that is going to go in the job. Looking at the columns in our data, it seems pretty cut and dried. How about a nice little report on all of the data, sorted by last name? Sounds like a plan. This is a very easy query to write.

Writing a Query for the Job

We have an example table and some data in place. Now we can write query against that data, and then schedule execution of the query through a SQL Agent job.

Here is the example query that we'll execute:

```
SELECT [userid],[firstname] + ' ' + [lastname] AS uname,[email],[phone],[admin]
FROM [dbo].[Users]
ORDER BY [lastname];
```

■ **Tip** If you constantly see the column and table names underlined when writing perfectly valid SQL, your IntelliSense cache probably needs to be refreshed. Press Ctrl+Shift+R to refresh the cache and get it back to how it should look.

Let's just go over the query really quickly, just to be sure that everyone understands what is going on. I am getting the concatenation of the firstname and lastname fields as a new field name called *uname*. This is specifically so that I don't return two columns for each name, with the last name and the first name separated. I would rather have them returned in a nice, readable format; hence, concatenate them together and call it a day.

So now we have the database mail setup correctly *and* we have a functional query to return our data. All that is left is for us to put them together in a SQL Server Agent job.

Creating a SQL Agent Job

In SQL Server Management Studio, expand SQL Server Agent (at the very bottom), right-click the Jobs folder and select New Job.… The first thing to notice on the General tab is that the Owner box isn't necessarily your logged in user name, but usually your Windows account name (your first and last name, usually, if using Windows Authentication). You need to change this to your actual Windows username, as shown in Figure 4-18, which is probably the owner of the database anyway.

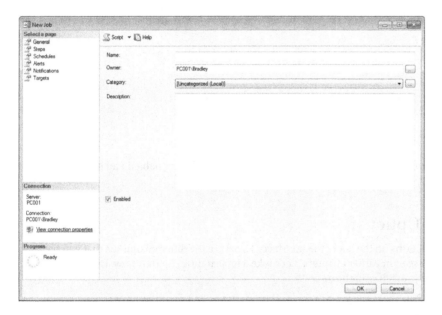

Figure 4-18. *New Job (initial interface)*

You need to add a name for the job, so just enter **Email User Information** in the Name field.

Change the Category to Database Maintenance and add a simple description. It should be something that is easily identifiable. You don't want to write *War and Peace* here, but you also don't want to write "does stuff" either. Short but concise is the key.

Your screen should now resemble Figure 4-19.

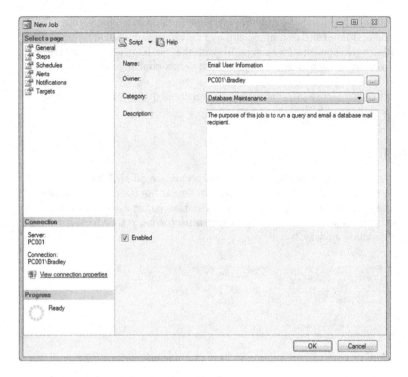

Figure 4-19. *New Job (updated interface)*

Make sure that the Enabled check box is checked; otherwise, the job is not enabled and it will not run as expected.

SQL Server Agent Options

Pay attention to the menu options on the left of the interface. These are the different options that you have to set in the job, as you have seen in earlier chapters. Let's take a look at those options now. Don't make any changes yet, just familiarize yourself with the options:

- **General**: This is the option that you are currently on. It lets you set the general options, hence the name.

- **Steps**: This option lets you define the steps that the job will take. You can also switch up the order of the steps, or define a different starting step. As always, once you add a step, you can always go back and edit or delete it.

- **Schedules**: This option lets you define a schedule to run the job. It can be set up almost any way you can imagine, so spend some time in this area to make sure that you got it right.

- **Alerts**: This option lets you choose from a wide variety of alerts that SQL Server maintains. Click the Add button at the bottom of the screen. When you first enter this option, you are on the General tab of the New Alert window.

Alerts are further broken down, as follows:

- **SQL Server event alert**: Choose the database to target and the severity or error number to look for. You can also set an alert to be raised whenever specific text is returned from any message, such as "error" or "failure", for example.

- **SQL Server performance condition alert**: This one is fun. You can choose the Object, Counter, and Instance to target here. For example, if you wanted to see the number of transactions as of the time that the job runs, you would choose Databases as the Object, Active Transactions for Counter, and your database name for the Instance. Change the value to "Alert if counter" to "rises above" and 0, and you will have a handy dandy performance monitor.

- **WMI event alert**: This area uses little-known WQL, or Windows Management Instrumentation (WMI) Query Language, to monitor SQL Server events. I think it may be beyond the scope of this book, since we can do what we need with the other two areas.

Next is the Response tab. Here is where you define what job you want to execute. You also have the option to Notify Operators by selecting the check box and choosing New Operator or choosing a predefined operator. Simply fill out the interface as needed and you are done! SQL Server makes this very easy to manage, don't you think? Select the E-mail check box and you will be all set up. It is important to mention here that this is not what we set up earlier. This isn't the database mail portion of the job; this pertains only to this particular Alerts area. We will get to the database mail portion next.

Notifications

Here is the part where we add the database mail. When you first open this tab, you see the E-mail, Page, and other options on the right. Select the E-mail check box and pull down the menu just to the right. You will see the operator name that you entered earlier. Leave it alone for now, since this is just an introduction to the options.

Targets

This is where you can choose which servers to target. Your options are—get ready for it—local or multiple. Note that the Multiple option is probably grayed out. This is because there are no other servers added as linked servers, and there is no contingency to have the server communicate with any other server.

Now that we've gone through the options, let's *finally* set up the job!

Steps Tab

Go back to the Steps tab. It should be blank, meaning that there are no steps listed yet. On this Steps tab, there is a button labeled New at the bottom of the screen. Click this to continue.

General

You should see the interface shown in Figure 4-20 open. Notice that you are currently on the General tab on this screen.

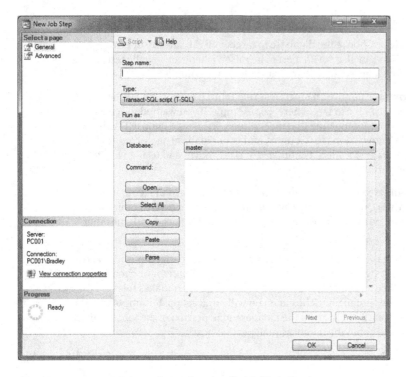

Figure 4-20. *New Job Step, General option (initial interface)*

This is what you see at this point. Enter **Run SQL Query** in the "Step name" box.

Coincidentally, the Transact-SQL Script (T-SQL) option is already selected for us. There are other options here that you can choose, but we will stick with this one for now.

There is a drop-down here labeled "Run as". You can leave it at the default (which is blank). This box is for if you have set up a proxy account, and would like the proxy account to execute this step instead of the SQL Server Agent account. The reason for this is that the current context of a running job is always going to be SQL Server Agent, but the current step can be executed by a different user. You can set a different user for a particular task, which I will show you next, but this can stay at the default.

Select your database name from the Database drop-down menu; master is currently selected.

The Command box is where you want to paste the SQL query we wrote earlier, so go ahead and put that in there. You can press Parse, if you would like. The interface should now look like Figure 4-21.

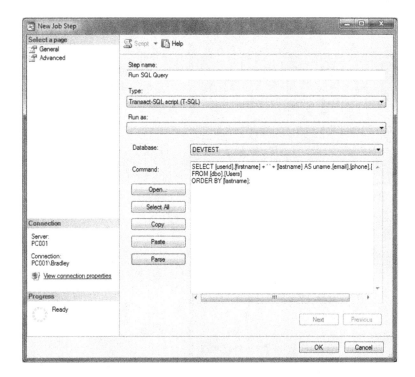

Figure 4-21. *New Job Step, General option (updated interface)*

When you're ready, click the Advanced tab to continue.

Advanced

The purpose of this screen is to set up the advanced options for this step. Initially, it should look like Figure 4-22.

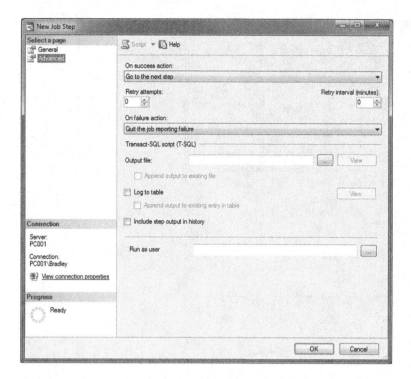

Figure 4-22. *New Job Step, Advanced option (initial interface)*

Note that there is a "Run as user" box. We just did that, didn't we? Well, yes and no. The correct option for this field is your current Windows login (if you have Windows Authentication and it is a user on the database), or the database owner (dbo) account. The reason is because this step needs to run under the context of the user account so that it can run. Typically, you can use dbo for just about anything, since it will most like be the account that owns the database and can therefore perform most of the necessary operations without any additional privileges.

If you want to log what happens, this is the place to do it. You have an option for On Success and On Failure, with retry and interval options. If you have chosen logging for this area, then go ahead and set it here.

You can also choose to output the SQL script, append the SQL script to an existing file, log to a table (you need to have the table already set up), and include the output in step history. Really, the only one that I want to see is the step output in history, so go ahead and select this option, as shown in Figure 4-23.

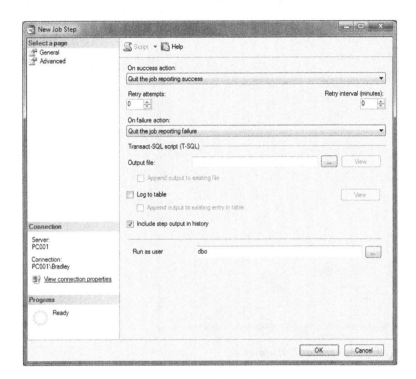

Figure 4-23. *New Job Step, Advanced option (updated interface)*

Now that this is all done, go ahead and click OK to move to the next area shown in Figure 4-24.

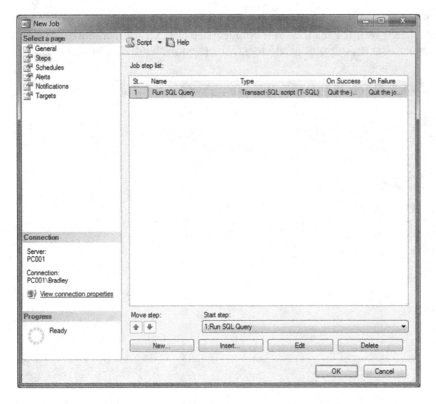

Figure 4-24. *New Job Step, Advanced option (updated interface)*

Note that after you clicked OK, you were brought back to the Job Properties window and Steps tab, and you can now see the newly entered step in there. Good job!

It looks good so far. Note that the Start Step option is set to the only value available, which is what we just entered. You now have the option to Insert, Edit, or Delete steps. Proceed carefully because it is not recoverable if you accidentally delete something.

Schedules Tab

Here is where you set the schedule. This is the part where you need to determine how often you want the job to run. You can set it for just about any value, just remember that you will greatly diminish your system resources if you constantly have a job cranking along. That's not really adding anything for you, is it? Remember, the purpose of this maintenance plan is to make your life as a database administrator easier, not more complicated. If this complicates your life, you're probably doing it wrong. Take the time to reexamine the requirements of the job, and implement a solution from there.

There are two options initially on the Schedules tab, as shown in Figure 4-25.

Figure 4-25. *Job Properties, Schedules tab*

Those options are New and Pick. New lets you create an entirely new schedule from scratch. Pick lets you pick from a previously existing schedule.

Pretty straightforward. You can go over the predefined schedules here, or create your own suited to your specific needs. For the purpose of this exercise, I have chosen Pick and I am going with the option CollectorSchedule_Every_6h. This plan will run all day, every day, every 6 hours, until the end of time. Choosing the option and clicking OK shows the option on the screen, as shown in Figure 4-26.

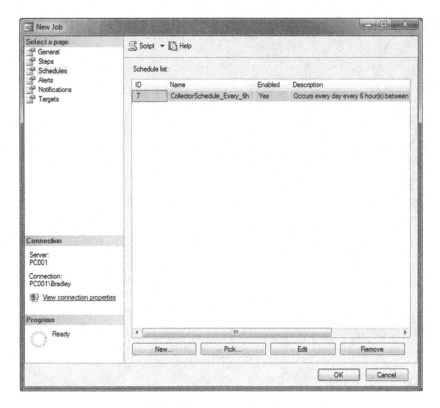

Figure 4-26. *Job Properties, Schedules tab (updated)*

So that's all set up. Moving right along!

Alerts Tab

Next is the Alerts tab. There is a ton of good information in here, and we will go over all of the menu options in detail. Let's look at a general overview of what happens after you press Add. You can always refer to the preceding information for a briefer introduction, because this is going to be a while.

The first thing you notice is that there are three tabs: General, Response, and Options.

General

The General tab lets you decide what event you are going to target. Now, even though we aren't going to use alerts in our job, I still wanted to go over how to set it up, so you can always come back and reference this when needed.

This area is for capturing events, and that is it. What types of events can be captured?

- **SQL Server event alert**: Choose the database to target, or leave the default as <all databases>. Then choose the alerts that will be raised; either by Error Number or Severity, with an additional setting to search any returned values for a specific string, as specified by selecting the Raise Alert check box and entering a string in the Message Text field.

- **SQL Server performance condition alert**: This area is much more complex. There are literally thousands of combinations of data fields here, and to outline each one with their specific attributes would take thousands of pages. A succinct definition of this area would be to capture specific performance conditions when they occur.

- **WMI event alert**: I have never once used this, so I am not going to focus on it. If you were hoping to see some cool WMI stuff, I'm sorry to disappoint!

Response

When you first click the menu option, you see the screen shown in Figure 4-27.

Figure 4-27. *New Alert*

If you have already saved the job, you will see that the Execute Job check box is defaulted to on. That's because it is a part of this job, like it or not. If you haven't, it won't be assigned to a job yet, but will still be disabled. You also have the ability to notify operators, though, and this is key. For this step, to notify operators of the event being targeted, this must be checked and a user must be selected. You can check the Notify Operators box and click New Operator to add a new operator to the Operator area of SQL Server Agent. An example of this is shown in Figure 4-28.

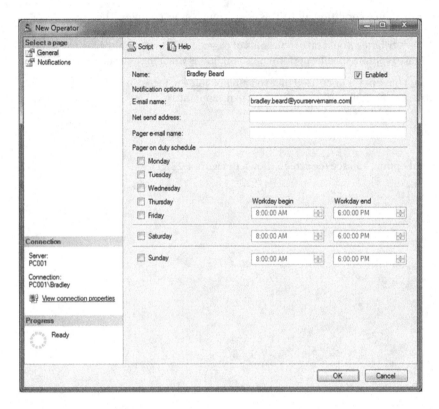

Figure 4-28. *New Operator*

Click OK at this screen. Notice that if you were to expand your server name, followed by SQL Server Agent, and then Operators, you would see the operator you specified in this area. Also note that you cannot delete an operator from this interface (within the Job Properties). If you need to delete an operator, it will need to be done from SSMS in the Operators section.

If you've already added an operator, we see that this operator is in the interface with a set of check boxes next to the name. The values are E-mail, Pager, and Net Send. If you've set a value for these options, then select them here (e-mail, at least). If you like, click View Operator and notice that there is another option on the left called History. Clicking that option reveals a new interface, as shown in Figure 4-29.

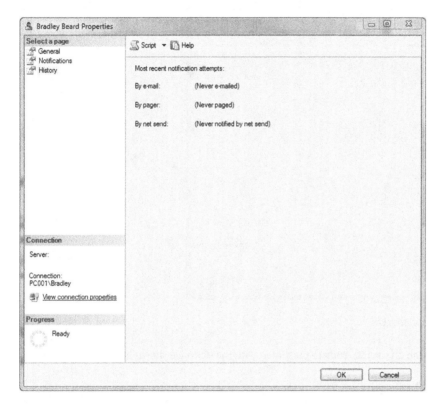

Figure 4-29. *New Operator, History tab*

Once there is data available for this job, that is, after it runs, then there will be data here. Since it has never run, it has no data. Click OK to go back to the New Alert interface.

You should now see where you left off; the Execute job option is disabled and no operators are selected, as shown in Figure 4-30.

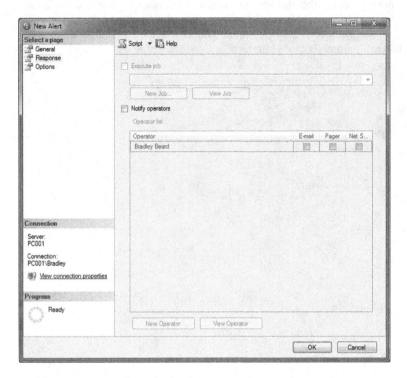

Figure 4-30. *New Alert, Response tab*

Next, click the Options tab on the left. You are presented with the interface shown in Figure 4-31.

Figure 4-31. *New Alert, Options tab (initial interface)*

This gives you the option to include the alert error text in e-mail, pager, or net send. You can specify any additional information here as well by entering it into the textbox. You can delay responses here as well. What is a delay response? Simply put, it's a sleep command for any additional occurrences of the same event within the specified time frame. Let's say that you didn't set this correctly and had the defaults set as we have them now. What that implies is that for every single targeted event that hits the database engine, an e-mail is created and sent to the operator listed. You can imagine that this would generate a ton of e-mail, and you would be correct. Setting a delay between responses—a time frame that SQL Server waits to respond to the next same event—takes care of this.

What does all this mean? Here is a good way to look at it.

When the specified alert happens, I want to notify this person via e-mail. I also want to add the text "I hope it's not a permanent error!" to the e-mail, so I'm going to add it here. I don't want to know about every single error of this type, just that this error occurred. I'm going to set a delay for this, so that even if the same event occurs that would normally trigger this event, I don't want the event to trigger this same job.

See how it works? An updated interface with suggested values is shown in Figure 4-32.

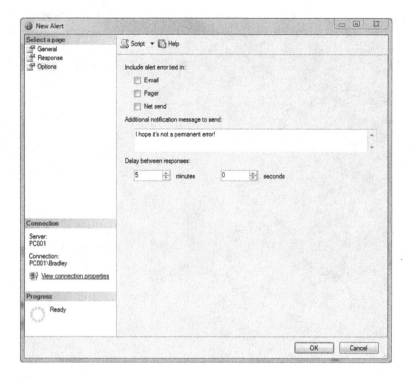

Figure 4-32. New Alert, Options tab (updated interface)

Now we can see that we are going to wait at least 5 minutes between e-mails.

We don't want to actually use these values, so just press Cancel to return to the Job Properties page. You should see a blank Alerts screen; we didn't want to set up any alerts here, remember. We did set up an operator, which is all we really needed out of this area. Yes, there are a few other ways to do it, but this way showed you around this area.

Notifications

Next is the Notifications tab, as shown in Figure 4-33. Notice that none of the options is checked and the drop-down values are defaulted.

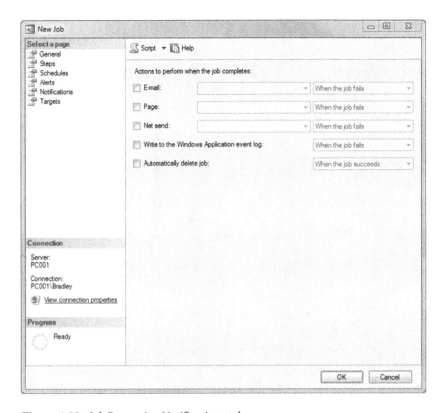

Figure 4-33. Job Properties, Notifications tab

This is where we actually get to define the database mail option we set up earlier. The following are the available contact options:

- E-mail

- Page

- Net Send

- Write to the Windows Application event log

- Automatically delete job

Any or all of these can be selected so that the users that need to be notified can be. I would usually suggest setting up a catchall e-mail for database issues, but that would ultimately depend on your setup and any security constraints. In any event, there really is no reason for this area to be left blank (besides e-mail being selected, since that's the point of this). For example, why wouldn't you want the job status to be written to the Windows event log?

This screen itself is pretty self-explanatory, as shown in Figure 4-34 with my recommended options and values.

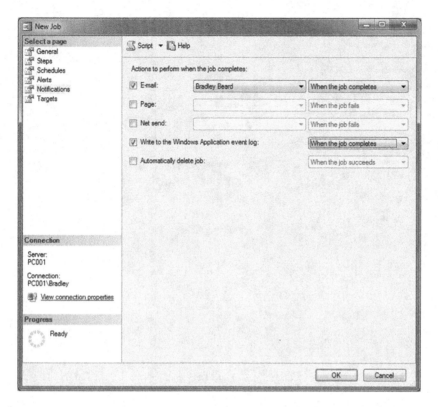

Figure 4-34. Job Properties, Notifications tab (updated)

■ **Tip** If you don't see your E-mail name in the box, save the job and open it again. Presto!

Note how my account name is in the e-mail field? That's because it was populated there from the Database Mail work we did earlier. Also notice that there are three different options for the drop-down menus: When the job succeeds, When the job fails, and When the job completes. Figure 4-35 illustrates this.

Figure 4-35. Job status meanings

What do these mean? What is the difference between them and which should I choose? The following heuristics will help answer these questions:

- If you want to know when a job completes successfully, choose "When the job succeeds"

- If you want to know when a job fails, choose "When the job fails"

- If you want to know that a job either succeeded or failed, choose "When the job completes"

That is literally the only difference between the options. The "completes" option is a catchall, where "succeeds" and "fails" are contingent on the pass or fail status of the job. Think of "completes" as an AND clause, and both "succeeds" and "fails" as OR clauses.

Targets

You can leave this screen defaulted to "Target local server". Click OK when you're done. The SQL Server Agent job is now set up!

■ **Note** This is a major chapter and there has been a lot of information. If you didn't get everything to work, then you really do need to go back and work it through again. If you've made it this far, don't give up now!

Test the new job to make sure it works. Right-click the job and choose Start Job at Step… to start it. Figure 4-36 shows what you should see at this point.

Figure 4-36. *Success!*

Success! Now, check your e-mail. Hey, look at that! You should have received an e-mail similar to what is shown in Figure 4-37.

```
JOB RUN:     'Email User Information' was run on 12/2/2015 at 2:09:26 PM
DURATION:    0 hours, 0 minutes, 0 seconds
STATUS       Succeeded
MESSAGES:      The job succeeded. The Job was invoked by User PC001\Bradley. The last step to run was step 1 (Run SQL Query)
```

Figure 4-37. *E-mail received*

There's something else that I need to add at this point... I set up the in an environment that did not have any contingencies for outside servers, so getting the connectivity was a piece of cake. In the real world, it will likely be much more complex, so I would suggest making sure that all your ducks are in a row before you start, so to speak. I went back and tried to get this to work using Gmail, and it effectively blew up in my face. There were a lot of settings that were specific to how Gmail operates that had to be set on Gmail's side. It is assumed that you will be working in a corporate environment of some type, and will have access to the SMTP information you need from a system or mail administrator. I will include a short and sweet guide to connecting to Gmail and using their SMTP service though.

Gmail's SMTP

This is actually a fairly convoluted process. There are very specific settings that you need to have set in order for Google to

- Allow access to their SMTP server
- Send e-mail through their SMTP server

Each of these items requires different steps to enable, and we will look at those in a minute. First, let's set up the new profile.

Setting Up a Profile

Double-click Database Mail from inside the Management folder in SSMS. You will see the interface shown in Figure 4-38.

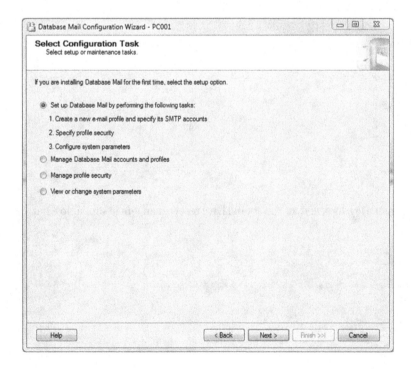

Figure 4-38. *Select Configuration Task*

This is the generic beginning screen, so choose the default option selected and click Next.

When you see the screen in Figure 4-39, enter **Gmail Profile** as the profile name, and something short and sweet for the description.

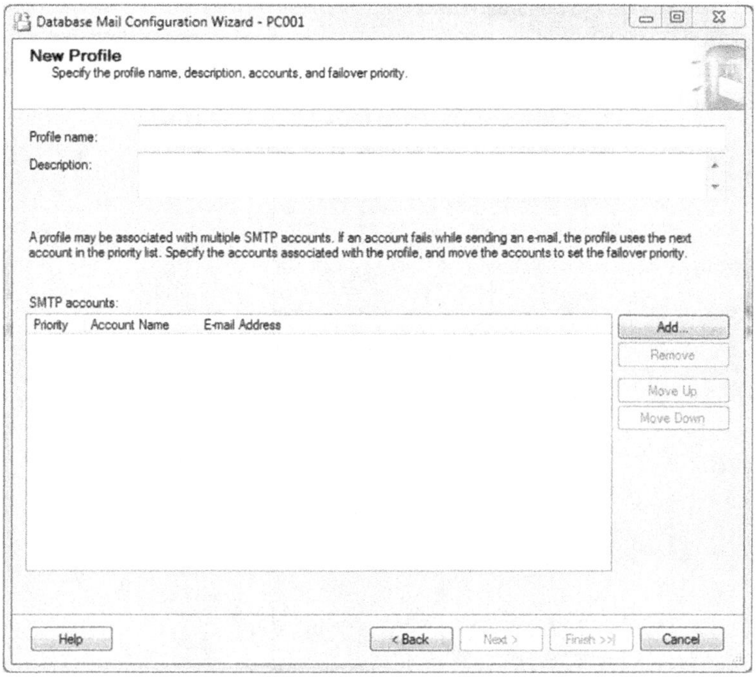

Figure 4-39. *New Profile*

Once you get that, click Add... to continue.

You should now see what is shown in Figure 4-40. Notice that our old profile is there. That's the other profile, not the new Gmail one.

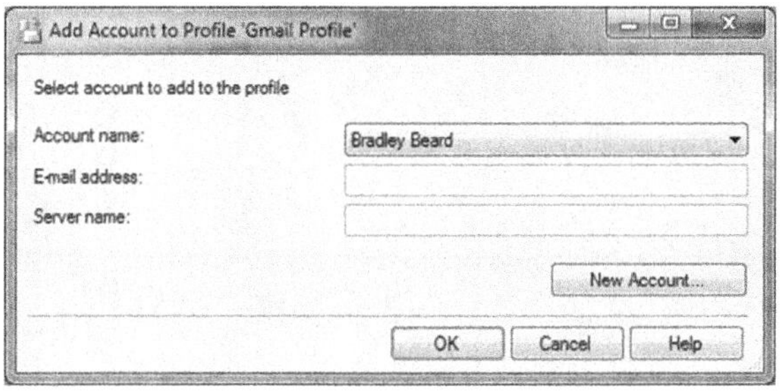

Figure 4-40. *Add Account to Profile*

Since we don't want to use this old profile because we are setting up a new profile, click the New Account... button. That will bring up the interface that you see in Figure 4-41.

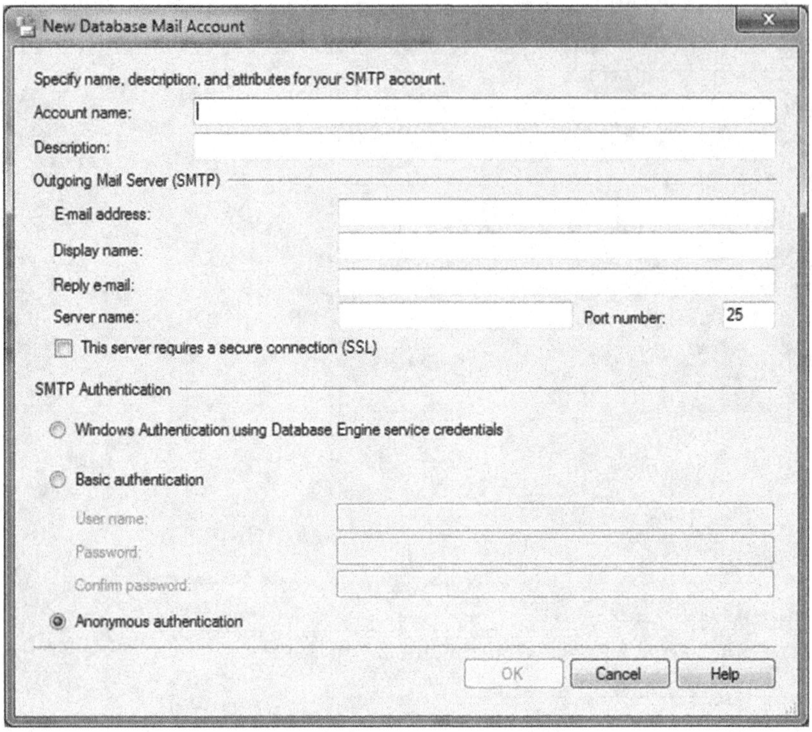

Figure 4-41. *New Database Mail Account*

This is exactly as we entered earlier, but now let's update that for the Gmail-specific settings. Complete your selections as shown in Figure 4-42.

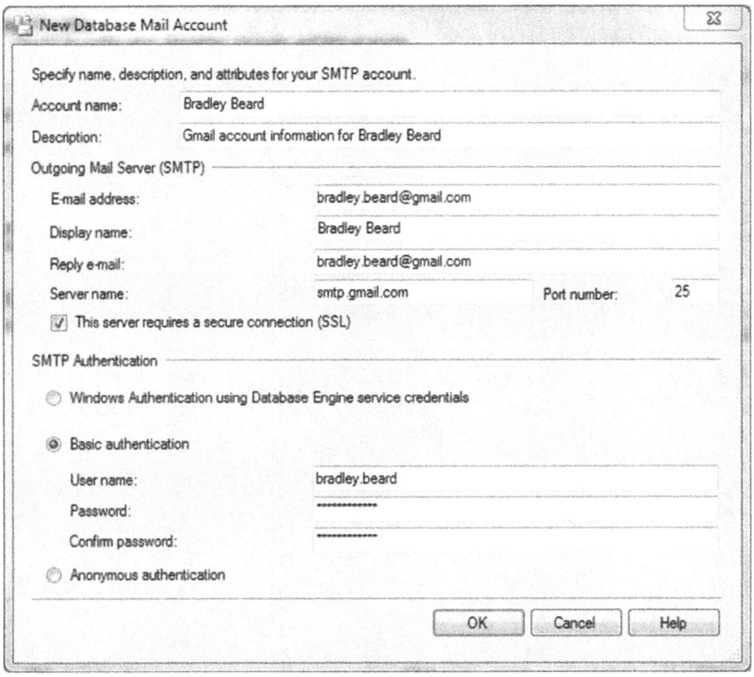

Figure 4-42. *New Database Mail Account (updated)*

The important bits are that the SSL check box needs to be selected and your account information needs to be correct, obviously. The SMTP server for Gmail is smtp.gmail.com and the port number is 25. Click OK when you're done. You will see the screen shown in Figure 4-43.

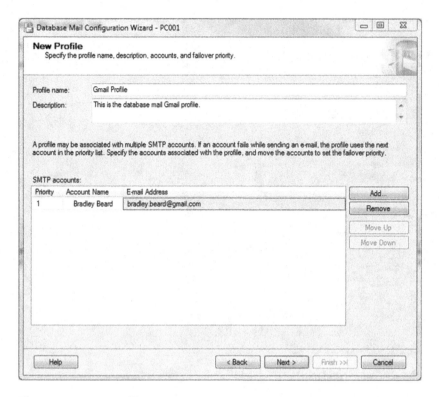

Figure 4-43. *New Profile*

Go ahead and click Next here. You will see the Manage Profile Security screen, as shown in Figure 4-44.

Figure 4-44. *Manage Profile Security*

Note that I have selected the Public check box. I also changed the Default Profile value to Yes. This is a pull-down menu, so pull it down and change the value. You don't need to go into the Private Profiles section, so don't worry about that. Click Next when you are ready to move on. You will see what is shown in Figure 4-45.

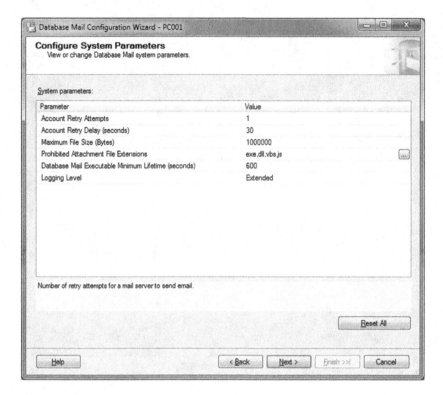

Figure 4-45. *Configure System Parameters*

This is the screen where you define the system parameters. Remember setting these options before? They're the same now, so leave them alone and click Next.

You will then see the Complete the Wizard screen, as shown in Figure 4-46.

Figure 4-46. *Complete the Wizard*

These settings are what we've done to this new profile, so go ahead and click Finish when you're done. You should see the green check boxes next, as shown in Figure 4-47.

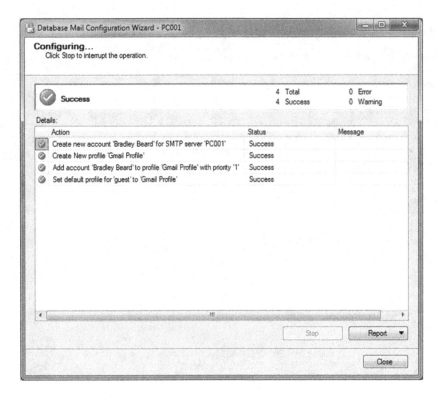

Figure 4-47. Configuring...

Testing E-mail Configuration

At this point, the first part is done. It probably won't work just yet. To test if it does, you can either manually send a test e-mail by right-clicking Database Mail and choosing Send Test E-Mail... or by using the following script.

```
EXEC msdb.dbo.sp_send_dbmail
@profile_name='Gmail Profile',
@recipients = 'bradley.beard@gmail.com',
@subject='This is only a test. We control the horizontal. We control the vertical.',
@body='Testing the Gmail profile'
```

This will send e-mail also. Either way you want to do it is fine. After you run it, check the Database Mail Log by right-clicking Database Mail and choosing View Database Mail Log. You will then see the screen shown in Figure 4-48.

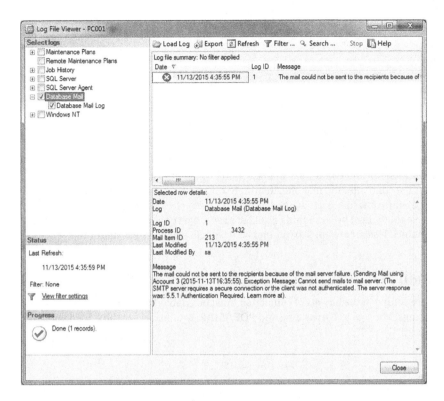

Figure 4-48. *Log File Viewer*

See that error? Let's look at that: "The mail could not be sent to the recipients because of the mail server failure. (Sending Mail using Account 3 (2015-11-13T16:35:55). Exception Message: Cannot send mails to mail server. (The SMTP server requires a secure connection or the client was not authenticated. The server response was: 5.5.1 Authentication Required. Learn more at)."

Interesting! The important part here is (and I can't stress this enough): *do not change anything yet.* Trust me. SQL Server is configured correctly. You have to finish setting up Google before anything is going to work.

Now, let's look at Google's settings.

Allowing Access to Google's SMTP Server

The first thing that we need to do is allow SQL Server to access Gmail's servers. This seems like it would be a trivial task, and it kind of is, but you need to change a few things on Google's side.

First off, log in to Google from your browser and go to `https://myaccount.google.com/security`. This is Google's main security page. You can handle just about any Google task from right here.

Once you get to this page, you want to look for a section labeled "Allow less secure apps". This is set to OFF by default. Just click the button and change it to ON, as shown in Figure 4-49.

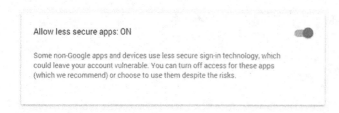

Figure 4-49. *Allow less secure apps*

Once that's done, go back to SSMS and check the Database Mail Log again. I only see one more error in there, which happened about 1 second after the first one. Remember how we set the interval to 5 minutes? We have to wait that amount of time now to see if it worked or not.

I don't see anything yet, so there must be something else! Let's see… we've set up the Database Mail task correctly (trust me), we've enabled less secure apps to interact with Google… what else is there?

Enabling POP E-mail

What else is there? An obscure setting in the bowels of Gmail that must be enabled, that's what. Open your Gmail account and go to Settings. Then go to Forwarding and POP/IMAP. You should see the screen shown in Figure 4-50.

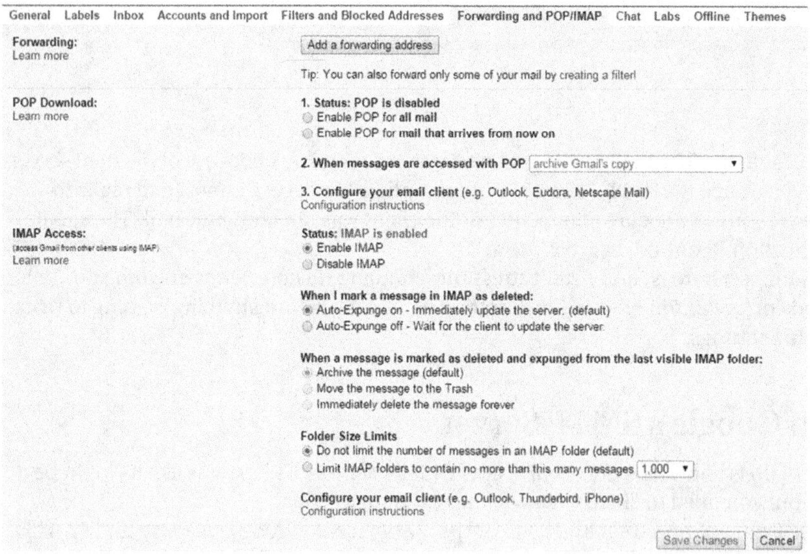

Figure 4-50. *Gmail settings*

See that bit there about POP? That's the stuff we need to look at next. Pop quiz: What is the difference between POP and SMTP? POP receives e-mail, whereas SMTP sends e-mail. So my settings say that POP is disabled, meaning I can't receive e-mail over POP. Change this to "Enable POP for all mail" and click Save Settings at the bottom of the screen. It takes a second to save, and then you go back to your inbox.

Go back to SSMS and send another test e-mail using the earlier script. Check your Gmail inbox. You should see what is shown in Figure 4-51.

This is only a test. We control the horizontal. We control the vertical.

Bradley Beard <bradley.beard@gmail.com>
to me ▾

Testing the Gmail profile

Figure 4-51. *Gmail received*

We can send test e-mails to Gmail now!

If you still have trouble connecting to Gmail from here, go back over this section again. I've read that the SSL port might need to be changed to 587 from 25, but my profile is set to 25 and it works just fine.

Summary

This was a *huge* chapter. If there's anything you didn't get, I strongly suggest rereading it again. There is a lot that can go wrong if everything isn't exact. I would much rather you took the time to understand exactly what we're doing so that you can see how the pieces all fit together, rather than get frustrated and quit halfway through because the concepts seem obscure or outside of your comfort zone. One of the reasons I wrote this book is to bring you out of your comfort zone, because you can never grow as a DBA if you aren't exposed to new concepts and ideas. How exciting to get the opportunity to learn more about the topics that will only serve to enhance your knowledge of a concept!

■ ■ ■

CHAPTER 5

Cleaning Up SQL Server Agent History

If you've been doing the exercises, you may have noticed that there is a lot of archival data, specifically in the realm of the history of the jobs. This can be both good and bad, depending on your point of view. It can be good because you want to know about the history of your jobs *if they fail.*

- If your job always succeeds, then you don't really need to know about it, except for your own edification.

- If your job always fails, then you *really* need to know about it to fix it.

A good way to think about this cleanup task is that this will unclutter the history of your jobs so that you will only see the information for the time period you specify. You can define any arbitrary time slice that you would like, but usually it's going to be something like three days. Only keep history for three days, in other words; otherwise, the history for a job will go on forever and not really give you anything.

The overall purpose of these exercises, if you remember, is to make your life easier. If I were your boss, you would be in deep trouble if you keep history, log everything, and you don't have any kind of cleanup tasks, but then come to me and ask for more storage because all your hard drives are full. Your next day would be spent reading this very book with a dunce cap on your head!

An important note for this chapter is that the task you learn here is about cleaning up SQL Server Agent's logs—and that's it. These aren't the .txt files generated by the maintenance plans; that is in Chapter 6. What this chapter's task does is clean out the logs that SQL Server Agent keeps regarding the status of the jobs. For many jobs, this can quickly grow to be a huge problem that is hard to sift through. Keeping it truncated to three days gives you plenty of time to look at any issues that may pop up, considering that you are checking your emails for any issues.

Setting Up the Maintenance Plan

Okay, down to business. This task is very easy to create. Go ahead and right-click the Maintenance Plans folder again from inside the Management folder, and select Maintenance Plan Wizard. The generic interface you are presented with in Figure 5-1 should be something you are familiar with by now.

Figure 5-1. *Select Plan Properties*

Update it to appear as shown in Figure 5-2.

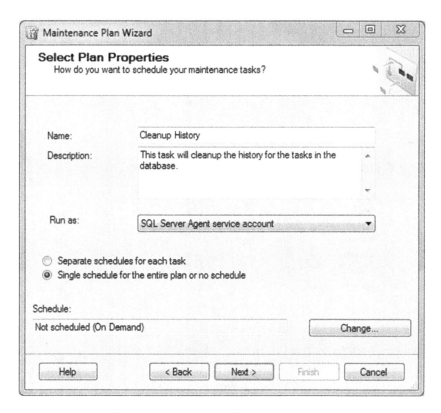

Figure 5-2. *Select Plan Properties (updated)*

That sets us up for the next section, which is …? That's right, the scheduling of the task. Remember, it makes no sense to have a task that isn't scheduled. That basically means that you intend to run the tasks manually, which completely defeats the purpose of using SQL Server Agent to automate these tasks for you.

Click the Change… button to set up the schedule. Initially, the schedule is incorrect, so let's change it to the settings shown in Figure 5-3.

Occurs: Daily

Occurs once at: 12:00:00 AM

You should see a result like that shown in Figure 5-3 when finished.

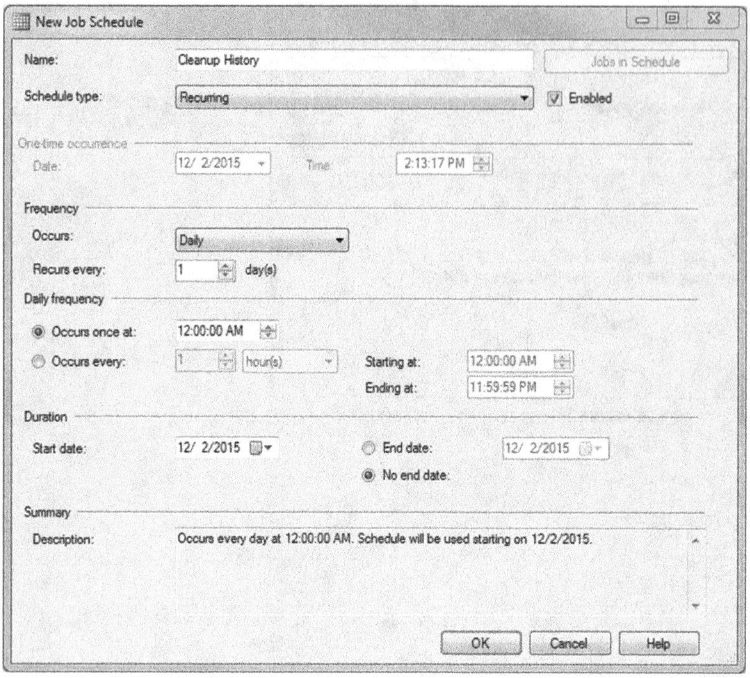

Figure 5-3. *New Job Schedule*

Told you this was easy. Click OK to move on. Notice that you go back to the screen you set the options on before, except now the schedule block is filled in. Click Next to continue.

Choosing Tasks

Now we actually have to set what we're going to do, because we didn't yet. Figure 5-4 shows the tasks that we are going to choose from.

Figure 5-4. Select Maintenance Tasks

Obviously, we're going to choose Clean Up History here and then click Next.

Figure 5-5 shows the next screen from which you choose the order for the tasks. Since we have just the one task, we can click Next here and move on. However, while we are here, you might want to look closer to see an interface error that, while humorous, can also cause you to lose work.

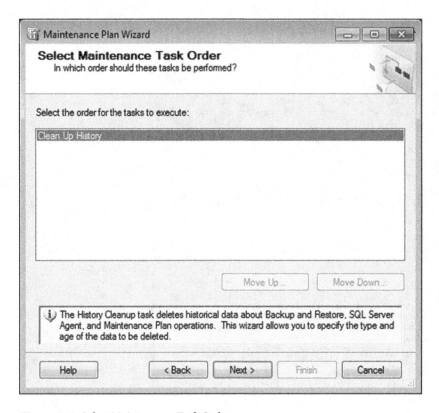

Figure 5-5. *Select Maintenance Task Order*

Are you seeing the screen in Figure 5-6 now? Click inside the area where the Clean Up History text appears. Notice that the Move Down… button becomes active.

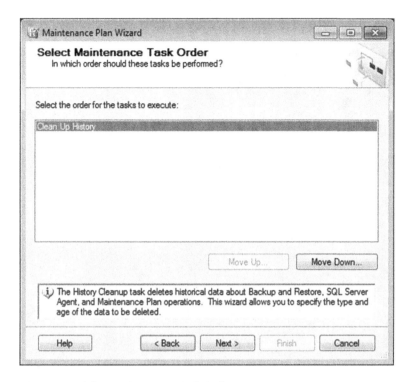

Figure 5-6. Select Maintenance Task Order

Weird. Go ahead and click the Move Down... button now. Nothing bad could happen, right? Figure 5-7 shows that something bad did indeed happen.

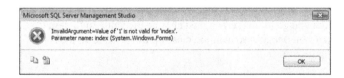

Figure 5-7. Error!

D'oh! Microsoft owes me a thank-you for debugging their interface! I expect to see this fixed in future versions of SSMS.

When you see the Define History Cleanup Task screen, you are ready to continue.

Define What to Clean

The next piece of the puzzle is to define what we want to clean up and how often, as shown in Figure 5-8.

Figure 5-8. *Define History Cleanup Task*

Initially, Figure 5-8 shows what you see when you go to this screen. Just change the value to "3 days" and you're good to go. Leave the three check boxes on because we want to cleanup those three areas. Your updated interface should appear as shown in Figure 5-9.

Figure 5-9. *Define History Cleanup Task (updated)*

Click Next when you're ready to continue.

The next screen gives you reporting options. You can write a report, email the report, or both. I suggest both in case you don't have access to either option. If you're going to use the text file option, make sure that you choose a folder location that is set up specifically for storing log files. I typically tend to use the folder structure that I described in Chapter 1, and point all the maintenance logs to the Backup folder; this means that transaction logs are the only logs that go in the Logs folder.

If you're going to choose to email the report, click the check box and select the operator that we set up back in the database mail discussion in Chapter 4.

Your interface should now resemble Figure 5-10, with your values in place of mine.

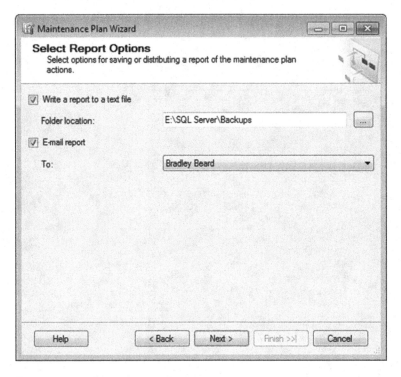

Figure 5-10. *Select Report Options*

Review

Click Next and get ready to finish this task. You will see the summary of what we've done so far in this task. Expand everything. You should see the information displayed in Figure 5-11.

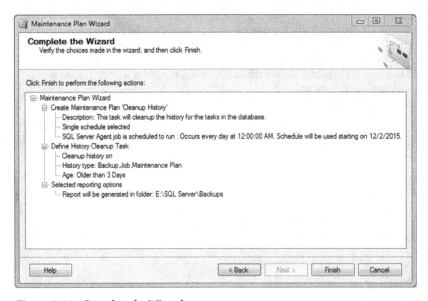

Figure 5-11. *Complete the Wizard*

To review, just run over the actions listed in the Complete the Wizard screen and make sure that everything is how you need it to be. If it isn't, just click the Back button and fix whatever you need to. When you're ready to implement, click Finish. You should see what is shown in Figure 5-12.

Figure 5-12. *Maintenance Plan Wizard Progress*

Have I mentioned how much I love the green check boxes? They tell us that everything checked out okay and that the maintenance plan has been added to the maintenance plan subsystem to be executed by SQL Server Agent on the set schedule.

Remember to change the default name of the Job now! Double-click the job name in the Jobs folder in SQL Server Agent and change it to something memorable. If you recall, we named the maintenance plan Cleanup History, so I named the job Cleanup History as well. The full name is now Cleanup History, as shown in Figure 5-13.

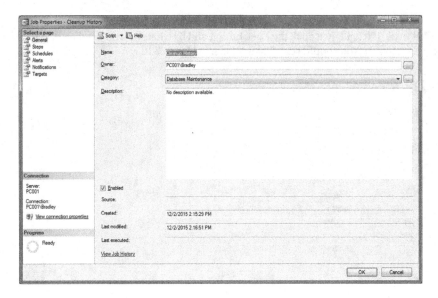

***Figure 5-13.** Job Properties*

Remember to set up the rest of the options in this Properties area as we did earlier. Your Jobs folder should now look like Figure 5-14.

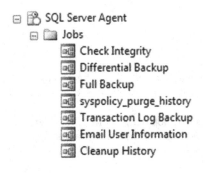

***Figure 5-14.** SQL Server Agent Jobs*

Your Maintenance Plans folder should now look like Figure 5-15.

- ⊟ 📁 Maintenance Plans
    - 📜 Backup Maintenance Plan
    - 📜 Database Integrity Plan
    - 📜 Cleanup History

***Figure 5-15.** Maintenance Plans*

Summary

Five chapters and three maintenance plans down so far. Notice that we didn't create a maintenance plan for the SQL Server Agent Job chapter. That is by design. We didn't want a maintenance plan for it because I just wanted to show how to create the job independent of the maintenance plan. In other words, there is a definite separation between the job and the maintenance plan, which you should recognize by now.

CHAPTER 6

███

Cleaning Up Maintenance Files

Very similar to the content of Chapter 5 is the topic of maintenance cleanup tasks. History and maintenance tasks probably could have been tied together, but I can understand why they are separate.

Separation of History from Maintenance

Why are cleanup tasks separate for history and maintenance? Let's look at the differences between the two tasks. Figure 6-1 highlights some of the key differences to be aware of.

Maintenance Cleanup Task

- The Maintenance Cleanup task removes physical files left over from executing a maintenance plan.
- These files, typically, are .bak and .trn files.

History Cleanup Task

- The History Cleanup task deletes historical data about Backup and Restore, SQL Server Agent, and Maintenance Plan operations. This wizard allows you to specify the type and age of the data to be deleted.
- These files make up the SQL Server Agent historical reference to the maintenance tasks.

Figure 6-1. *Differences between Maintenance and History Cleanup Tasks*

What do these differences mean in layman's terms? Here is what you need to know:

- The Maintenance Cleanup Task cleans up the physical files left after executing a maintenance plan. When you view the file system where you are logging the maintenance plan steps, you will likely see quite a few files. These files are deleted when the Maintenance Cleanup Task is run (subject to the period of time specified).

- The Maintenance Cleanup task cleans up the .bak and .trn files in the file system, but you need to have two separate maintenance plans for each file type, since we have our file system set up like I do (meaning that we are storing the .bak files physically separate from the .trn files).

- The History Cleanup Task cleans up history in the tasks themselves, and not the physical files. When you right-click a job and select View History, that history goes away when the History Cleanup Task is run (subject to the period of time specified) because these rows are removed from the msdb database.

© Bradley Beard 2016
B. Beard, *Practical Maintenance Plans in SQL Server*, DOI 10.1007/978-1-4842-1895-2_6

Now that we understand the difference between the two types of cleanup tasks, let's look at setting up the Maintenance Cleanup Task.

Setting Up the Maintenance Plan

Remember that we need three separate tasks for this: one for the .bak files, one for the .trn files, and one for the .txt files. Why? Because SQL Server makes you choose a file extension to look for and delete if it is beyond a certain age, and database backups (.bak) and transaction log backups (.trn) are both physically and logically different.

We are going to name these plans Backups Cleanup, Logs Cleanup, and Text Files Cleanup. This should keep it nice and clean for us to easily see what goes where.

We are going to set up Backups Cleanup first, followed by Logs Cleanup, and finally Text Files Cleanup. Remember that if something goes wrong with your maintenance tasks, the .txt files referenced in the Text Files Cleanup task are a great place to start troubleshooting.

Backups Cleanup

The purpose of cleaning up backups is fairly simple: you don't want to have multiple copies of a large database in a file system, keeping space from other applications or operating system functions that may need the space. For this reason, it is far easier to configure a default retention period and clean the backups automatically based on that retention period. The Backups Cleanup task allows us to create an automatic method to clean up these backups files.

Right-click the Maintenance Plans folder under Management and choose Maintenance Plan Wizard to get started. Enter **Backups Cleanup** as the Name, and something short and sweet in the Description box, and then click the Change... button to set the schedule. Change the Occurs drop-down to Daily but leave the rest alone, and then click OK. Your interface should resemble Figure 6-2.

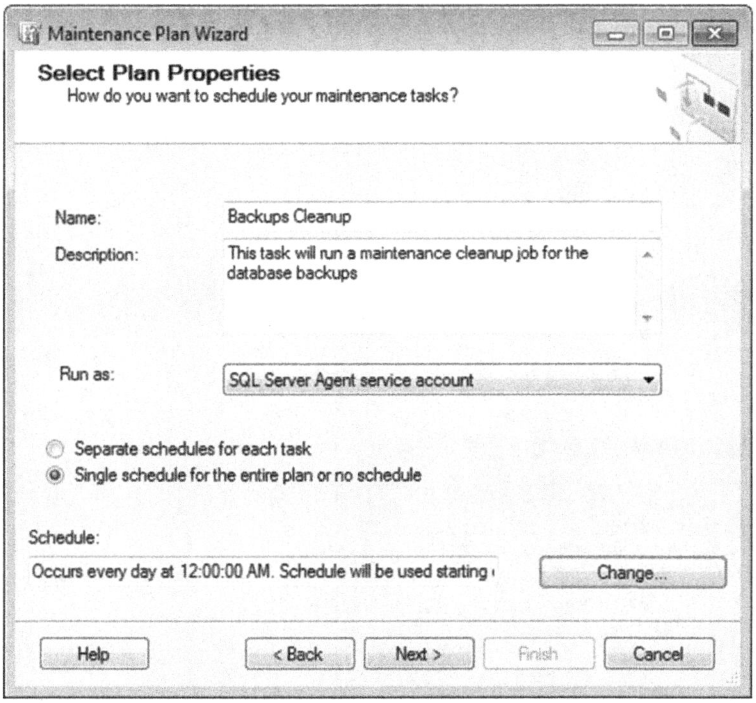

Figure 6-2. *Select Plan Properties*

Good start. So, just like before, we've given it a good Name and Description, left Run As set to the default, and set the schedule to fire at midnight every night. Click Next and let's set up the next part, as shown in Figure 6-3.

Figure 6-3. *Select Maintenance Tasks*

Obviously, you're going to choose Maintenance Cleanup Task here and then click Next. You will then see the interface shown in Figure 6-4.

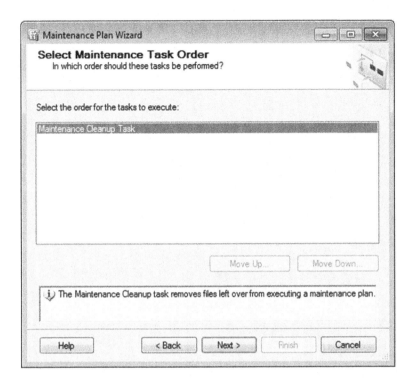

Figure 6-4. *Select Maintenance Task Order*

You can stop and generate the interface error, as we did in Chapter 4, but you need to start over if you do. Click Next when you're ready.

The next screen is the meat and potatoes of this task. If you're vegetarian, it's the tofu and kale. Either way, the initial interface appears as shown in Figure 6-5.

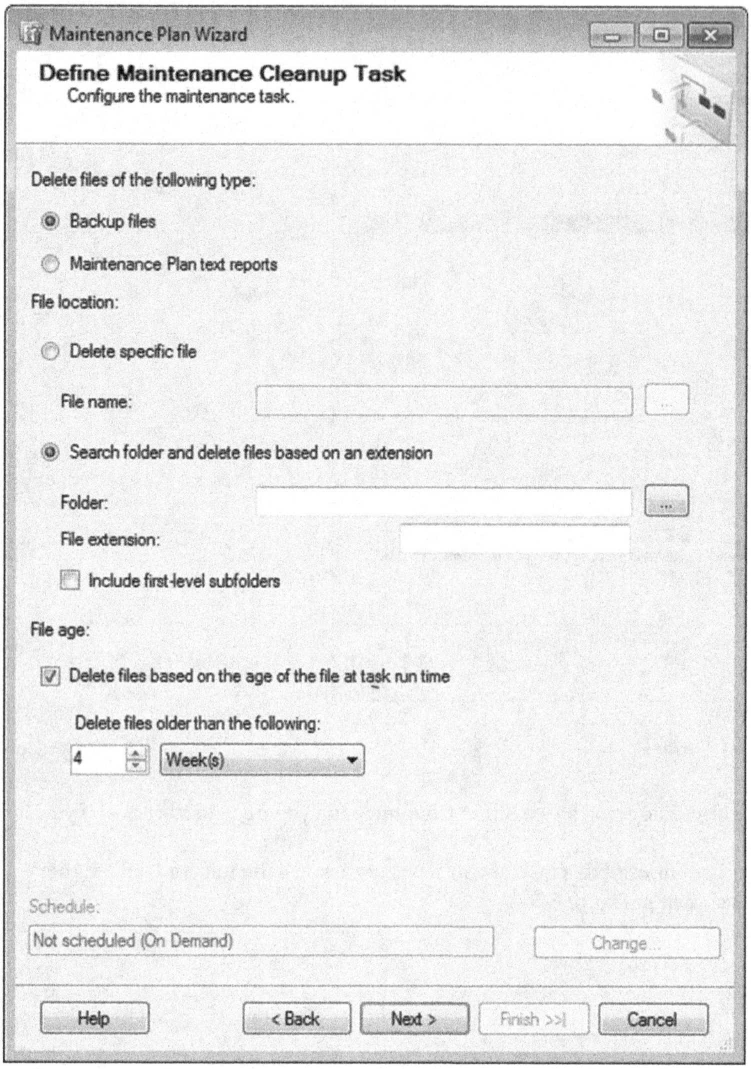

Figure 6-5. *Define Maintenance Cleanup Task*

The first thing you notice is that there is a radio option at the top of the screen that gives you two options: "Backup files" and "Maintenance Plan text reports". Does this imply that you can't do both at the same time in the same task? In a word, yes. If you want to do both, you need to set two maintenance plans or jobs for each type of file that you want deleted. The reason for this is because in one area, you are deleting the actual backups of the database, and in the other, you are deleting the text reports for the maintenance plan operations. They're different cleanup tasks, in other words, and behave differently. I would like to see Microsoft split these up into two separate tasks in future versions of SQL Server, but I won't hold my breath.

For now, let's concentrate on the "Backup files" option. The "Maintenance Plan text reports" options are next.

Deleting Backup Files

You have the option to delete the actual database backup files. Note that if you have the backup schedule in place as described in Chapter 1, then you are running a full backup, followed by a differential backup, and then by transaction log backups. With this in mind, if you were to implement this solution, you would only retain backups for a certain period of time. But the kicker is this: *there is no difference, from a file system point of view, between full and differential backups*. Read that part again. There is no difference, because they both have the .bak file extension by default. So, if you delete the full backup, but not the differential, you will not be able to restore the differential, because it depends on the full backup to restore. Without it, it cannot restore the data to the database and it is, in essence, completely useless.

▪ **Tip** Obviously, any time you delete data, it should be done very carefully. Please take the time to go through this thoroughly to alleviate any future headaches from accidentally deleting a backup that you may need.

Okay, so referring to Figure 6-5, make sure that "Backup files" is selected. The area under that, "File location", determines if you want to delete a specific file or all the files in a folder with a certain extension. Although this sounds cut and dried, let's look at the two options presented.

Deleting a Specific File

Let's say that you have set up your logging to "Save all to the same file". I can't imagine why you would want to do this, but let's say that you have a valid reason. This option finds and deletes a specified file in a specific location. Does that make sense? It will not traverse directories to find the file; it will only delete the file specified.

Searching and Deleting Based on Extension

Much like the backup options, this option lets you delete all the files in a specific location, including the first-level subfolders. Why the first-level subfolders? Because this option was presented when you set up the backup section way back in Chapter 1, and they want you to be able to properly manage your backups. It wouldn't make much sense to let you write backups to a directory, and then not give you the power to manage the backups in that directory.

With those two nuggets of wisdom in mind, we are going to leave the default of "Search folder and delete files based on an extension" selected, and make sure to check the "Include first-level subfolders" as well. The default file extension should still be set to bak. The folder location needs to be set to where you defined the backups to be stored. This same location is where we are going to search for backup files and delete them based on the age of the backup. Figure 6-6 should be what you see at this point.

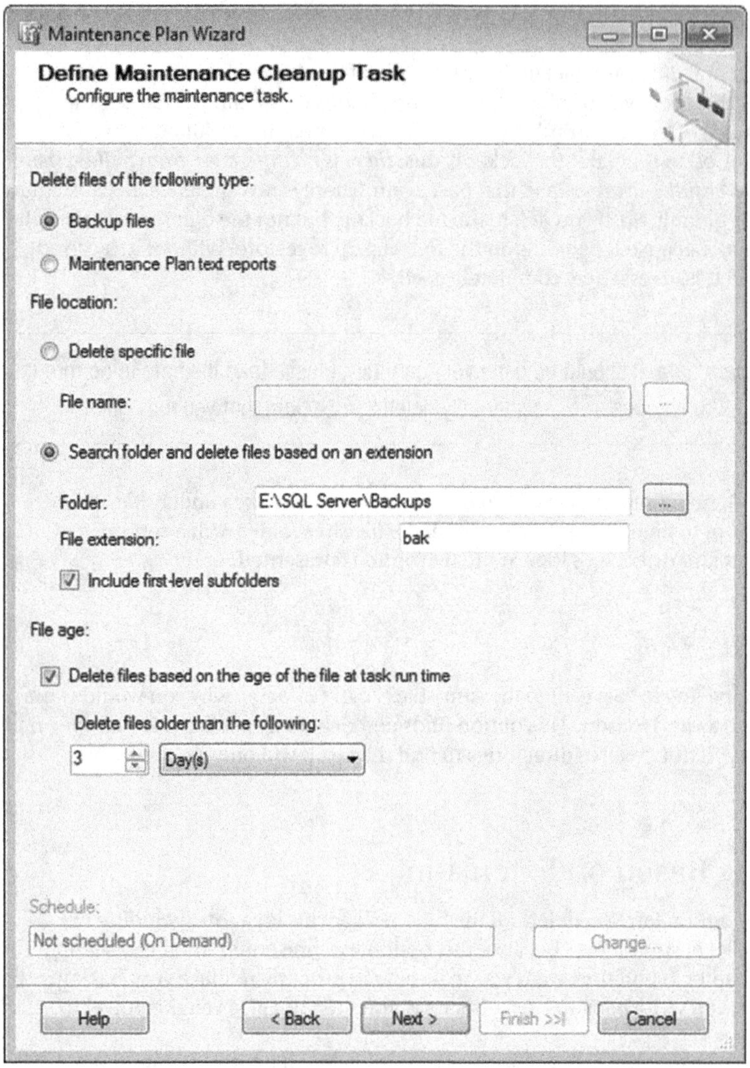

Figure 6-6. Define Maintenance Cleanup Task (completed)

The last bit is the "File age" part. You want to leave the "Delete files based on the age of the file at task run time" check box selected. The standard that I try to stick to is three days of file retention, so update the selections to match this or whatever your requirements are.

Be careful about this area. As I said before, this needs to be taken very seriously. You can't undo a file deletion at this level. Be absolutely sure that you realize the implications of deleting these files. Once you make your selections, click Next to move on.

Once again, you are met with the option to either "Write a report to a text file" or to "E-mail report". I recommend selecting both options; that way, you are aware of what is happening to your database as it happens. Make the changes you see in Figure 6-7, substituting your operator in the e-mail step.

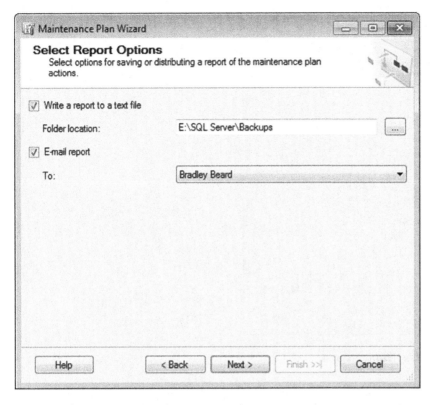

Figure 6-7. Select Report Options

Click Next here and you will be shown the Summary page. Again, this is where you need to make absolutely sure that these settings are correct. Figure 6-8 shows what my Summary looks like.

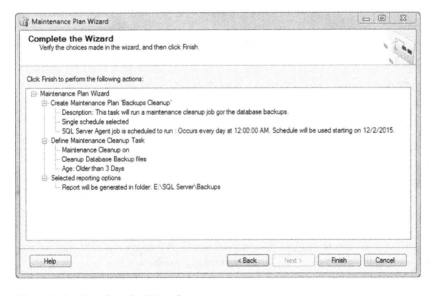

Figure 6-8. Complete the Wizard

Click Finish when you're ready. Hopefully, you see the green boxes shown in Figure 6-9.

Figure 6-9. *Maintenance Plan Wizard Progress*

I see all green check boxes. Very good!

Make sure that you update the job using the techniques from earlier chapters by double-clicking the job in the Jobs folder under SQL Server Agent. I changed mine to bak Files, but you can pick another name if you want. After you update it, your interface should look something like Figure 6-10.

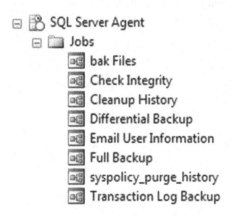

Figure 6-10. *SQL Server Agent Jobs*

Next, we need to re-create the same job, but for .trn files (transaction log backups). Basically, this next part is going to be a cut-and-paste of the previous information, but updated for the .trn files.

Logs Cleanup

Much like before, the Logs Cleanup task is going to allow us to delete the .trn files present in the file system. Why do this? Aren't the transaction log backups important? Yes, they are. But they are only relevant as long as they relate to a current backup set. Recall that backed up transaction logs can only be restored to a differential backup. Well, if the differential or the full backup file has been deleted, then there is no reason to keep the transaction logs for that backup. That's what this task gives us: the flexibility to delete the transaction logs that just aren't needed anymore.

Begin the same as before. Right-click the Maintenance Plans folder under Management and choose Maintenance Plan Wizard. Enter **Logs Cleanup** as the Name, and something short and sweet in the Description box, and then click the Change... button to set the schedule. Change the Occurs drop-down to Daily and leave the rest alone, and then click OK. Your interface should resemble Figure 6-11.

Figure 6-11. *Select Plan Properties*

Good start. So, just like before, we've provided a good Name and Description, left Run As set to the default, and set the schedule to fire at midnight every night. Click Next. Now let's set up the next part, as shown in Figure 6-12.

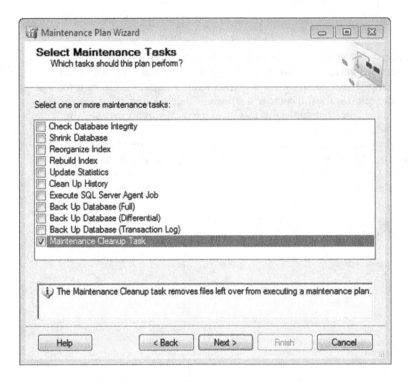

Figure 6-12. *Select Maintenance Tasks*

Choose Maintenance Cleanup Task here and then click Next. You will then see the interface shown in Figure 6-13.

Figure 6-13. *Select Maintenance Task Order*

Click Next when you're ready and you should see what is shown in Figure 6-14.

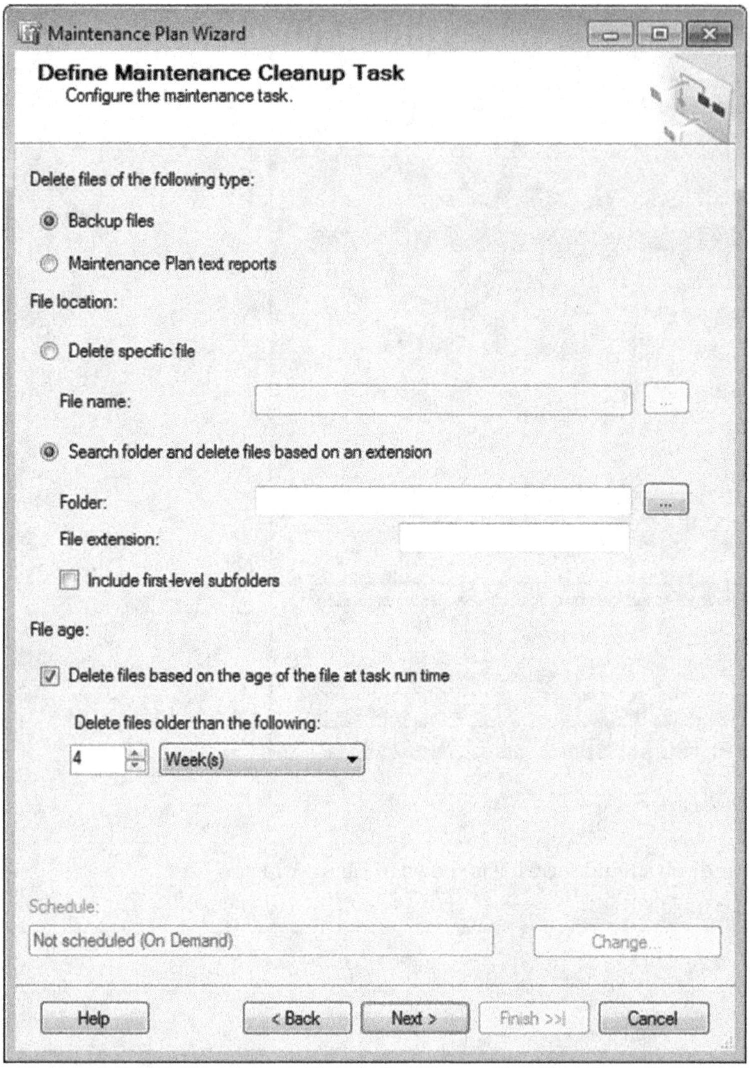

Figure 6-14. *Define Maintenance Cleanup Task*

Choose the "Backup files" option here. Choose your transaction log location and enter **trn** in the "File extension" field. Notice that we have selected our logs location this time, because this is where the transaction logs are being stored.

Figure 6-15 should be what you see at this point.

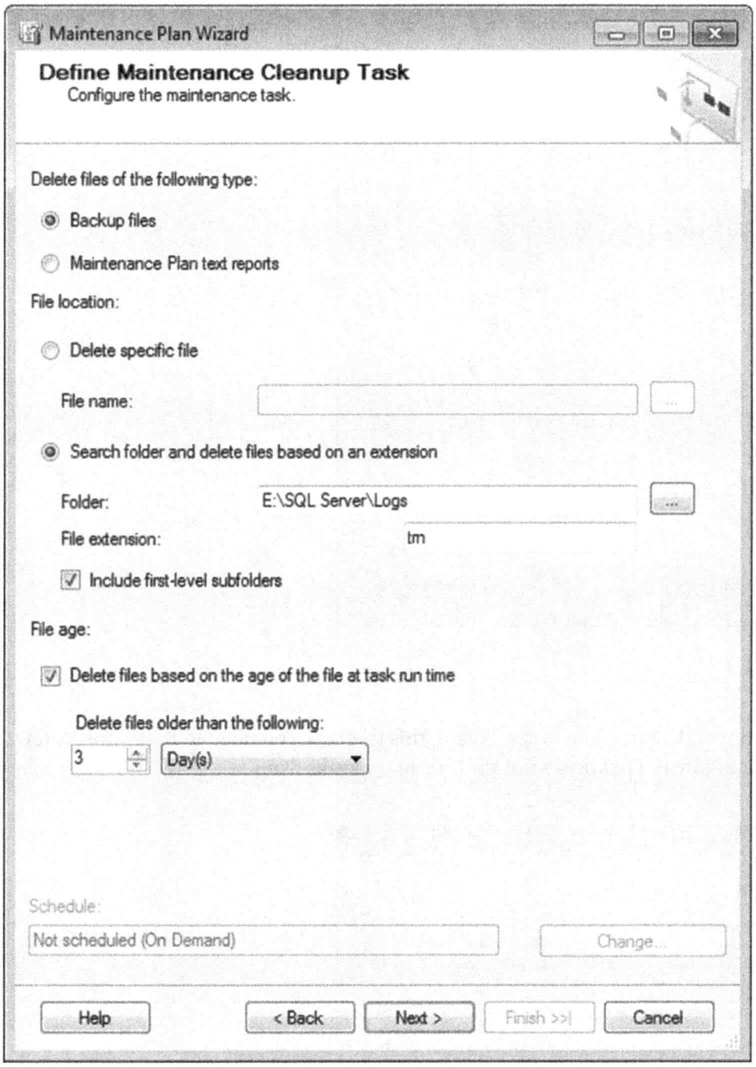

Figure 6-15. Define Maintenance Cleanup Task (completed)

Notice that we've selected 3 Days; the same as with the .bak option. The reason for this is that you won't be able to restore a transaction log without the corresponding differential backup, so we're going to delete all of the files by day so that we are always in sync. You want to leave the "Delete files based on the age of the file at task run time" check box selected. Click Next at this point.

Once again, you are met with the option to either "Write a report to a text file" or to "E-mail report". I recommend selecting both options; that way, you are aware of what is happening to your database as it happens. Make the changes that you see in Figure 6-16, substituting your operator in the e-mail step.

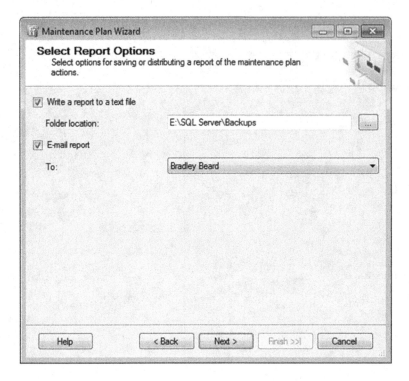

Figure 6-16. *Select Report Options*

Click Next here. You will be shown the Summary page. Again, this is where you need to make absolutely sure that these settings are correct. Figure 6-17 shows what my Summary looks like.

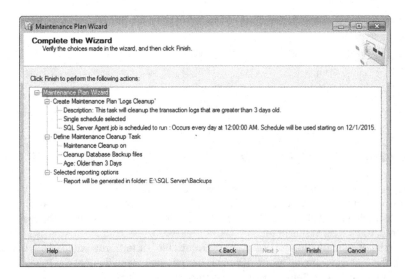

Figure 6-17. *Complete the Wizard*

Click Finish when you're ready. Figure 6-18 shows what you should expect to see at this point.

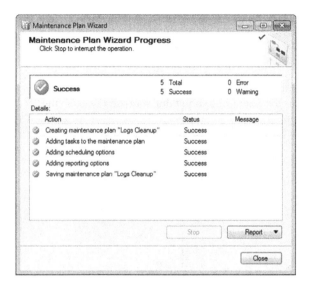

Figure 6-18. *Maintenance Plan Wizard Progress*

When you see only green check boxes, you have successfully configured this part of the maintenance plan. Excellent work so far!

Make sure that you update the job by double-clicking the job in the Jobs folder under SQL Server Agent. I changed the name of mine to trn Files, but you can pick another name if you want. After you change it, your interface should look something like Figure 6-19.

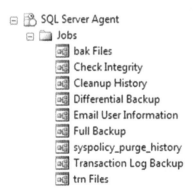

Figure 6-19. *SQL Server Agent Jobs*

Do you remember that we created two sections in the maintenance plan to delete files? The first part was Backup Files, which let us delete .bak files. The second part was Logs Cleanup, which let us delete .trn files. The next part is to clean up the text files left over by the backup operation.

Text Files Cleanup

When SQL Server runs maintenance operations using SQL Server Agent, it creates text reports for troubleshooting or general light reading. The Text Files Cleanup operation we're going to set up will allow us to clean those files out after a certain amount of time. This is fine because a well-maintained database alerts a database administrator when there is trouble, which is the only real purpose of holding on to the maintenance text files generated by the tasks.

Starting fresh again, just right-click the Maintenance Plans folder under Management and choose Maintenance Plan Wizard. Enter **Text Files Cleanup** as the Name, and something short and sweet in the Description box, and then click the Change... button to set the schedule. Change the Occurs drop-down to Daily and leave the rest alone, and then click OK. Your interface should resemble Figure 6-20.

Figure 6-20. *Select Plan Properties*

Click Next at this screen. You can choose Maintenance Cleanup Task from the interface, as shown in Figure 6-21.

Figure 6-21. *Select Maintenance Tasks*

Choose Maintenance Cleanup Task here and then click Next. You will then see the interface shown in Figure 6-22.

Figure 6-22. *Select Maintenance Task Order*

Click Next here, since we only have the one task.

Previously, we chose Backup files. This time, we're going to choose Maintenance Plan text reports. This is because we needed to set up a different task to delete different types of files, if you recall.

We are going to set this to point at our Backups directory, because that's where we saved the maintenance plan text reports. These were stored as .txt files (defined back in Chapter 2 for report options). Your completed interface should look like Figure 6-23 when you are finished.

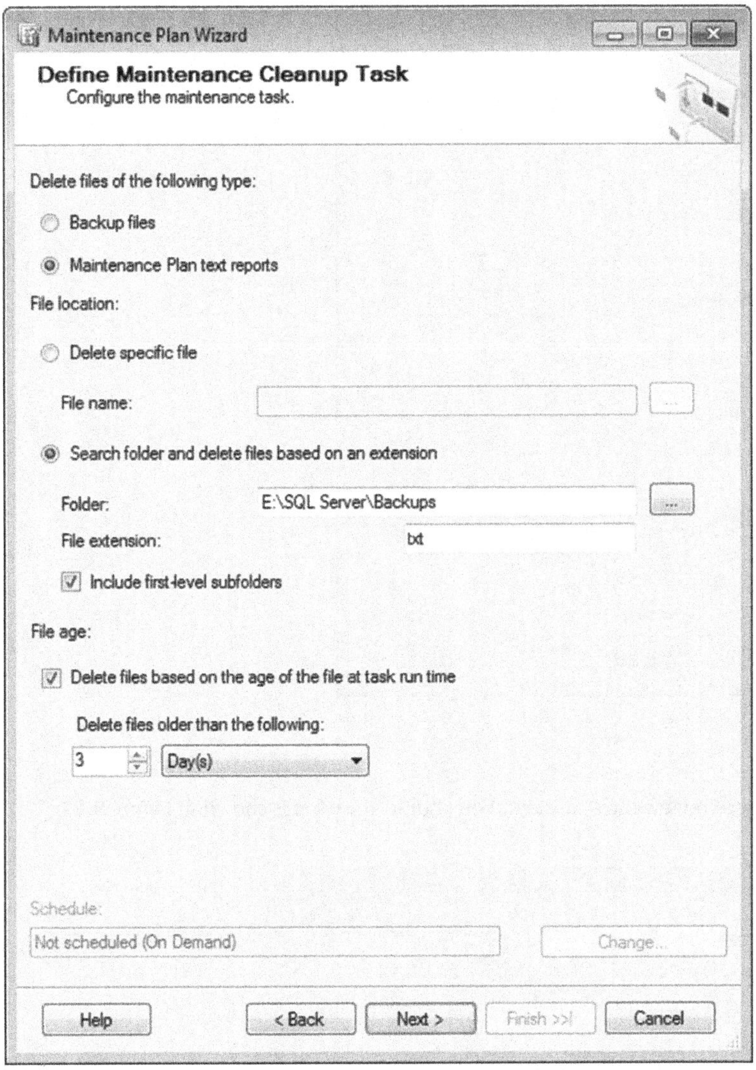

Figure 6-23. *Define Maintenance Cleanup Task*

Going through the options, you can see that the folder is defined to our Backups location, and the .txt file extension specified. Remember that this is the default extension for text reports generated by SQL Server. Also note that I changed the time selection to three days instead of four weeks. What does this mean? It means that I want to delete all .txt files in the E:\SQL Server\Backups directory and those files in the first-level subdirectories that are older than three days when the task is run.

Click Next when you are ready and you will see the Select Report Options interface shown in Figure 6-24. Modify it as we did before (to write the detail log to our Backups directory) and alert us by email.

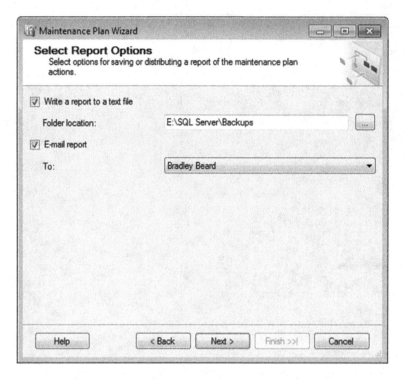

Figure 6-24. *Select Report Options*

Once you see this, click Next and review the summary. You should see what is shown in Figure 6-25.

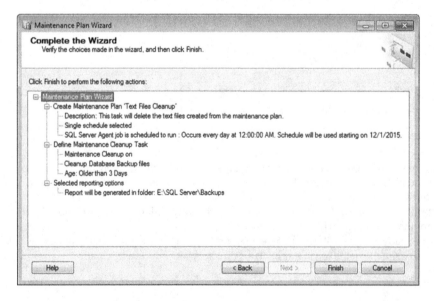

Figure 6-25. *Complete the Wizard*

Go over these options carefully. Everything looks good, so click Finish again. You should (hopefully) see what is shown in Figure 6-26.

Figure 6-26. *Maintenance Plan Wizard Progress*

It's a thing of *beauty*.

Again, make sure that you change the job name as described earlier—and update the job while you're at it. I named mine `txt Files`. It's up to you what you want to name yours, as long as it is easily recognizable. When you are finished, you should see the Jobs layout shown in Figure 6-27.

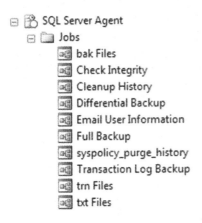

Figure 6-27. *SQL Server Agent Jobs*

Your Maintenance Plans folder should appear as shown in Figure 6-28.

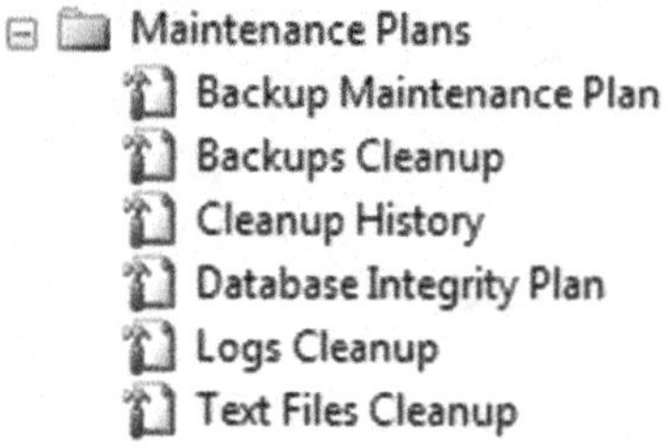

□ 📁 Maintenance Plans
 📄 Backup Maintenance Plan
 📄 Backups Cleanup
 📄 Cleanup History
 📄 Database Integrity Plan
 📄 Logs Cleanup
 📄 Text Files Cleanup

Figure 6-28. *Maintenance Plans*

This all looks really good so far. Notice how we have separated each task into its own maintenance plan or task. This is going to be important in later chapters.

Let's review what we did in this chapter, because this was perhaps the one chapter that could really screw up your database.

Summary

We learned that there are two different types of maintenance cleanup tasks that can be run: one that cleans up the files necessary for restoring data to the database (.bak and .trn files), and one for the maintenance plan text reports (.txt files). We also created three maintenance plans: Backups Cleanup (which deleted the .bak files), Logs Cleanup (which deleted the .trn files), and Text Files Cleanup (which deleted the .txt files). These three maintenance plans are going to be run separately and will delete the files specified by the individual plan.

If any part of this chapter is unclear, I urge you to go back and redo the exercises so that you can really get a grasp of what is going on and why. I want to take a moment again to stress how important it is to understand *exactly* what is being backed up and deleted, and why. It makes no sense to have a backup plan that constantly fails, so if you see failures in yours, troubleshoot them until you find the issue. Work to resolve them as soon as possible, because if you can't restore the data that you've been entrusted to protect, you are pretty much redundant. This concept is absolutely vital to the success of any database administrator.

■ **Tip** Theory is important, but unless it's put in practice, it is almost useless.

■ ■ ■

CHAPTER 7

Rebuilding Indexes

What is an *index* and why does it need to be rebuilt? An index is what SQL Server uses to retrieve rows from a table. The obvious similarity is to the index of a book; if you need to know about a certain topic, flip to the back and check the index. It tells you right where to find exactly what you're looking for.

You can have a table without an index defined. In this case, it's just a heap of data, so it's termed a *heap table*. Storing data as a heap isn't very efficient, as the entire table must be scanned in order to return the data you are requesting in a query. Instead, when you use indexes, the data is retrieved much quicker and more efficiently.

If you have a small database, is it worth it to create an index on a table? In short, yes. It is always worth it, because databases often tend to grow. When the administrative work is done at the beginning, it doesn't need to be done later. And when you define indexes early on, and then set up a maintenance task to automatically rebuild those indexes, you are coming out *way* ahead of the game, because over time, the indexes start to "drift." They may reference obsolete data, or large parts of the pages may be missing. Rebuilding the indexes makes sure that these things don't happen, because they are all organized (which, if you ask my wife, is not my greatest strength).

For the first part of this chapter, I am going to go briefly into indexes in SQL Server. I say *briefly* because there isn't enough room in this book to explain every single concept, so I'm going to assume that you have at least heard of indexes. Then in the second part of this chapter, we will actually get to the maintenance task to use to maintain your indexes.

Indexes Explained

Maybe you don't really know or understand what indexes are or how they work. Believe it or not, that's okay! Not long term, but the first step is realization, right? More than likely, if you're not very familiar with indexes, then you're either a new database administrator or a seasoned DBA that just hasn't had the time or inclination to get into the weeds of how indexes work.

The best way that I can think of to describe indexes is to say that they are ways that SQL Server can access table data quickly by assuming certain things about how the data is accessed. You can have zero indexes on a table; that is completely acceptable. Not efficient at all, but acceptable. Think if you wanted to search for a certain word or phrase in this book, a standalone word like *interface*. I've said that word a lot, right? Can you imagine going through every page of this book just to find the locations where the word "interface" was used? That would take a long time! Imagine instead if you had an index that told you exactly where you could find these occurrences. That's what indexes do for your database.

© Bradley Beard 2016
B. Beard, *Practical Maintenance Plans in SQL Server*, DOI 10.1007/978-1-4842-1895-2_7

From this point on, there are two things about every single reader. Every one of you will fall into one of these two categories:

- You already have indexes on your tables. You also need to manage them, either willingly or reluctantly.

- You don't currently have indexes, but recognize a need for them.

That's it. Either you have them and want to manage them, or you don't and want to implement them. For the rest of this section, I'm going to work from the assumption that you don't currently have indexes. Skip ahead if you are solid in your understanding of indexes and how they work.

Beginning Indexes

Let's start from the very beginning. How do you know if you even have an index? Simple. Go to SQL Server Management Studio and expand your database. Then expand a table that needs an index. Look at that—a folder named Indexes. Click the little plus-sign there. If it expands, there are indexes and the type is shown to you. If it doesn't expand, there are no indexes on that table.

At this point, you may be surprised to find that you had an index all along. If you inherited the database, then it may well be a custom index defined by the previous DBA. More than likely, it's a *primary key*.

How to tell if it's a primary key index? Just right-click the table name and choose Design, and then look for the little key next to a column name. That's your primary key.

If you had a primary key index, then let's look at what you can do with it from here. Right-click the index and choose Properties. You should see something similar to Figure 7-1.

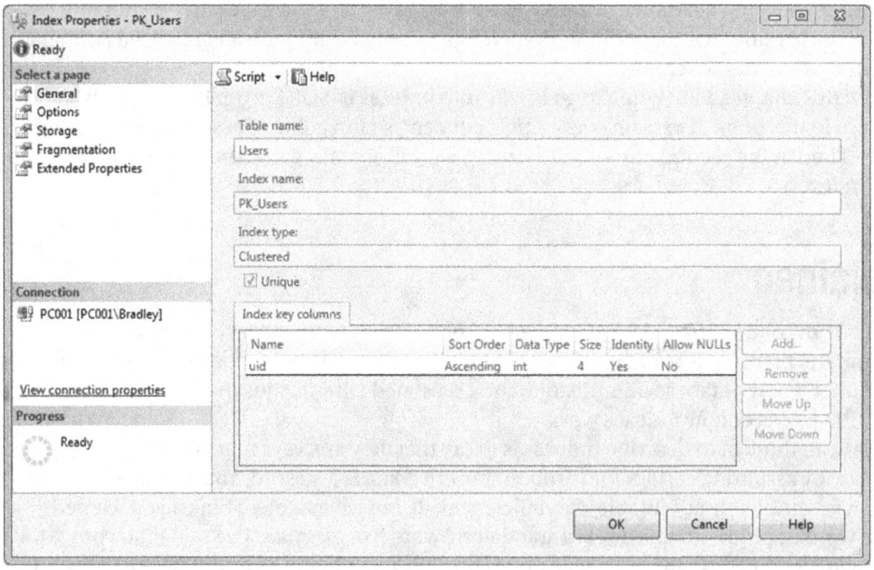

Figure 7-1. *Index Properties*

Look at that! You have a clustered index on that table. Look at the part that says "Index key columns" there. It says that the UID is sorted in ascending order as an integer, it is an identity field, and it does not allow NULL values. What that tells us is that, with this index in place, data is returned sorted by the UID field in ascending order—smallest to largest values.

Let's say that you wanted the values to be returned in descending order, though. What can you do? You can't edit the index from this screen. You could always add another index, but you can't add another clustered index; it has to be nonclustered (more on the differences between those later), so that doesn't make any sense. The last option is to delete this index and create a new one.

Go ahead and close the Index Properties screen, if it's still open. Right-click the index in the Indexes folder and choose Delete. You're going to get a screen that looks like Figure 7-2. When you do, just click OK.

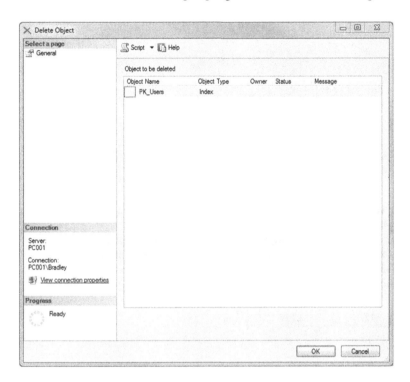

Figure 7-2. *Delete Object*

It is now deleted.

Again, right-click the Indexes folder and choose New Index ä Clustered Index. You will get an interface, as shown in Figure 7-3.

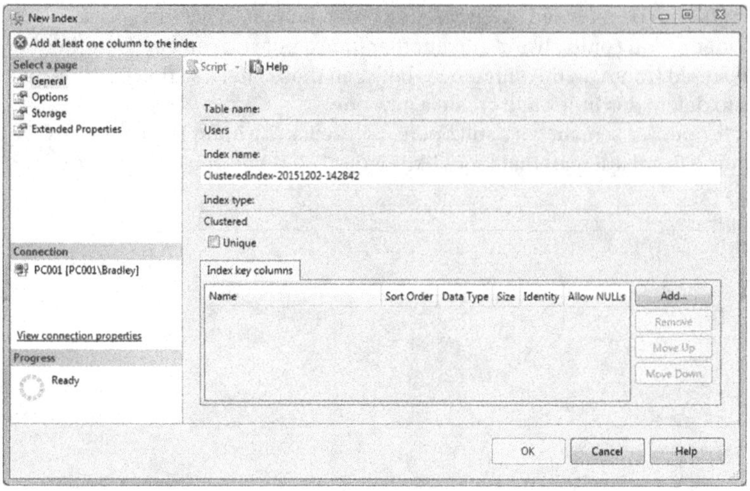

Figure 7-3. *New Index*

This lets you set up the index. When you choose a primary key, this is all done for you. This way gives you slightly more control, as you will see.

You can see that the table name is automatically added for you, but then a great big ugly Index name is defined. Go ahead and change that to IX_Users. Click the Unique check box as well. Next, click the Add button there on the right. You are shown a list of the columns in the table, so choose the column that you want to index and click OK. You should then see the screen shown in Figure 7-4.

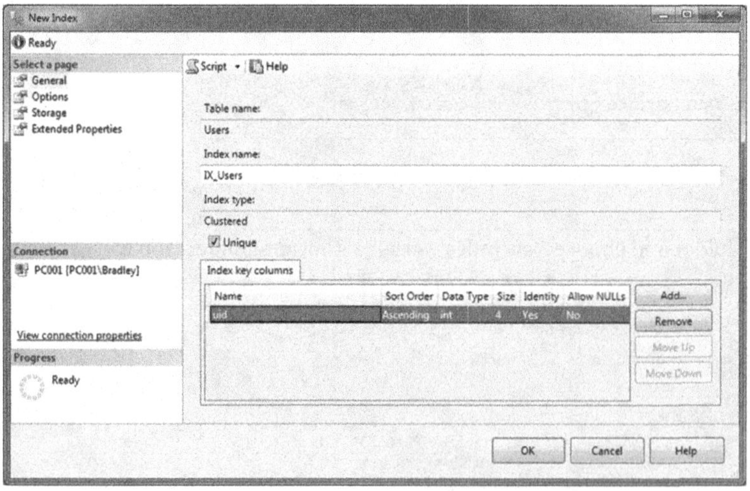

Figure 7-4. *New Index (updated)*

I said earlier that we wanted to show the values sorted in descending order. This is where we define that value. Pull down the menu under the Sort Order column shown in Figure 7-4 and select Descending. You should now see what is shown in Figure 7-5.

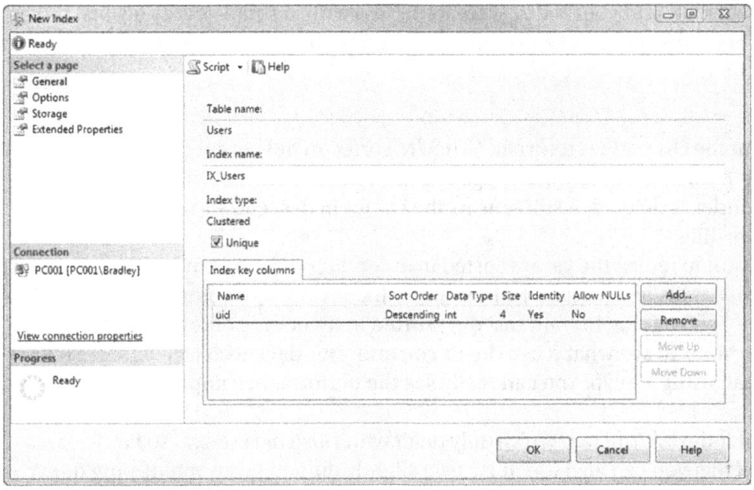

Figure 7-5. *New Index (updated)*

The only other thing we have to do is define where the index should live, so click the Storage option on the left. You should now see what is shown in Figure 7-6.

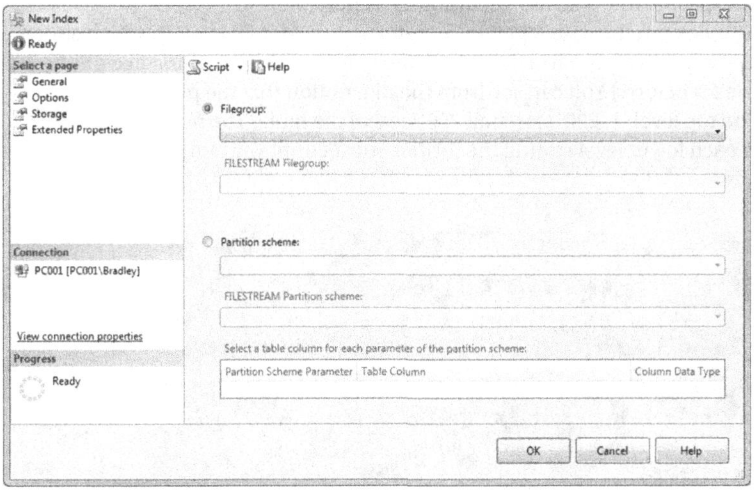

Figure 7-6. *New Index, Storage option*

Since we have to give the index a home, pull down the Filegroup menu and choose PRIMARY. This means that we are defining the index to be performed on the PRIMARY filegroup. It wouldn't make much sense to define an index and then not define what to index. Defining the table wasn't enough, in other words; we had to actually specify the filegroup. Why? Because you can have multiple filegroups for multiple databases. You can also choose to select a partition scheme here, but I didn't want to get that far into it, and I've honestly never had to deal with this before. For 99% of installations out there, you won't be using this option anyway.

Once you choose PRIMARY, click OK and your index is created. Now write a simple query against the table you just wrote the index for. Something easy, like the following, should suffice.

```
SELECT uid FROM [dbo].[Users];
```

Did you notice anything about the UID values returned? They're sorted in descending order, that's correct. It is important to note that *from now on*, any query against this table is returned with descending UID values by default. Even if the index is deleted, it still returns the values in descending order until told to do otherwise by a new index. Interesting!

So what happens when you want to return the values sorted in ascending order again? I will leave that as an exercise for the student, but it entails deleting the current index and setting up another one. Review the previous steps to get going on that. You're going to want this data sorted in ascending order, more than likely.

That's a great start to indexes. You can see what it can do for you and your data, which is organize it for you and return it much quicker than using a heap. You can really see the performance improve when you get into much larger tables and joins.

So, are there different types of indexes? You bet. We've only dealt with *clustered* indexes so far. There is another type called *nonclustered* that you can also use. It is just a slightly different way of returning query data quickly. I'm not going to get into the definitions for these in this book. If you are still unclear on the purpose of indexes at this, read on.

B-Tree Structures

You can't really talk about clustered and nonclustered indexes without first bringing up the concept of *B-Tree* structures, which are used to return specific row data as expeditiously as possible.

Simply put, a B-Tree helps the index put the data together for return. Consider Figure 7-7, which shows the relationship between the different nodes of the structure. (I'm sure you've seen something like this a million times, if you've studied indexes before.) You can see from the illustration that the pages make up the traditional B-Tree structure. The top level, 1–200, stores all 200 rows of the table. The next level stores a subset of the original value, with each lower level storing the further subset until you actually get to the physical row of data.

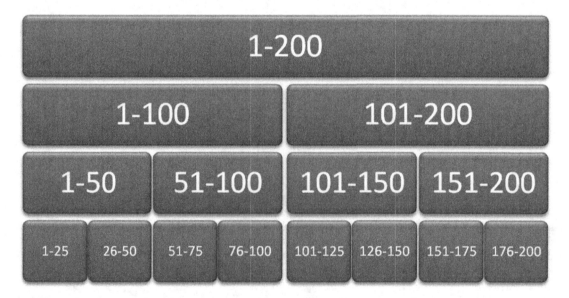

Figure 7-7. *B-Tree structure example*

The B-Tree structure can be a great way to physically figure out how your database is returning the data it needs. It's important to note that each page (or little box, as shown in Figure 7-7) references the lower pages until you get to the data. These pages are what become corrupted over time, so reorganizing and rebuilding the indexes is ideal for proper maintenance of your database.

You can use the B-Tree structure for both clustered and nonclustered indexes; both indexes work the same way. Yet there is another important thing to remember: you can't have more than one clustered index on a table, but you can have (almost) as many nonclustered indexes as you want on a table.

■ **Tip**   Keep in mind that although you *can*, whether or not you *should* is ultimately the issue.

There will be performance hits with too many indexes on a table, a classic example of too much of a good thing. Yes, indexes will definitely boost your query performance, as long as they are used sparingly. Don't index just for the sake of indexing, in other words.

I could have written about ten more pages on the different types and usages of indexes, but that's really sort of outside of the scope of this book. If you are still unclear on indexes at this point, you should probably seek some supplemental reading on the topic. It is important for a good DBA to be absolutely clear on this subject of indexes.

Rebuilding vs. Reorganizing

For this chapter, we are focusing on rebuilding your indexes. You may have noticed that there was another task very similar to rebuilding that is named Reorganize Index. The major difference between rebuilding and reorganizing is quite simple: the Rebuild Index task drops and re-creates the indexes when the task is executed, while the Reorganize Index task simply shuffles the indexes to be better organized. They both return unused space to the operating system, they both will compress to an optimal size, and they both will leave the index functional during the operation (if selected).

Because they are so similar, Rebuild Index and Reorganize Index can be treated almost alike. More consideration should be given to the Rebuild task, though, because as I noted earlier, the index is dropped (destroyed) and re-created. This is probably optimal because it means that the index does not have a chance to become fragmented or have much "drift," as opposed to an index that has only had the Reorganize task run against it. The Reorganize task is essentially the same as when insert, update, and delete statements are executed by the database engine. Essentially, the Reorganize task is an additional layer on this same functionality. While it certainly isn't meaningless, it carries less weight in my book than the Rebuild task.

Setting Up the Maintenance Plan

Here we go again! Right-click Maintenance Plans under the Management folder in SSMS and choose Maintenance Plan Wizard. You then see what is shown in Figure 7-8.

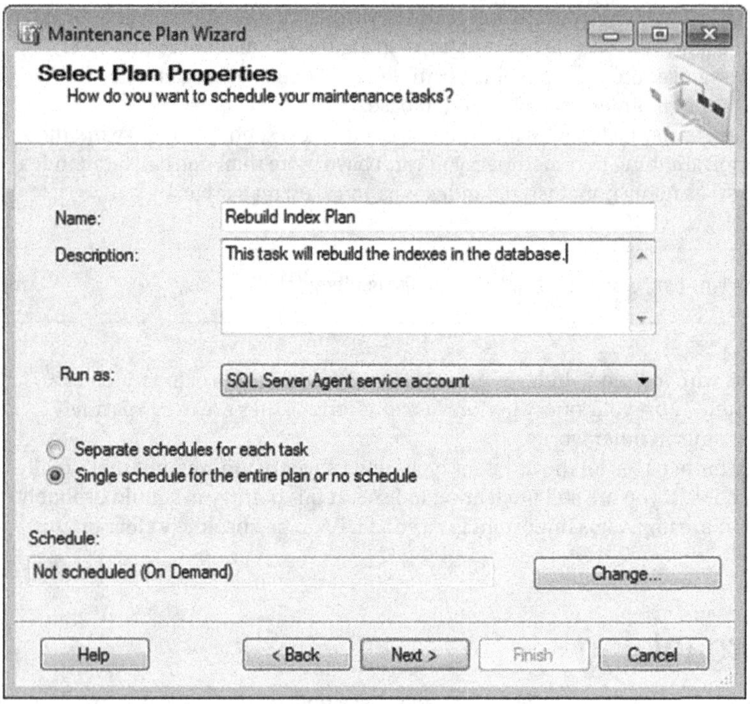

Figure 7-8. *Select Plan Properties*

Change the default values to what is shown in Figure 7-8. Click the Change... button to set the schedule, as shown in Figure 7-9.

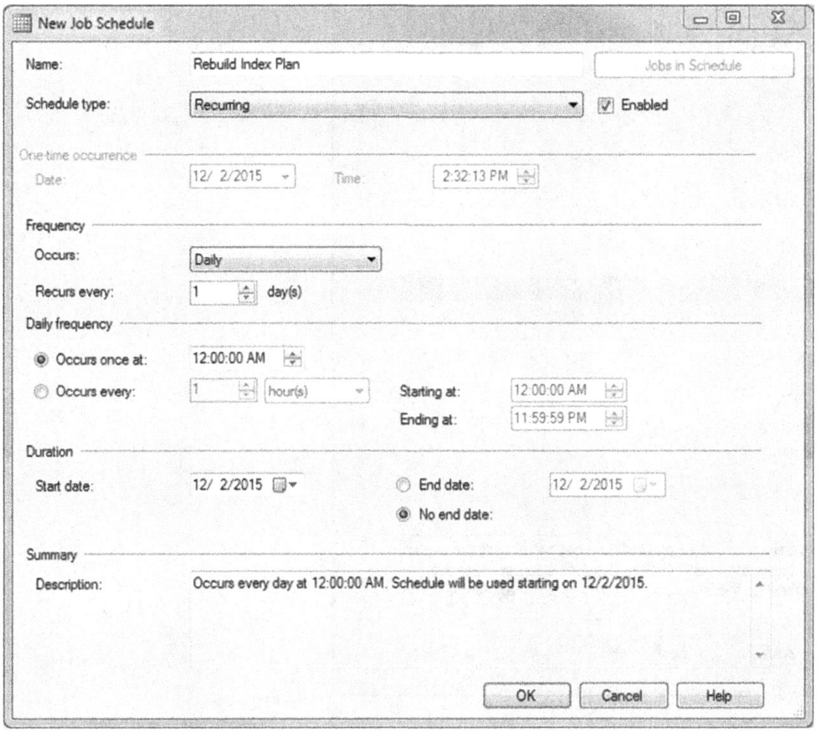

Figure 7-9. *New Job Schedule*

You only want it to run once a day, so change the Occurs drop-down menu to Daily and click OK. Your schedule is now set to run at 12:00AM every day. Click Next to continue.

You now see the screen shown in Figure 7-10, where you can choose the task you want to perform.

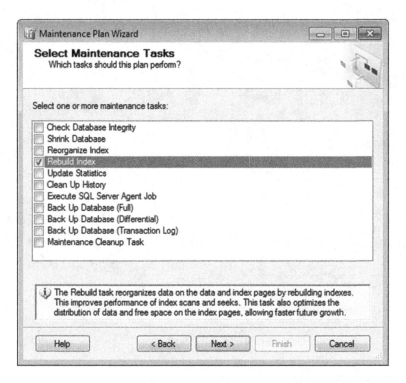

Figure 7-10. *Select Maintenance Tasks*

Choose the Rebuild Index check box and note the definition given: "The Rebuild task reorganizes data on the data and index pages by rebuilding indexes. This improves performance of index scans and seeks. This task also optimizes the distribution of data and free space on the index pages, allowing faster future growth."

See how that relates to what we went over earlier in this chapter? Those indexes eventually drift; this task gets them back in line by rebuilding them from scratch. Does it take time? Yes. And it takes resources as well, so this is going to be an important one to keep an eye on. Luckily, we can do that.

Click Next when you're ready to move on. You will now see the screen shown in Figure 7-11.

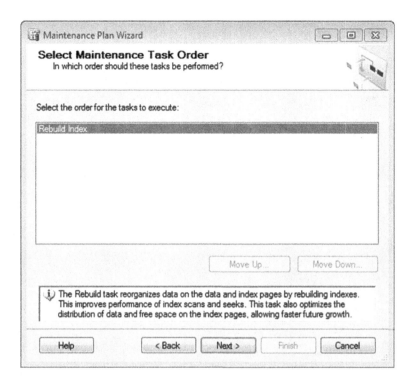

Figure 7-11. *Select Maintenance Task Order*

Since we just have the one task in here, don't worry about it; click Next.
You are then shown the default screen to define the task. It should look like Figure 7-12.

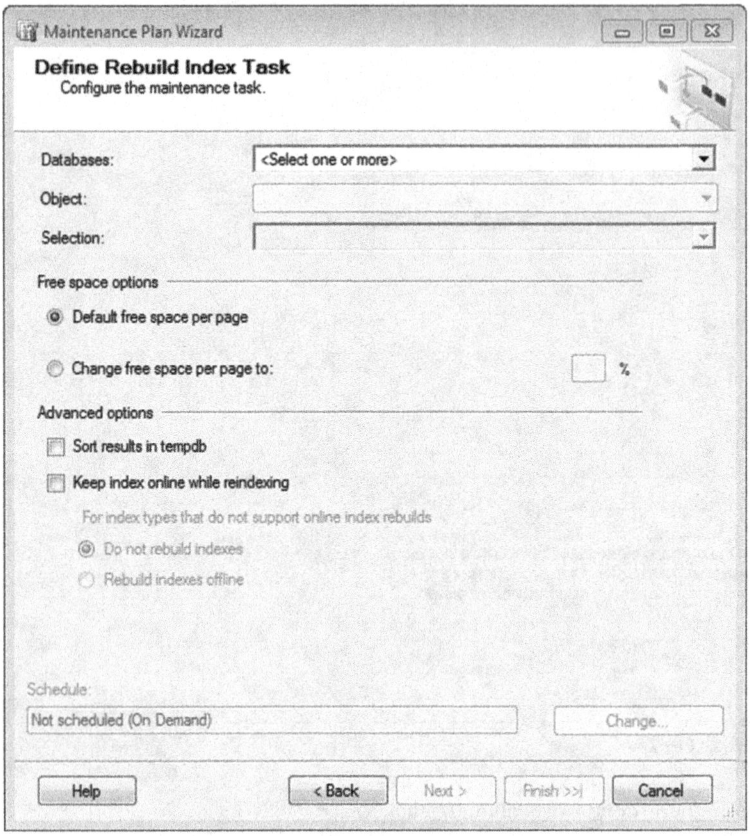

Figure 7-12. *Define Rebuild Index Task*

This should look familiar by now. You want to choose your database from the drop-down menu first. You are then shown the option for Object, which has the values Tables, Views, and Tables and Views. Choose the object that you want to set the task on, or leave the default of Tables and Views selected. This is absolutely everything that can be indexed: tables and views.

- If you choose Tables, you have to manually define the tables you want to rebuild indexes on.

- If you choose Views, you have to manually define the views you want to rebuild indexes on.

- If you choose Tables and Views, all indexes are automatically rebuilt.

In the "Free space options" area, keep the "Default free space per page". This is optimal for the database.

Under Advanced options, there are two selections: "Sort results in tempdb" and "Keep index online while reindexing". What on earth…?

"Sort results in tempdb" gives you the option of keeping the indexes as they are built in tempdb, and then outputting the completed and rebuilt index to the specified filegroup. This doesn't really give you anything beyond sorting and storing them directly in the filegroup. Selecting this option stores the sort results in tempdb and then the filegroup. Leaving it unselected runs the sort only against the filegroup. That's about it.

The "Keep index online while reindexing" option is somewhat apparent. Do you want to keep it online while you're rebuilding it? Chances are you want to enable this; otherwise, the index is not available when it is being rebuilt. Select the "Rebuild indexes offline" radio button also, in case there are indexes that cannot be rebuilt while online.

Your screen should look like Figure 7-13 when you are finished.

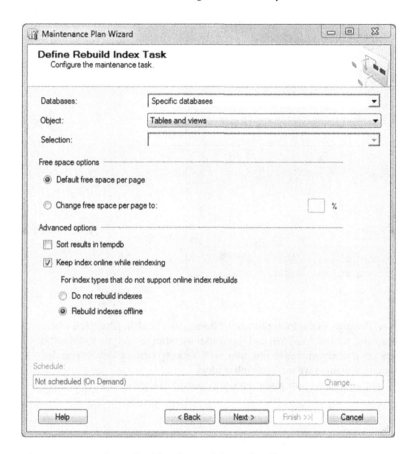

Figure 7-13. *Define Rebuild Index Task (completed)*

Click Next here. Now we get to define our reporting options. Go ahead and set your text file report location and the operator that we already set up. Your screen should now look like Figure 7-14.

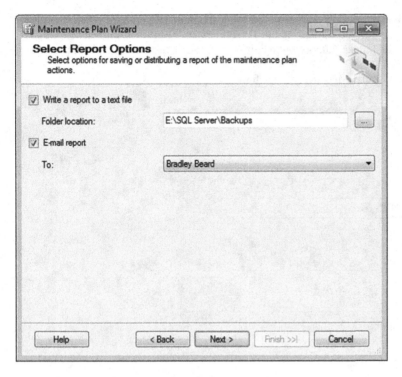

Figure 7-14. *Select Report Options*

Why did I choose E:\SQL Server\Backups as the folder location? Remember back in Chapter 5 when we defined the maintenance cleanup task for text files? We had this folder location set as the location that we wanted to clean up because we were already writing to this area. So if we keep writing to this area, the maintenance cleanup task will clean up any mess we leave, which is ideal.

Click Next when you're ready. You will see the summary screen, as shown in Figure 7-15.

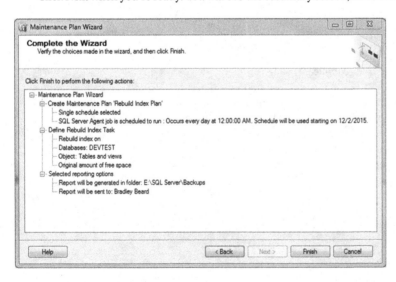

Figure 7-15. *Select Report Options*

Fingers crossed. Hit Finish. Figure 7-16 should appear, complete with all those wonderful little green check boxes.

Figure 7-16. *Maintenance Plan Wizard Progress*

Beautiful.

Before we go on, make sure that you update the job as described before. I named mine Rebuild Index. Your Jobs folder should now look like Figure 7-17.

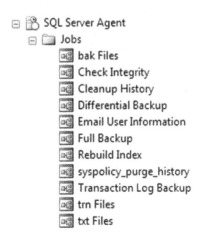

Figure 7-17. *SQL Server Agent Jobs*

Your Maintenance Plans should now look like Figure 7-18.

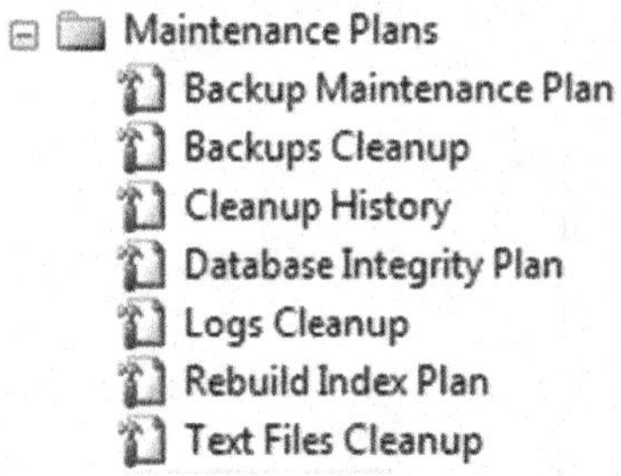

```
⊟ 📁 Maintenance Plans
        📄 Backup Maintenance Plan
        📄 Backups Cleanup
        📄 Cleanup History
        📄 Database Integrity Plan
        📄 Logs Cleanup
        📄 Rebuild Index Plan
        📄 Text Files Cleanup
```

Figure 7-18. *Maintenance Plans*

Summary

Let's quickly review this chapter.

We learned how to set up an index on a table and demonstrated the successful indexing by showing how data is returned in descending order based on the index values.

We briefly learned about indexes and B-Tree structures, and we now understand the importance of indexes as it relates to data retrieval.

Here is something else to remember, as an aside: if you have a high-volume database, then you should probably rebuild at least once a week. I know we set this as once a day in the task, and that's fine too, as long as it fits your needs. I mentioned in an earlier chapter that "high volume" is a relative term, and I appreciate that it may not mean the same to all users. To alleviate that, I'm going to just say that once a week is enough for probably 99% of the readers of this book. Of course, you are free to do it as often as you like, but if you truly have a high-volume database, you will experience performance degradation if you rebuild too often.

That's a pretty solid start for indexing. If you still are unclear, I highly recommend Mike McQuillan's book *Introducing SQL Server* (Apress, 2015) as supplemental reading material on this topic.

CHAPTER 8

Reorganizing Indexes

Building on what we just did in Chapter 7, we are now going to reorganize our indexes. Is this necessary, since they would have just been rebuilt? Let's take a look find out.

Reorganizing vs. Rebuilding

Think about a hotel. It's a nice building, sitting there all built and stuff. It has a structure and multiple floors, with each floor having lots of rooms. You know that you can get right to the room you're supposed to go to by going into the correct hotel first, and then up the elevator to the floor with the room on it, and then to the actual room. This is exactly how indexing works.

With this hotel scenario in mind, does it make sense to destroy and rebuild the entire hotel, or just maybe reorganize the way you can find your way to the room that you want? Ultimately, that depends on your interpretation and needs. It might not be necessary to rebuild, but it is absolutely necessary to reorganize, at a minimum. Sometimes, all you need to do is update the map to the room that you need to get to, and not destroy the whole hotel.

■ **Tip** Reorganizing indexes keeps the existing indexes as they are. Rebuilding indexes drops and rebuilds the indexes every single time.

Clearly, there are differences in the time and effort it takes to destroy and rebuild a hotel vs. doing the same to an index. The principle is the same, though, and that is what needs to be understood. Just because you *can* do something doesn't always mean that you *should*, in other words.

Again, depending on your scenario, it might be advantageous to do either of the options, or even both options. There really isn't a need to do both at the same time, since they both accomplish the same goals of a clean index.

Another interesting point about indexes is that indexes are automatically maintained whenever update, insert, or delete queries are made. This causes modifications to the data itself, which is what causes fragmentation of the data. Excessive fragmentation is what leads to long query times, because the data is physically separated on the disk and not in contiguous pages. Reorganizing and rebuilding puts these pages back in order, so that the queries run faster and your database behaves better.

© Bradley Beard 2016
B. Beard, *Practical Maintenance Plans in SQL Server*, DOI 10.1007/978-1-4842-1895-2_8

Setting Up the Maintenance Plan

The process of creating a maintenance plan should be very familiar by now. Right-click the Maintenance Plan option under Management in SSMS and choose Maintenance Plan Wizard. Change your interface to match what you see in Figure 8-1.

Figure 8-1. *Select Plan Properties*

Click the Change... button to set the schedule to Daily, as in previous chapters, and click OK. You really don't want to reorganize your index during usage hours, if at all possible, although it won't hurt anything. Click Next when you are ready.

You are now shown the interface where you can select the task, so choose Reorganize Index, as shown in Figure 8-2.

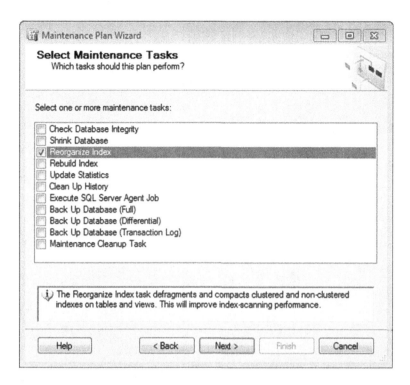

Figure 8-2. *Select Maintenance Tasks*

Notice the definition for Reorganize Index given by Microsoft: "The Reorganize Index task defragments and compacts clustered and nonclustered indexes on tables and views. This will improve index-scanning performance."

Recall the definition for Rebuild Index: "The Rebuild task reorganizes data on the data and index pages by rebuilding indexes. This improves performance of index scans and seeks. This task also optimizes the distribution of data and free space on the index pages, allowing faster future growth."

They sound sort of alike, right? So why have two different options that do basically the same thing? Because it makes more sense from a DBA point of view to be able to point a task at a small or medium table with an index and say "go rebuild that index," as opposed to doing the same thing to a massive table with billions of rows. You may want to just reorganize this index, since rebuilding the index will definitely take some time to run. Rebuilding that single massive index is something that will take a bit of time, more than likely a few seconds at least, but remember that this is an eternity in computer time.

Click Next at the Select Maintenance Tasks screen (shown in Figure 8-2) and then click Next again at the Select Maintenance Task Order screen, as shown in Figure 8-3.

Figure 8-3. *Select Maintenance Task Order*

You then need to define the task on the Define Reorganize Index Task screen. Exactly like in Chapter 6, choose your database and keep Object set to "Tables and views". Leave the rest as is. You should see what is shown in Figure 8-4.

Figure 8-4. *Define Reorganize Index Task*

Click Next here and you can start setting up the reporting options. Again, exactly like in Chapter 7, change the folder location to where you are writing your logs, and enable the operator, as shown in Figure 8-5.

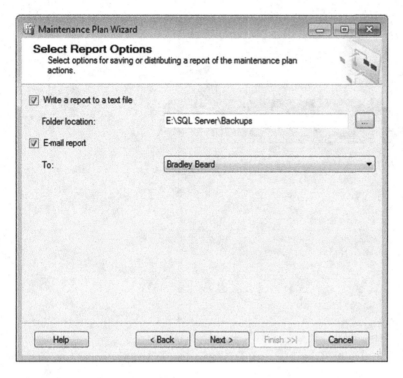

Figure 8-5. *Select Report Options*

Click Next at this screen to go to the summary screen, as shown in Figure 8-6.

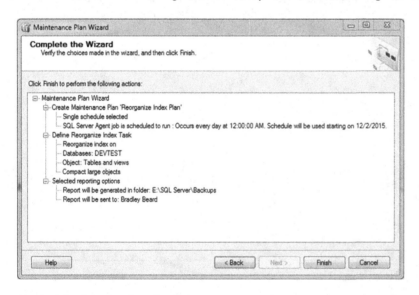

Figure 8-6. *Complete the Wizard*

This shows us the breakdown of what is happening. Everything is pretty much the same as in Chapter 7, so click Finish and wait for those green check boxes, as shown in Figure 8-7.

Figure 8-7. Maintenance Plan Wizard Progress

Great job!

Don't forget to update the job, like in previous chapters. To do this, double-click the job named Reorganize Index Plan.Subplan_1 and rename it Reorganize Index, and then make the other necessary changes. Your Jobs folder should now look like Figure 8-8.

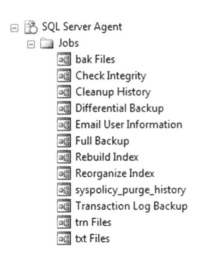

Figure 8-8. SQL Server Agent Jobs

Your Maintenance Plans should look like Figure 8-9.

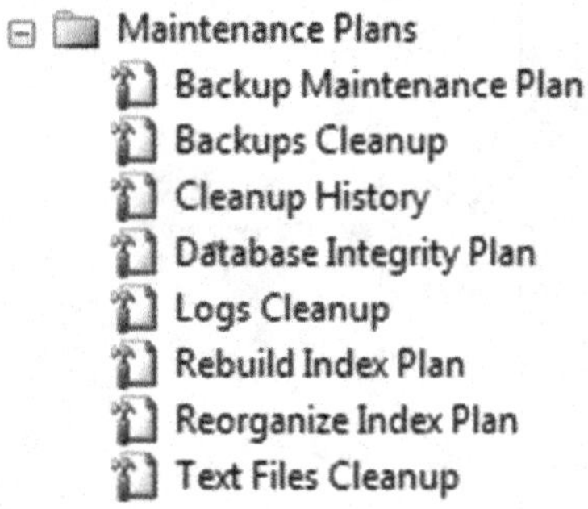

- Maintenance Plans
  - Backup Maintenance Plan
  - Backups Cleanup
  - Cleanup History
  - Database Integrity Plan
  - Logs Cleanup
  - Rebuild Index Plan
  - Reorganize Index Plan
  - Text Files Cleanup

Figure 8-9. *Maintenance Plans*

Summary

If you've gotten this far, congratulations on the progress that you have made! Keep reading to learn about the other cool ways that we can manipulate our database in anticipation for the ultimate goal of heightened data integrity.

CHAPTER 9

Shrinking the Database and Files

Ever get the feeling that things are just getting too big for you to handle? Wondering why your database, which doesn't seem very big, all of a sudden is much larger than you remember? There are lots of reasons why this could be, not to mention that there is simply more data in there than you realize. Do you need to add a shrink task to your maintenance plan? Let's take a look and find out.

Disk Usage Reporting

Right-click your database name and choose Reports ➤ Standard Reports ➤ Disk Usage. It takes a second to run, and then you get a cool little graphic similar to the one shown in Figure 9-1.

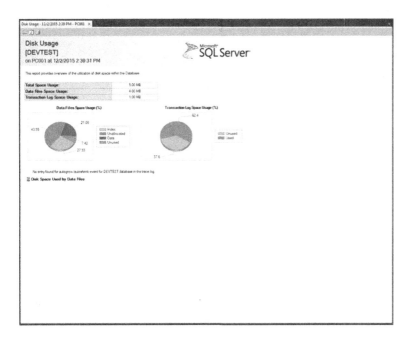

Figure 9-1. *Disk Usage Report*

© Bradley Beard 2016
B. Beard, *Practical Maintenance Plans in SQL Server*, DOI 10.1007/978-1-4842-1895-2_9

This first thing that I noticed was the pie charts. Looking at those, you can see that they are representative of the percentage of space usage for the data files and the transaction logs, respectively. Now, as I said before, my database is tiny and only has the one table, so these results are probably very different from yours. The information is still important, though, and what it can tell you. Read through this report carefully.

■ **Tip**   Believe it or not, you actually do want a bit of unused space in the database.

Why do you want unused space in the database? That makes no sense! The database should be as streamlined as possible, right? In one sense, this is correct. But what is the primary purpose of a database? To provide an organized place for data to live, of course. And what happens when you need to add more data to an extremely compact database? It has to add more space from the available disk space.

Disk Space Considerations

When a database is created, there is a setting to add storage either as a factor of the size of the database or as a percentage. This setting is invoked when space is needed to keep the database functional. Right-clicking the database name and choosing Properties, and then choosing the Files option on the left will show you the settings for the Autogrowth/Maxsize options. The settings for my DEVTEST database are shown in Figure 9-2.

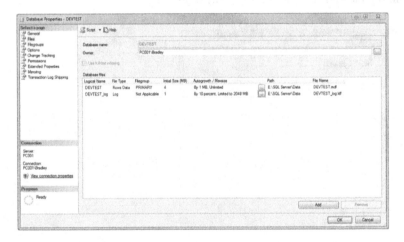

Figure 9-2. *Database Properties*

Note that I have selected an initial size of 4MB for both the PRIMARY filegroup and the transaction log. This is because I didn't want to make it too small and then have the database almost immediately request more space. I gave it some room to play, in other words. My PRIMARY filegroup will grow by 1MB as needed, to unlimited growth. Careful monitoring of this database is required, since we said it will have unlimited growth. The transaction log will grow by 5% until it is 2GB, and then a new transaction log will be created, and these will work in conjunction until the logs are truncated. Also note that my Path and File Name sections are set to where I actually want my data, and not buried in the default SQL installation folders.

Consider these options carefully, depending on the expected data insertion and retrieval rate for the intended database purpose.

To alleviate any issues with database size, the Shrink Database option is available. It basically says to the database, "Okay, here's the deal. You can have as much disk space as you want during the day, but at night, you're on a diet. I'm taking back any room you haven't used and returning it to the file system. If you need it later, you know to ask, but you can't just hold on to it." In other words, the database maintenance plan needs to run at night or when there are as few users on the system as possible. When it runs, it takes the unused space previously claimed by SQL Server and returns it to the file system. If the database needs it later, it requests the chunk of space from the file system, and if there is room available, then it takes it. The process is then repeated the next time the maintenance plan is set to run.

Consequently, when setting up the Shrink Database option of the maintenance plan, there is an option where you can set the amount of unused space to remain in the database. It is important to remember that this setting works in conjunction with the setting to determine how much space is actually granted to your database on the file system.

Using an 800GB database as an example, when the database is shrunk and 50% of the database size is chosen, our 800GB database reserves 400GB, or 50% of the space. So the 800GB database with maybe 70GB of free space turns out to be 730GB primary database size and 365GB in reserve. See how that works? That will quickly eat up disk space without proper management and oversight. That is where we, as the database administrators, come in.

The Transaction Log

An important part to consider is how the transaction log interacts as a part of the database, specifically in regards to how the shrinking of the database takes place. The purpose of a transaction log is to, um, log the database transactions. It literally keeps a record of the DML statements (SELECT, UPDATE, INSERT, DELETE) that manipulate the database. If you imagine that this will get very big, then you're absolutely right. In a database with a lot of transactions, this log can get *huge* very quickly. When shrinking the database, you can shrink it as much as you want, but you'll never touch the transaction log size unless you shrink the transaction log. Remember, it's a completely separate entity with a separate file designation, and it needs to have the same attention as the primary data file. Given this, it is still a part of the database and can't be shrunk without being explicitly told to shrink. Otherwise, your log will either continue to grow until the disk is full or get to its limit and cause an error. Either way, it is not a good thing!

To alleviate this issue, simply set up another database backup task to shrink and truncate the transaction log. Let's look at how to do that.

Setting Up the Maintenance Plan

This plan is one of the easier ones to set up, honestly. It's almost exactly the same as the plans in Chapters 7 and 8, so most of this should start to look familiar at this point.

Right-click Maintenance Plans from the Management folder in SSMS and choose Maintenance Plan Wizard. The initial interface needs to be changed to show what you see in Figure 9-3.

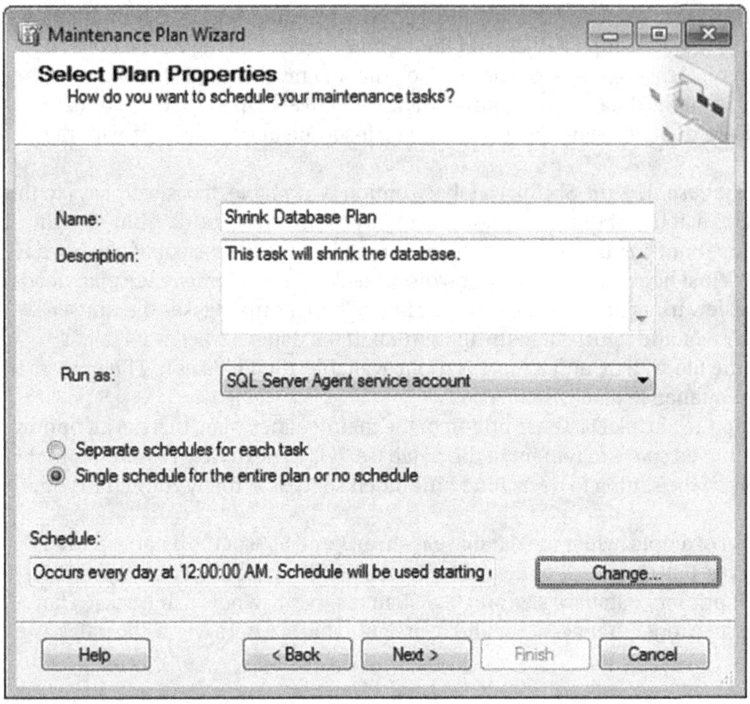

Figure 9-3. *Select Plan Properties*

Change the schedule by clicking the Change… button and set the Occurs option to Daily to make it run once a day. Shrinking the database takes some time, so I wouldn't set it any more frequently than that. Click Next to continue. You will see the page where you choose the tasks, so choose Shrink Database as shown in Figure 9-4.

Figure 9-4. *Select Maintenance Tasks*

That's an interesting definition there as well. It removes empty data and log pages. Recall what this means in terms of the indexes discussed in Chapter 6 and 7. Reorganizing and rebuilding indexes would probably make this task more relevant, don't you think? If the maintenance plan didn't have to run and find the empty pages, it would certainly be more efficient.

▪ **Note**   The Shrink Database task shrinks both the transaction logs and the data file for the selected database. Transaction logs are shrunk first, with the filegroup shrunk afterward.

Click Next to continue. You are taken to the Select Maintenance Task Order screen, shown in Figure 9-5, so click Next here since we are only doing the one task.

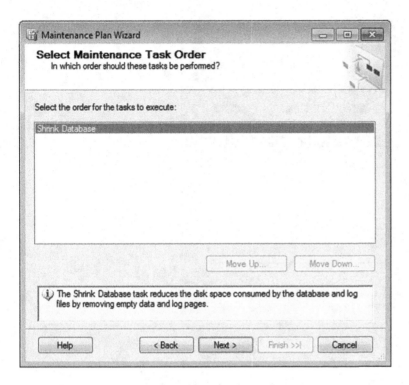

Figure 9-5. *Select Maintenance Task Order*

It seems that we are always bypassing this screen, but we will definitely be using the concept of ordering tasks later, and you will see where this can become quite important. For now, though, just click Next at this screen and you will see the Define Shrink Database Task interface shown in Figure 9-6.

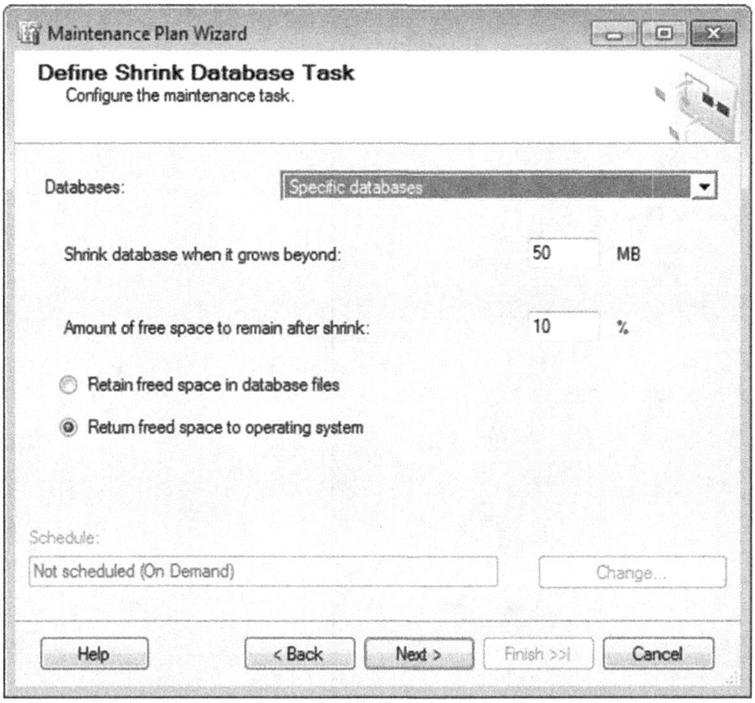

Figure 9-6. *Define Shrink Database Task*

Go ahead and choose your database from the drop-down, but leave the rest of the options alone.

What this means is that you want to shrink the database if it grows beyond 50MB. Otherwise, do nothing. So even though the maintenance task will run, if the database is 49.9MB, it will not execute. Interesting, huh? So make sure that you change this to a setting you can deal with.

The amount of free space to retain after shrink is important. You don't want to set this to 0. That would be silly because the first thing your database is going to do is request space from the operating system. You can leave this set to 10%, which shouldn't be very much depending on the size of the database.

Click Next and you will see the reporting options screen, and just like before, set these to the settings shown in Figure 9-7.

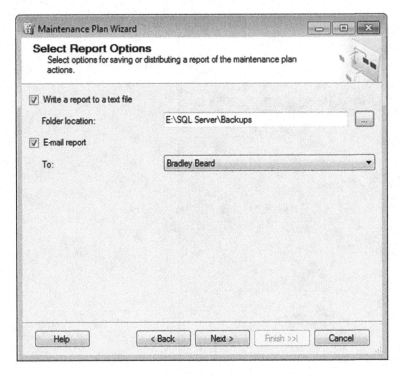

Figure 9-7. *Select Report Options*

Again, the folder location is set to where we are writing our maintenance text files, so that the maintenance cleanup task can take care of them for us later.

Clicking Next will show the summary, as shown in Figure 9-8.

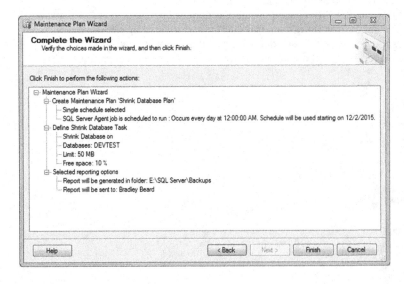

Figure 9-8. *Complete the Wizard*

So we defined our Shrink Database task to run every night at midnight on our DEVTEST database when it grows beyond 50MB. We want to leave 10% free space, and write the results to a file in E:\SQL Server\ Backups. Looks pretty good! Click Finish and hope for the best, which, coincidentally, is shown in Figure 9-9.

Figure 9-9. *Maintenance Plan Wizard Progress*

Always good to see those green check boxes!

Don't forget to update the job like in previous chapters. I named the job Shrink Database, as shown in Figure 9-10.

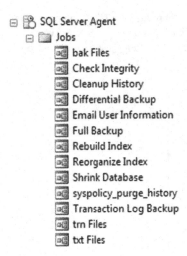

Figure 9-10. *SQL Server Agent Jobs*

Your Maintenance Plans folder should now look like Figure 9-11.

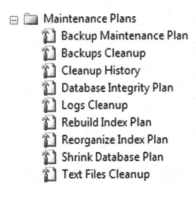

Figure 9-11. *Maintenance Plans*

Summary

This chapter was short and sweet, but there is actually a lot to it. Let's do a quick review.

- We looked at how important it is to set up the database initially as far as space requirements are concerned.

- We saw how quickly large databases grow, and how important it is to have a good maintenance plan in place to keep the size of the database in check.

- And we set up the actual maintenance plan to enforce the shrinking of the database.

If you've gotten this far, you're doing really well. I hope that you've learned something in this book so far, instead of just knowing where to click to make things happen.

CHAPTER 10

■ ■ ■

Updating Object Statistics

Don't worry; this book isn't really about math. I'm not going to trick you into doing any statistics homework or anything. When SQL Server refers to statistics, what does that mean?

Statistics, in this reference, means *distribution statistics*.

Great… so what does *that* mean? If you remember back in Chapters 7 and 8, we talked about indexes. Remember how we said that, for the B-Tree structure, there were different levels and how each level fed the next higher level? Distribution statistics is what defines those levels.

Distribution Statistics Explained

Let's say that you have a table that is used to store user data. Almost everyone has a Users table in their database. When you're in development, you may have five or ten test accounts that you use to test your functionality under different roles. And when you move to production, what happens? You all of a sudden get a huge influx of user accounts. But if your statistics are still showing that you have a very small number of records, and you actually have a very large number of records, the indexes would be outdated, and it would actually take longer to return the correct information. Distribution statistics allows SQL Server to both manually and automatically recompute and optimize the values for these indexes so that they return the correct information quickly.

When we discussed the B-Tree structure in Chapter 7, we had a pretty graphic that showed the various levels of the tree. Remember how they lined up nice and pretty? Well, what happens when records are moved around, deleted, updated, and inserted? Fragmentation of the physical files will occur, and the indexes will begin to drift. Does SQL Server do anything to automatically mitigate this? Yes. SQL Server will manually recompute these statistics as needed when some DML actions are performed (delete, update, and insert). This doesn't take care of the fragmentation; that's what our reorganize and rebuild tasks do, if you recall. But it does do a quick cleanup of the index.

Remember when you were younger and company would drop in unannounced to your crappy apartment? (Maybe it was just me.) How fast would you get it cleaned and how thorough of a job was it? The same principle applies here, believe it or not. It's not a perfect job, it's not 100% complete, or as thorough as a maintenance task designed for this exact task, but it's enough to keep the indexes in shape for the next query.

© Bradley Beard 2016

B. Beard, *Practical Maintenance Plans in SQL Server*, DOI 10.1007/978-1-4842-1895-2_10

■ **Tip**   The important thing to remember about statistics is that they constantly change.

Statistics won't stay the same in a large database for very long. In order to provide the highest level of data integrity possible, we need to be able to return the requested data quickly and correctly. Recomputing and optimizing the statistics for the indexes and tables regularly goes a long way in helping achieve this goal.

Setting Up the Maintenance Task

To set up the task to update the statistics on the database, begin as normal. Right-click Maintenance Plans under the Management folder in SSMS, and choose Maintenance Plan Wizard, as shown in Figure 10-1.

Figure 10-1. *Select Plan Properties*

Change the default values to what you see in Figure 10-1 and then click the Change... button to set the schedule. You only want it to run once a day, so change the Occurs drop-down menu to Daily and click OK. Your schedule is now set to run at 12:00AM every day. Click Next to continue.

You are now shown a screen where you can choose the task you want to perform. Figure 10-2 details the tasks and shows the correct option for this area.

Figure 10-2. *Select Maintenance Tasks*

Choose the Update Statistics option, as shown in Figure 10-2, and notice the definition. Just as I summarized before, this task "ensures the query optimizer has up-to-date information about the distribution of data values in the tables."

Click Next when you're ready to move on. You will see what is shown in Figure 10-3.

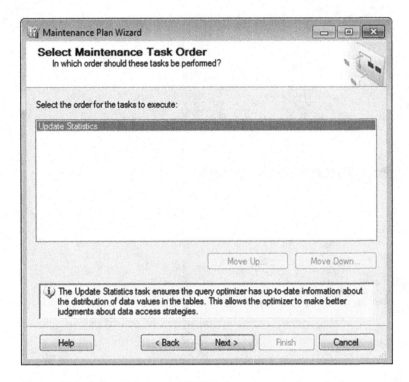

Figure 10-3. *Select Maintenance Task Order*

Since we just have the one task in here, don't worry about it and click Next.

You are then shown the default screen to define the task. It should look like Figure 10-4.

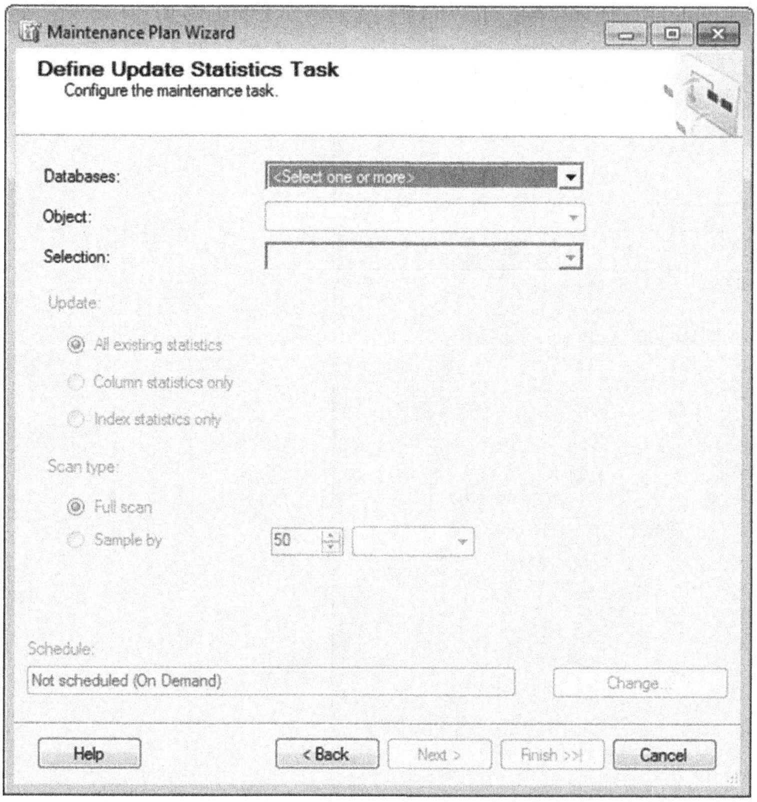

Figure 10-4. *Define Update Statistics Task*

This is where we want to define the parameters of our task. Choose your database from the drop-down menu, with Object set to Tables and Views.

If you recall from Chapters 6 and 7, leaving the Object set to Tables and Views lets us update the statistics on all available objects in the database. You are free to choose just Tables or View if you would like, but you will need to go in and change this setting if you ever want to make any changes to the maintenance plan later.

There are two other options under there:

- *Update* allows you to choose between All, Column, or Index statistics. Keep the default at All.

- *Scan type* lets you define either a full scan (recommended) or you can also choose a sample size to run the scan under. What this means is that SQL Server takes a sample size of the specified number and extrapolates the extent of the scan from there. It doesn't do a full scan, but it gets sort of close. The full scan option scans the entire catalog instead of just a sample of the data, and then updates the statistics based on the results of that scan.

I recommend leaving these two options set to the default values, as shown in Figure 10-5.

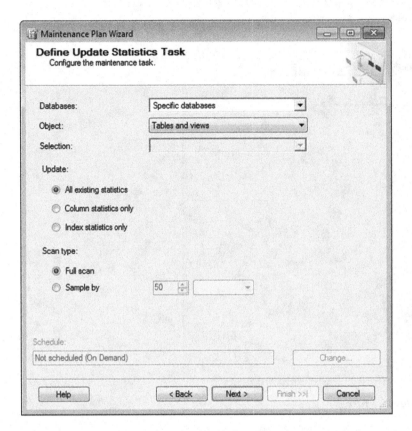

Figure 10-5. *Define Update Statistics Task (completed)*

Click Next when you are ready to move on.

Here is the old familiar interface where we define our reporting options. Set it up as you see in Figure 10-6 and click Next to move on.

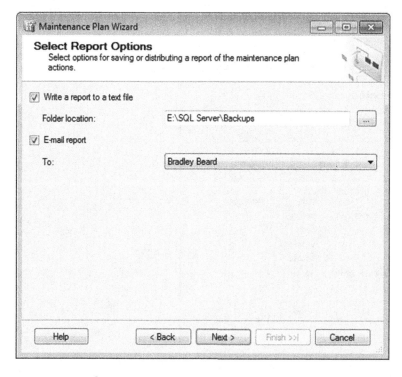

Figure 10-6. *Select Report Options*

Now you see the summary screen shown in Figure 10-7. Review this, as always, just to be sure that you didn't miss something.

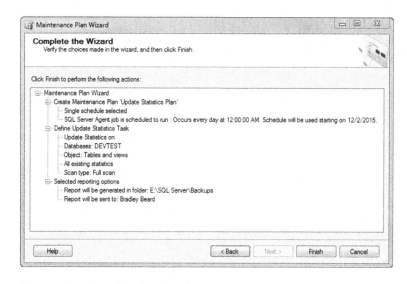

Figure 10-7. *Complete the Wizard*

When everything is copacetic, click Finish and wait with baited breath for what is shown in Figure 10-8 to appear.

Figure 10-8. *Maintenance Plan Wizard Progress*

Once again, another maintenance plan is all set up.

Make sure you update the Job, like in previous chapters. I updated the name of mine to Update Statistics. Your Jobs folder should now look like Figure 10-9.

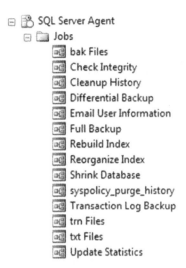

Figure 10-9. *SQL Server Agent Jobs*

That's a lot of jobs in there! Don't worry, I know this looks daunting right now, but I promise that this will all start to make more sense in the very near future.

Your Maintenance Plans folder should also look like Figure 10-10.

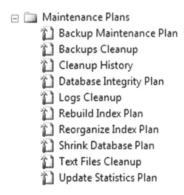

Figure 10-10. *Maintenance Plans*

Summary

Let's take a quick look at what this chapter was all about.

- We learned how a database uses statistics to recompute what it "knows" about a database.

- We saw how, when properly managed, recomputing the statistics on a database works in conjunction with the rebuilding and reorganizing of the indexes to provide a heightened level of data integrity and query completion time.

- We learned how to set up the task and went through the specifics of the task portions.

Great job! This was a quick chapter, but still very important. We are starting to wind down now, so keep going and finish up your maintenance plan learning.

CHAPTER 11

Executing T-SQL Statements

The Execute T-SQL Statement Task is one of the easiest tasks to set up. All you have to do is have an SQL query that you want to run, paste it in the box—and you're done.

But wait... what if the query is in an .sql file? And what if that file may change? Does that mean that you have to update this task every time the query changes?

Nope. This is a great example of how SQL Server swoops in to save the day. You can select from direct input, file connection, or variable inputs for the SQL query.

We're going to set up this task differently than the previous plans, because this task is specific to the SQL Server Integration Services (SSIS) subsystem, and not the SQL Server Agent subsystem. Even though SQL Server Agent is going to execute this and all the other jobs, this specific task (and the Notify Operator Task) can only be created here.

Setting Up the Maintenance Plan

Since we're going to be working within the design surface and not the wizard interface, setting up this plan is different from what you have seen. The essence of the task is the same, in that we are setting up a job to be run and defining the characteristics of that job within the interface presented to us. The simple fact is that we can't run a T-SQL statement in a regular maintenance plan that we have already set up without a lot of extra work that really wouldn't have anything to do with the original maintenance plan. It would need to be run as an addition to an existing plan, in other words, which makes no sense since we want to keep these maintenance tasks logically separated. Working this task up in the design surface, and not the wizard, gives us the opportunity to specifically create a T-SQL task.

Right-click Maintenance Plans and choose New Maintenance Plan... and enter **T-SQL Plan** as the name, as shown in Figure 11-1.

Figure 11-1. *New Maintenance Plan*

Click OK. You should see the interface shown in Figure 11-2.

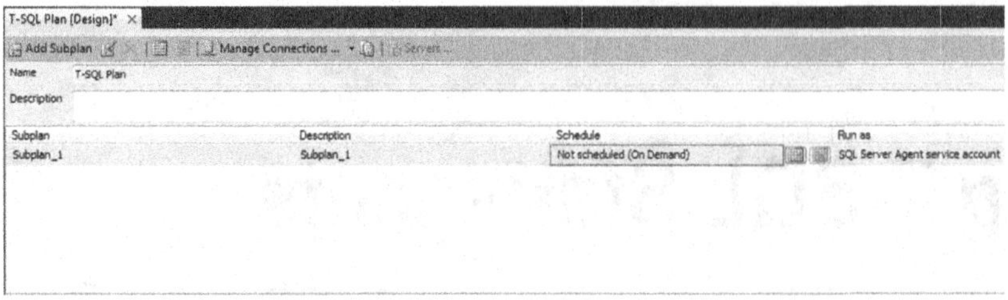

Figure 11-2. *Design surface*

At this point, you can enter a description in the large box at the top of the screen. When you're done with that, double-click the subplan that was created (Subplan_1) and fill it in like you see in Figure 11-3.

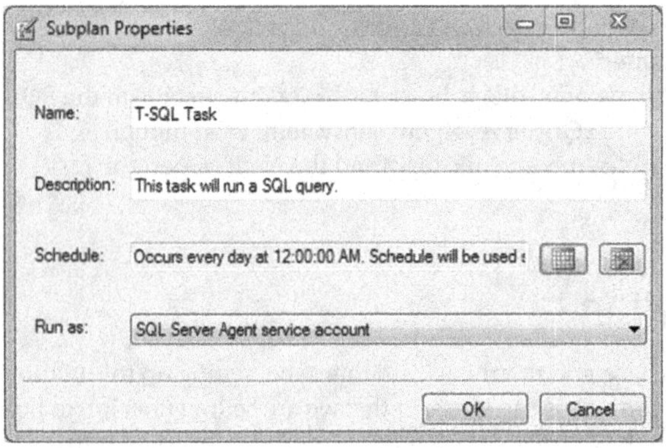

Figure 11-3. *Subplan Properties*

Looks sort of familiar, doesn't it? This is the other way to enter a task. Change the schedule the way that we did in the other chapters and leave the "Run as option" to the default.

Like I said before, this doesn't mean that it is any more or less powerful, or that it does anything different, it is just a different way of doing basically the same thing. In the Maintenance Plan Wizard, we didn't have the option to just run an SQL query without going into the SQL Server Agent Job and running an SQL script from there.

Click OK when you are done with this screen. You are then shown the interface you were at before, with the values you entered in place. You should be looking at something similar to Figure 11-4.

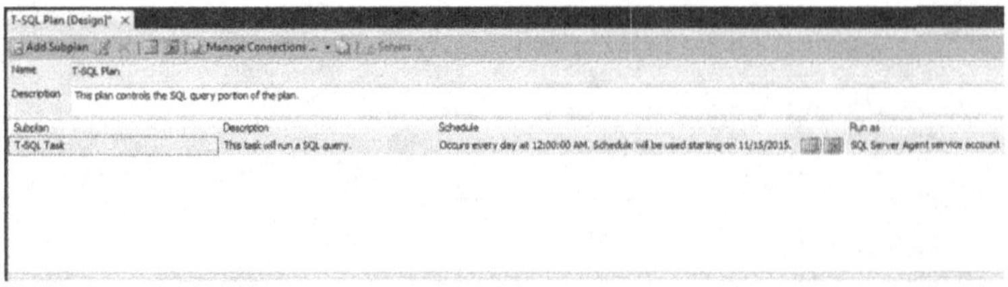

Figure 11-4. *Design surface*

I know what you're thinking. How do we add the SQL to this? There doesn't seem to be any place to add anything. That's because we haven't shown the Toolbox yet. Remember way back when we discussed the differences between setting up the maintenance plan using the wizard, and by using the design surface? This is one of those big differences.

On the left side of your screen, you should see a menu that says Toolbox. If you don't, press Ctrl+Alt+X to show it. Figure 11-5 shows what the Toolbox should look like.

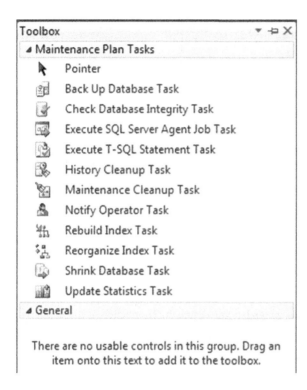

Figure 11-5. Toolbox

That's the Toolbox. Note that the majority of things in there are what we've already been through.

What you want to do here is the old "click and drag" technique. Click Execute T-SQL Statement Task and drag it into the gray area underneath the subplan information. What you will see is shown in Figure 11-6.

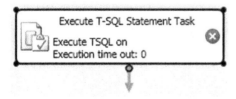

Figure 11-6. Execute T-SQL Statement Task (initial)

This is the first step, so don't worry that the red X is there. That's just because we haven't finished setting it up yet. Speaking of that, go ahead and double-click anywhere on the Execute T-SQL Statement Task box to go to the next step, as shown in Figure 11-7.

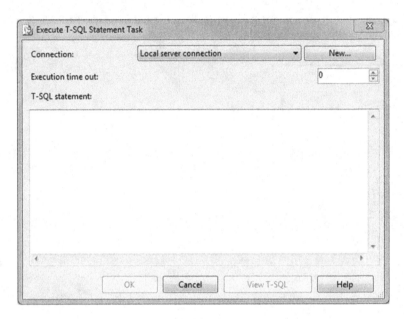

Figure 11-7. *Execute T-SQL Statement Task detail*

This is what you see when you first get there. This screen lets you define the connection, if you happen to have more than 1, and enter the T-SQL statement. You can also define the execution time out here as well. This value is in seconds, with 0 meaning that it will run until it finishes execution.

The T-SQL statement we are going to enter is going to be something short and sweet:

```
SELECT firstname + ' ' + lastname FROM users ORDER BY userid;
```

This gives us the concatenated user names from the Users table in our database.

Click OK when you are ready to move on. Notice that in Figure 11-8, the red X went away and the screen looks more complete.

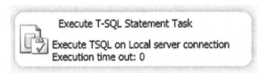

Figure 11-8. *Execute T-SQL Statement Task Detail (completed)*

Notice here that you can either keep the generic text of Execute T-SQL Statement Task in there, or you can enter a new value. To do this, just long-click the text and wait for it to become editable, enter the new value, and press Enter. I did this and changed it to Run Some SQL, as shown in Figure 11-9.

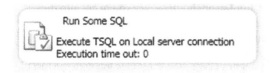

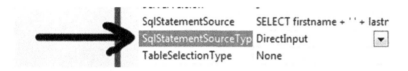

Figure 11-9. *Execute T-SQL Statement Task Detail (updated)*

Now that that's set up, let's look at some of the settings. Right-click and choose Properties. Holy cow, that's a *lot* of properties. To define them would take another whole chapter, so we're just going to assume that everything is okay in here and move along to one interesting bit.

Look for the property that says SqlStatementSourceType, as shown in Figure 11-10.

SqlStatementSource	SELECT firstname + ' ' + lastr
SqlStatementSourceTyp	DirectInput ▾
TableSelectionType	None

Figure 11-10. *SqlStatementSourceType*

That property is the key to this. The SqlStatementSourceType property is set to DirectInput by default. The other values are FileConnection and Variable. Let's look at these separately in Figure 11-11 before we go on.

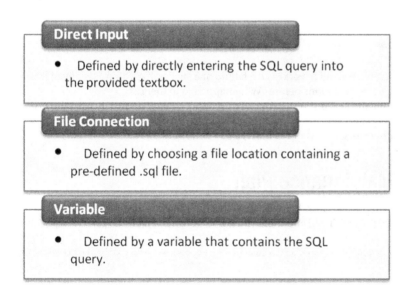

Direct Input

- Defined by directly entering the SQL query into the provided textbox.

File Connection

- Defined by choosing a file location containing a pre-defined .sql file.

Variable

- Defined by a variable that contains the SQL query.

Figure 11-11. *Source types overview*

Make sense? Those are the three ways that you can define the SQL that needs to be run. If you can't do it with one of these three methods, then I don't know what to tell you. I can't think of any other way that it can be run, honestly; except if it were a Stored Procedure, which can be set to a Boolean value by changing the IsStoredProcedure value to True from False (the default).

For this exercise, we are going to stick with DirectInput, but I strongly encourage you to get into the other two methods of doing this step, if you haven't already.

Save the plan and close it, and then go back to the Maintenance Plans section and refresh the Maintenance Plans folder to see the plan.

Open the Jobs folder. The plan is right near the bottom. Figure 11-12 shows this new job with the rest of the jobs.

Figure 11-12. SQL Server Agent Jobs

Interesting! So now, we have a job... but did it work? Is it a failure or a success? We didn't do any of those things this way. Remember setting all those options before? What happened to them?

Well, think of it like this. Creating the task this way gave you the chance to operate strictly from the *task* side and not the *schedule* or *reporting* side. This way allowed us to focus in on what, specifically, we wanted to do. Implementing it will be another story, but it isn't as hard as you may think.

Implementing the Maintenance Plan

Now that the task is set up, let's put it to work. How do we do that? Just double-click the job name under SQL Server Agent (mine is T-SQL Plan.T-SQL Task) and there you go, as shown in Figure 11-13.

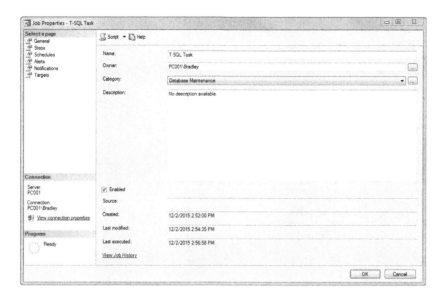

Figure 11-13. *Job Properties, General tab*

Oh, thank God. We're finally back to familiar territory! From here, set it up like you would normally; give it a new name and update the description, if you would like. I changed mine to T-SQL Task. Notice that we are on the General tab on the left. Let's step through the other tabs now.

We are now on the Steps tab. Initially, this interface appears similar to what you see in Figure 11-14.

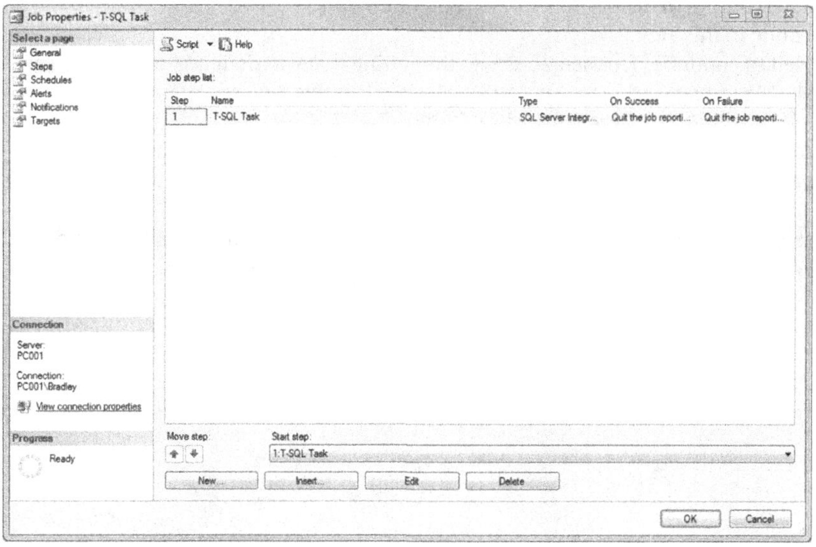

Figure 11-14. *Job Properties, Steps tab*

Everything is all set up for us! There are a couple of little things that I would like to change, though, so click Edit and then Advanced. You should see the interface shown in Figure 11-15 at this point.

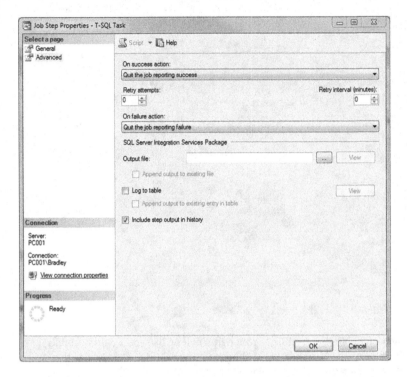

Figure 11-15. *Job Properties, Steps tab, Advanced option*

Just select the "Include step output in history" check box, and that's it.

Click OK when you are done in this area.

Click Schedules on the left to continue. This screen shows the setting that was defined for the task, which was Daily at 12:00 AM. Remember setting this earlier? It can stay like this, unless you need to change it.

The Alerts tab is next, so go ahead and click that. We don't really need to set any alerts on this, since we are just running a simple query. Again, if you need to run something here, feel free. This is your maintenance plan, after all!

Notifications is the next to last. It is the important bit. Make sure that you check the E-mail box, choose our operator, and set it to "When the job completes". Figure 11-16 shows the recommended settings.

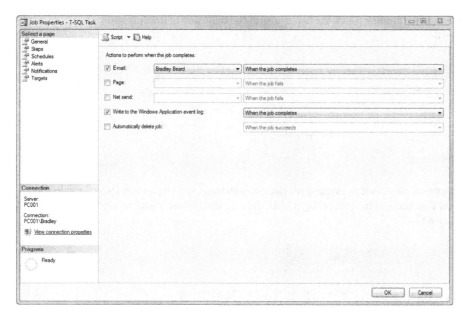

Figure 11-16. *Job Properties, Notifications tab*

On the Targets tab, just leave everything blank. We haven't defined anything at all for this section. When you are ready, go ahead and click OK to save the changes to this Job.

This setup routine should have been familiar to you if you read through Chapter 4. If you haven't, then you should certainly read that so you get an understanding on what we're doing and why.

Remember when I asked how would we know whether it had succeeded? Well, let's find out now.

Executing the Maintenance Plan

Right-click the job and choose Start Job at Step… to run it. More than likely, it failed. Mine did! Figure 11-17 shows this failure.

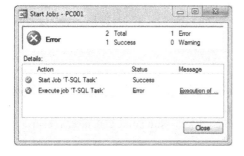

Figure 11-17. *Start Jobs*

It's time for some troubleshooting. Click the hyperlink on the right side of this box and you will see what is shown in Figure 11-18.

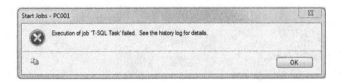

Figure 11-18. *Start Jobs error*

Wow. Thanks, Microsoft. That tells us nothing useful, except to read the history log. Okay, let's do that then. Close the window that showed the failure, right-click the job, and choose View History. This opens the interface shown in Figure 11-19.

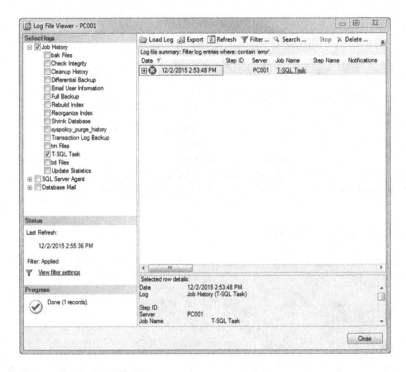

Figure 11-19. *Log File Viewer*

Interesting. Expanding this error message shows us "Invalid object name 'users." Hmm. Close this window and open the T-SQL Plan, as shown in Figure 11-20. Double-click the Run Some SQL task, as also shown in in Figure 11-20.

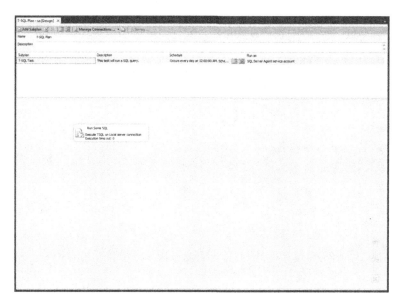

Figure 11-20. *T-SQL Plan*

Since the error specifically said that 'users' was an invalid name, let's change the query to the following, complete with a perfectly valid name:

```
SELECT firstname + ' ' + lastname FROM DEVTEST.dbo.users ORDER BY userid;
```

Click OK when you're done and then save the maintenance plan. Go ahead and right-click the T-SQL Task job and select Start Job at Step... to fire it off. Did it work? It sure did for me. This is a great lesson in how SQL Server Agent isn't looking at our specific database, but is instead looking at master as a default.

If your query is still failing, I'm going to give you a major piece of advice here. You can specify the account you want to execute the SQL instead of the SQL Server Agent, even though you cannot choose another option in Job Properties ä Steps ä Edit ä Run as. Want to know how?

Recall that our original query was as follows:

```
SELECT firstname + ' ' + lastname FROM users ORDER BY userid;
```

And then we updated that query as follows:

```
SELECT firstname + ' ' + lastname FROM DEVTEST.dbo.users ORDER BY userid;
```

That's the extent of our query. And it is failing. So at this point, we have a choice to make: we can either chase down a system administrator and demand heightened permissions for the SQL Server Agent account on the server, or we can create another domain account for the SQL Server Agent to be running as (with heightened permissions as well). Perhaps there's a third option, though? Tell me, can you successfully run this query by itself? Yes. So why can't you be set as the "Run as" value? Oh, but you can!

Double-click the T-SQL Plan maintenance plan and then double-click the Run Some SQL task in the gray area shown in Figure 11-21.

Figure 11-21. *Run Some SQL*

This brings up our T-SQL statement box, with the query listed earlier. We're going to change that around just slightly by entering the following SQL instead.

```
USE DEVTEST
GO

SELECT firstname + ' ' + lastname FROM users ORDER BY userid

EXEC AS LOGIN = '[DOMAIN]\[USERNAME]';
```

Take a look at the first bit… it's essentially the same as how we defined the SQL earlier, isn't it? That's right. Choosing to use the USE keyword or defining the database in the SQL as we did earlier accomplishes the same goal.

An important note to this is that the *package* is still executed by SQL Server Agent. The *task* is executed under the context of my user account. Does that make sense?

Save this maintenance plan and close it. Right-click the job and select Start Job at Step… and watch what happens in Figure 11-22, just by changing that SQL query to include my login.

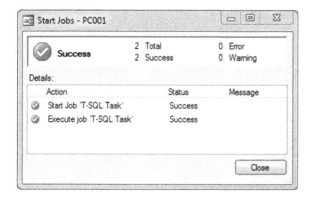

Figure 11-22. *Success!*

I love seeing that.

Summary

Let's do a quick recap here...

- We set up another plan using the "other" way (design surface).

- We edited that plan using SQL Server Agent's Job Properties.

- We discovered a possible failure in the query, so we rewrote the query and now it works.

Your Jobs folder should now look like Figure 11-23.

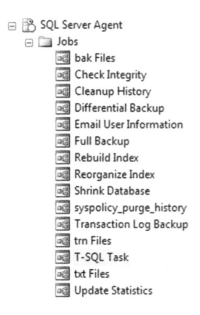

Figure 11-23. *SQL Server Agent Jobs*

Your Maintenance Plans folder should now look like Figure 11-24.

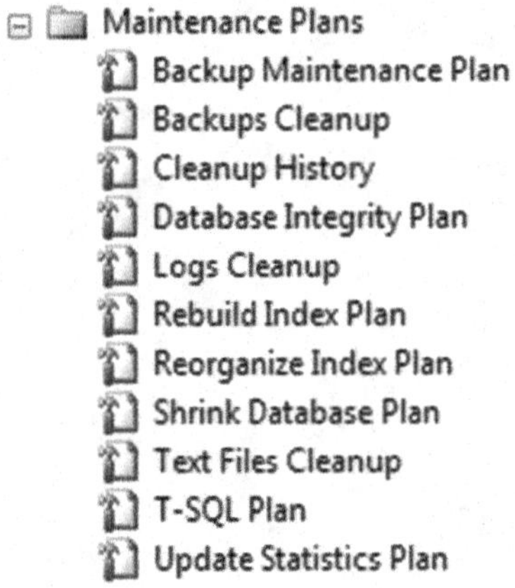

⊟ 🗀 Maintenance Plans
　　🗎 Backup Maintenance Plan
　　🗎 Backups Cleanup
　　🗎 Cleanup History
　　🗎 Database Integrity Plan
　　🗎 Logs Cleanup
　　🗎 Rebuild Index Plan
　　🗎 Reorganize Index Plan
　　🗎 Shrink Database Plan
　　🗎 Text Files Cleanup
　　🗎 T-SQL Plan
　　🗎 Update Statistics Plan

Figure 11-24. *Maintenance Plans*

Excellent job on this chapter. Reread what you didn't understand, though, especially the part about how to run the query with your user account instead of SQL Server Agent. Next, we will look at the Notify Operator Task, and then wind everything down for the conclusion. If you've made it this far, excellent job! You are well on your way to having the tools and the knowledge to create or maintain your own maintenance plan.

CHAPTER 12

Notifying Database Operators

The purpose of the Notify Operator Task is specifically to set up a notification task. It can be for any event within the plan; that is, the takeaway for this one. It doesn't have to be tied to any specific task either. You could conceivably have this task, by itself, and all it will do is notify an operator. What good could that possibly do? If this task is tied to nothing else, what could a simple notification do? Let's look at how to set it up and I will explain the answer to that question as we go.

Setting Up the Maintenance Plan

Right-click Maintenance Plans and choose New Maintenance Plan… to continue. Enter **Notify Operator Plan** as the name, as shown in Figure 12-1, and click OK.

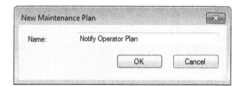

Figure 12-1. *New Maintenance Plan*

Make sure that the Toolbox is open at this point (Ctrl+Alt+X). The first bit to do is update the default options for the plan, so double-click the Subplan name (Subplan_1) and update your interface, as shown in Figure 12-2.

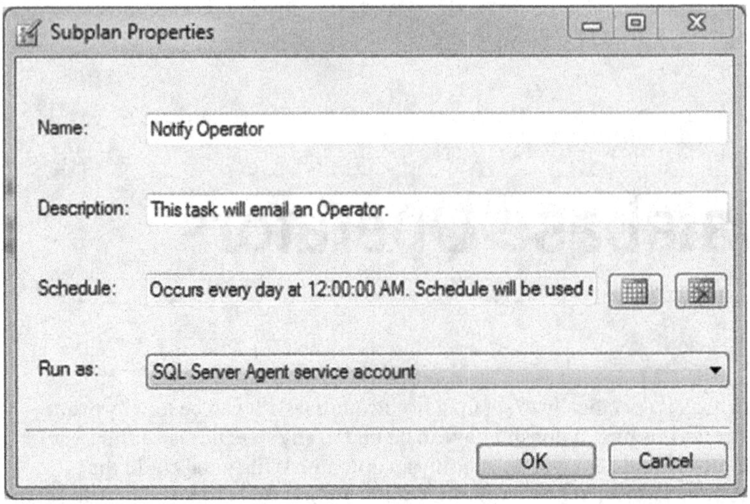

Figure 12-2. *Subplan Properties*

Notice that the Schedule box is not set yet. Change this to Daily at 12:00 AM, click OK on the Schedule page, and then click OK when you get back to the Properties window. This leads us to the updated interface, as shown in Figure 12-3.

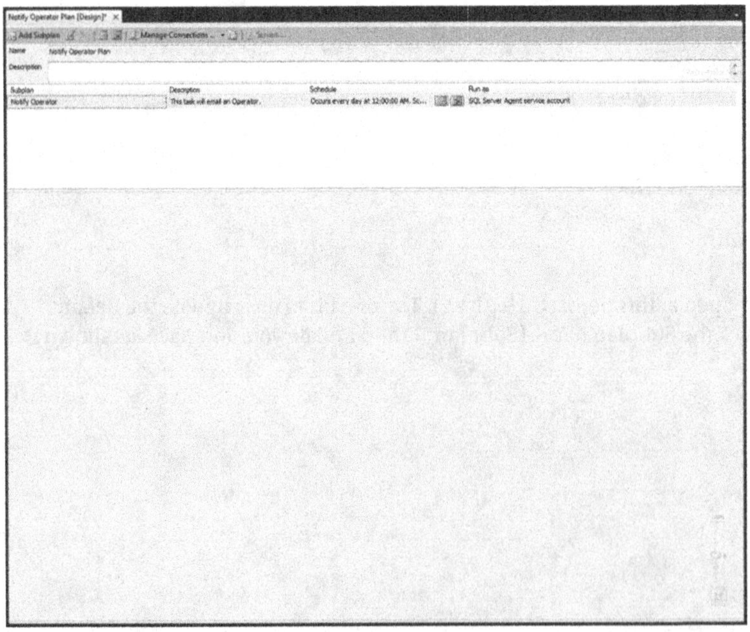

Figure 12-3. *Notify Operator Plan stage*

At this point, we are ready to add the Notify Operator Task, so click and drag the Notify Operator Task from the toolbar into the stage.

The first thing that you notice is the big red X. Just like in Chapter 11, we need to define the parameters of this task. Double-click the Notify Operator Task. You will see what is shown in Figure 12-4.

Figure 12-4. *Notify Operator Task*

Guess what we have to do here? Thankfully, Microsoft makes this fairly easy to ascertain. You can see that "Local server connection" is already selected, so that's fine. Underneath that, you have the available operators on the system.

Notice that you don't have the option here to create a new operator, or edit the current operator. I believe this is by design, as it shows a definite disjoint between the process of adding a new operator and using an existing operator. Keeping those two tasks separate forces the user to understand the ramifications of their decision, as well as reinforces the idea of proper flow within a maintenance plan. I believe that Microsoft said something like, "You can't add an operator that doesn't exist, now can you? Therefore, you must add an operator first. And don't think we're going to let you do it the Microsoft Lite way either. You're going to have to do this from the operator's area in SSMS. Once you do that, *then* you can come back in here and add an operator." Does that make sense? Think of it as Microsoft sort of *forcing* the user to make the conscious decision to follow a prescribed method for using this particular task.

At this point in the flow, you want to select the operator we already set up. Under that, you can see that there are boxes for subject and body. Sounds like an e-mail, doesn't it? That's because it is. Why else would we use the operator that we already set up? Now, granted, in the operator settings, we can specify e-mail, net send, or pager notifications. What happens if we don't specify an e-mail address for an operator, but choose them to be notified here? Short answer: you can't. This task is *specifically* for e-mail addresses. Want proof?

Let's quickly set up two more operators. Cancel the current open window and right-click Operators (inside of SQL Server Agent; you may need to click Object Explorer at the bottom of the screen to show this) and choose New Operator... Enter the information shown in Figure 12-5. We will call this one Net Send Operator, with the "Net send address" being in the format of DOMAIN\username.

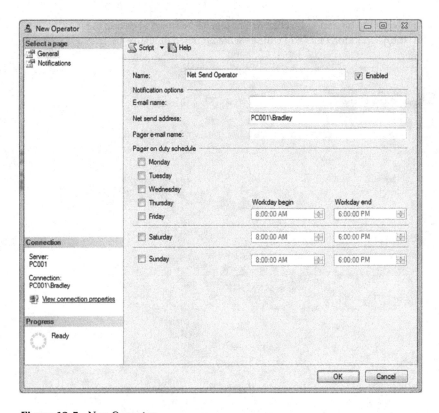

Figure 12-5. *New Operator*

Click OK when you're done, open another New Operator... window, and enter the information shown in Figure 12-6. We will call this one Pager Operator, with all days selected.

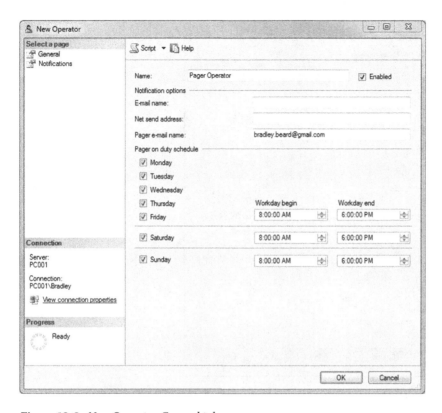

Figure 12-6. *New Operator, General tab*

Click OK when you're done. At this point, you should have three operators, as shown in Figure 12-7.

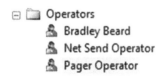

Figure 12-7. *Operators*

Easy enough. So with the Notify Operators task, let's determine which of these operators we should choose to notify.

Double-click the Notify Operator Task (it should still be up in SSMS) and notice that only the initial operator is listed, as shown in Figure 12-8.

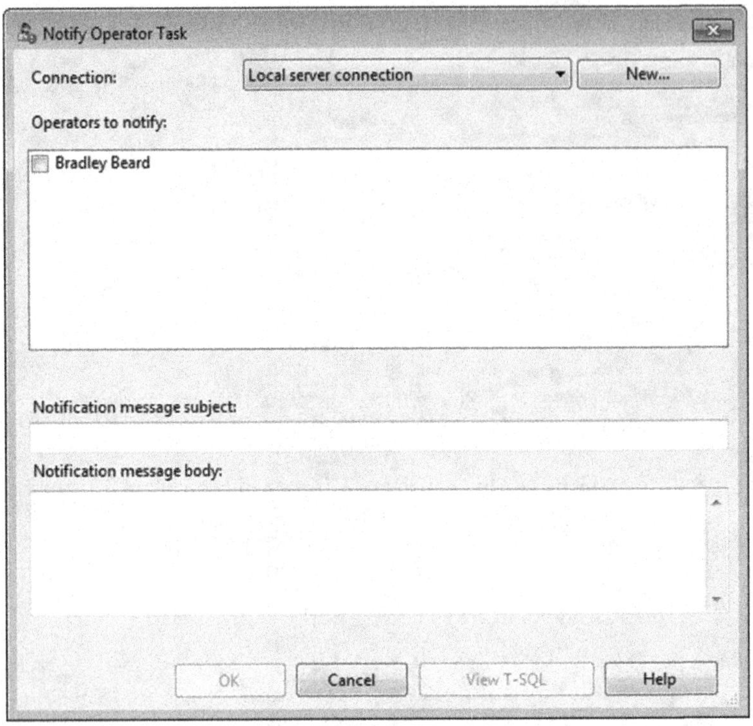

Figure 12-8. *Notify Operator Task*

Hmm. That means that none of the others are valid operators in this context. Want more proof? Double-click either the Net Send Operator or the Pager Operator and notice that the e-mail field is blank. I picked the Pager Operator to work with. Copy and paste the e-mail address in the "E-mail name" box. You should now see what is shown in Figure 12-9.

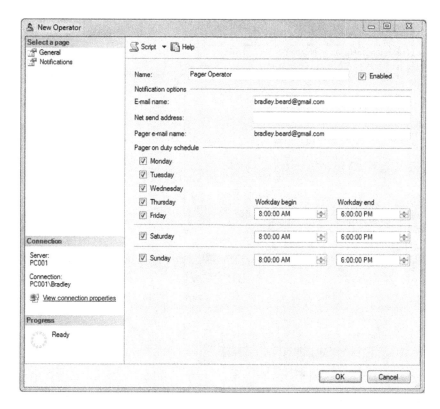

Figure 12-9. Pager Operator properties

So now we have an e-mail address specified for the Pager Operator. Click OK. Go back to the Notify Operator Task and double-click it. Figure 12-10 shows the updated interface.

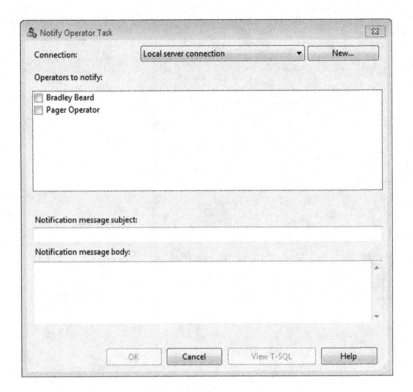

Figure 12-10. Notify Operator Task (updated)

Would you look at that? The Pager Operator is added.

Therefore, we can positively assert that an operator must have an e-mail address specified in order to be included in the Notify Operator Task in any capacity.

You can remove the Pager Operator and Net Send Operator now by right-clicking and choosing Delete, and then accepting the deletion operation. You should then be left with just the original operator.

On with the task! We left off with the specification of the interface, so update it to look like Figure 12-11.

Figure 12-11. *Notify Operator Task (updated)*

All we did was add the operator and define a generic subject and body. Click OK at this point. Notice that our interface has changed to display the information shown in Figure 12-12.

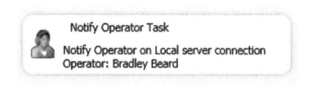

Figure 12-12. *Notify Operator Task*

This says that we are using our local server connection and Bradley Beard is our operator.

Perfect so far. So what is next? We need to test it. Either we can wait until midnight, when we scheduled it to fire, or we can run it now. Let's run it now.

First of all, you want to save the plan so far. Once you save it, the Notify Operator Plan.Email Operator job appears in the SQL Server Agent ➤ Jobs folder in SSMS, as shown in Figure 12-13.

Figure 12-13. *SQL Server Agent Jobs*

There are other jobs, but I want to focus on just this one for now. Right-click it and choose Start Job at Step... and watch what happens. Figure 12-14 shows what to expect.

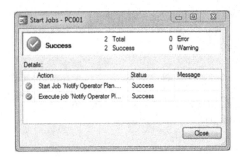

Figure 12-14. *Success!*

Success! I love it. If you got an error like the one shown in Figure 12-15, read on. If not, skip ahead to the end of this chapter.

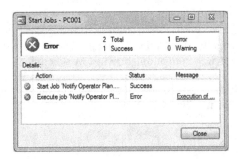

Figure 12-15. *Or not...*

It failed, you say?! Now why would it fail? In a nutshell, it failed because we haven't set up a profile for the operator yet. Let's look at how to do that now.

Creating an Operator Profile

We need to create an operator profile for our job to be able to run. Double-click Database Mail and click the "Manage profile security" radio button, as in the interface shown in Figure 12-16.

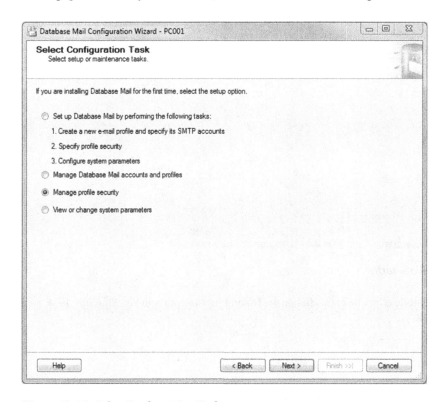

Figure 12-16. *Select Configuration Task*

Click Next to continue.

You are brought to a screen that has Public Profiles and Private Profiles as tabs across the top of the window. The default screen is Public Profiles, as shown in the interface in Figure 12-17.

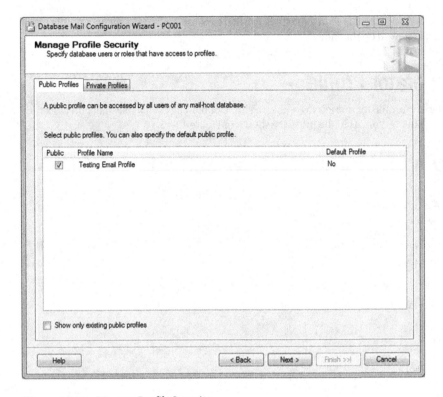

Figure 12-17. *Manage Profile Security*

At this point, click the Public check box and change the Default Profile option to Yes. Your interface should look like Figure 12-18.

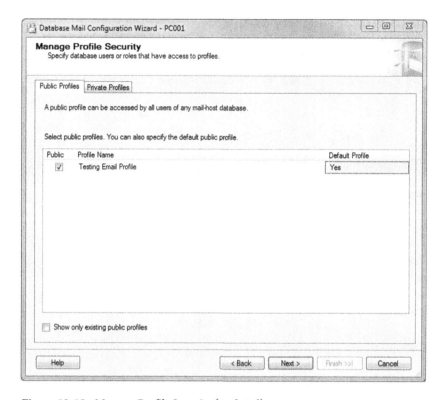

Figure 12-18. *Manage Profile Security (updated)*

Click Next to continue, and then click Finish to wrap it up. You should get a Success message, as shown in Figure 12-19. Close the window, right-click the job again, and choose Start Job at Step... to see what happens next.

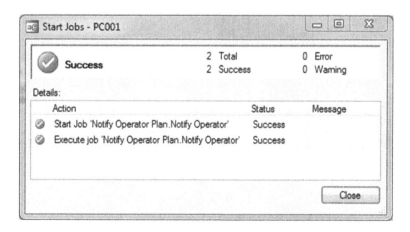

Figure 12-19. *Success! (again)*

Check your inbox now. Hey, look at that! Pretty fancy, huh?

Go ahead and rename the job to Notify Operator and update it as we did in the previous chapters. At this point, you should have all the jobs shown in Figure 12-20.

Figure 12-20. *SQL Server Agent Jobs*

Your Maintenance Plans folder should look as shown in Figure 12-21.

Figure 12-21. *Maintenance Plans*

Summary

Let's recap this chapter really quickly.

- We learned about the Notify Operator Task.

- We learned that the operator must have an e-mail address to be notified using the Notify Operator Task.

- We learned that the Database Mail profile security needed to be enabled for this to work correctly.

- We confirmed our settings by receiving an e-mail.

Excellent work so far. Really, you've done a great job if you've gotten this far in one piece; even more so if you've gotten here in one sitting. Press onward and we will *finally* bring everything to a close with the creation of our custom maintenance plan.

CHAPTER 13

■ ■ ■

Tying It All Together

At this point, we've been through each of the specific tasks to create a maintenance plan for each task. We've followed practical examples to lead us to the culmination of this book, which is to have you, the user, create your very own maintenance plan. From here on, we move from theory to application; we're going to apply what we know.

Checking Your Environment

If you've followed along, you've probably gotten quite a few test e-mails in your inbox. Go ahead and delete those since you don't need them anymore.

Figure 13-1 shows the jobs listed in SQL Server Agent.

Figure 13-1. SQL Server Agent Jobs

© Bradley Beard 2016
B. Beard, *Practical Maintenance Plans in SQL Server*, DOI 10.1007/978-1-4842-1895-2_13

Additionally, we should have the following maintenance plans available, as shown in Figure 13-2.

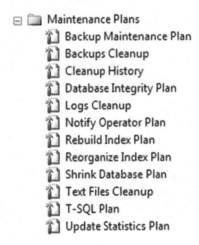

Figure 13-2. Maintenance Plans

Now, the important thing here is that, for the most part, we are done. That's right! You could conceivably leave the plans as they are and call it a day. However, there are important considerations that must be taken into account with regards to maintenance plans, and the most important one to remember is that some tasks need to be run before other tasks, and some maybe don't need to be run every hour or even every day. This next section is going to focus on what tasks actually need to be run, when they should be run, and in what order they should run.

Ordering of the Maintenance Tasks

That's right; there is a preferred order to the maintenance tasks. Why? It doesn't make much sense to back up the database, and then rebuild the indexes, now does it? There has to be an order to the tasks, so let's look at them in regards to the main task to be run—backing up the database.

Think about it like this. You don't want to back up bad data, but you also want to provide for a longstanding backup mechanism. To achieve this, you want to take care of the legwork up front, meaning the tasks that deal with the data integrity. After the backup, you want the cleanup.

Check out Figure 13-3. Ideally, this is how I would structure my new maintenance plan.

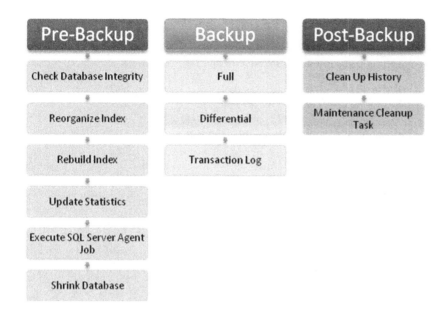

Figure 13-3. *Maintenance Plan Structure*

To summarize this even further, think of it like this.

- The Pre-Backup phase is made up of all the things that need to happen *before* the database is backed up.

- The Backup phase is what runs to actually back up the data.

- The Post-Backup phase is made up of what needs to happen *after* the backup is complete.

See how that works? We run tasks before, during, and after. The result is a fresh, clean backup of the database, and properly maintained tasks and logs.

So now we know the order that we need to run the tasks in. Next, we need to decide how robust we want this to be. We can decide to do as much or as little as needed for our security plan. Remember that, as a DBA, you have to follow the guidelines set forth for data retention and availability. You may be subject to different requirements than I am, so it is best to remember to use this as a guideline to creating your own database maintenance plan within the confines of your security principles.

Determining Complexity of the Maintenance Plan

Like I just said, this can be as simple or as complex as you want. I tend to try and keep things as simple as possible, so in this case, I'm not going to stray too far from that logic.

There are four main areas of database maturity, as shown in Figure 13-4.

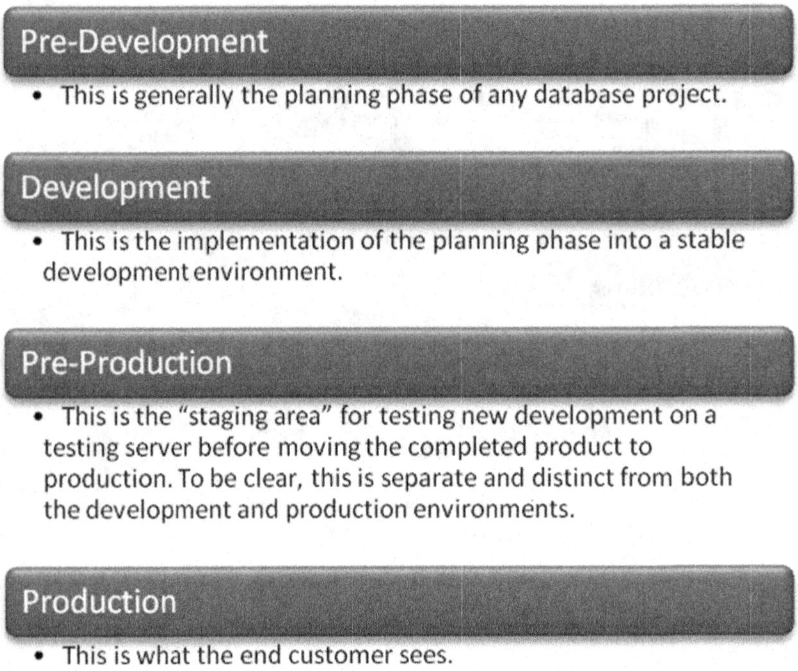

Pre-Development

- This is generally the planning phase of any database project.

Development

- This is the implementation of the planning phase into a stable development environment.

Pre-Production

- This is the "staging area" for testing new development on a testing server before moving the completed product to production. To be clear, this is separate and distinct from both the development and production environments.

Production

- This is what the end customer sees.

Figure 13-4. *Database Maturity Phases*

■ **Tip** Database maturity is the developmental process from when a new database is created, until it is to be implemented into a production environment for transaction processing to fulfill a business need.

Whether you are creating a database to simply store user and session information, or logging billions of transactions per second, you will always start with a fresh, clean database. That database must therefore mature before being ready to be used as it is intended. The only way that it matures is by going through the processes to ensure that it will meet the needs of the application and, ultimately, the end user. Part of those processes is going to be what maintenance needs to be done to the database and at what interval.

The interesting part here is that the planning for the database, ideally, should *only* be done at Phase 1. Now, obviously, this isn't always realistic because the requirements of the application or the database may change. In this event, Phase 1 begins again. See how that works? Anytime new development happens, it must go from 1 to 4 and not skip any steps. This is the only way to ensure absolute integrity and cohesion of the systems. In other words, when new functionality is being developed, it needs to be planned first in Phase 1, shown Figure 13-4, and then progress through the workflow until it hits production.

This may be a bit too complex for your needs. This is how I do things at my job, so that's how I'm used to doing it. You may find another way of doing things that fits your needs, and that's fine. For now though, we are going to work using this method.

This doesn't mean that we are going to create four different databases or anything like that. Instead, we are going to create one maintenance plan and then I will show you how to port the logic behind that maintenance plan, that is, what you learn from this book, into other databases.

Planning the Maintenance Plan

Plan the plan? Sounds like a plan. Always plan ahead, whenever you can. Seriously. Yes, there's a lot of alliteration in this paragraph, but it's a concept that will save you more times than not. Always err on the side of caution, especially when dealing with databases. And here is the cardinal rule of dealing with databases: *when in doubt, do a backup first.* All it takes is that one time when you blow something up on accident, but you didn't take a backup. That is probably all you need to happen to become a firm believer in backing up as often as possible.

■ **Tip**   When in doubt, *always* do a backup first!

So how do you plan a plan? You determine which steps you need, and then you plan how to implement them. Let's look at two different scenarios and determine the best way to implement a maintenance plan from there.

For the first scenario, let's say that you have a small database that doesn't handle a lot of data at once. This might be in instances like a home database that is used to record kids' chores or a CD collection.

For the second scenario, let's say that you are the DBA for a medium or large company running their database that handles a fairly large number of transactions per hour.

Scenario 1

The first scenario is going to be for a small database that doesn't handle a lot of data. Since this isn't a very large database, and it probably isn't mission critical (meaning it can be recovered quickly and easily and will not affect any portion of a mission or objective in its absence), then we can leave some of the tasks to the database engine to run. What tasks does SQL Server run automatically when those three magic DML statements are encountered? Rebuild Indexes, Reorganize Indexes, and Update Statistics. We can leave those out for this scenario, since we would effectively just be repeating what SQL Server has already done. For this reason, Scenario 1 might have a maintenance plan that looks like Figure 13-5.

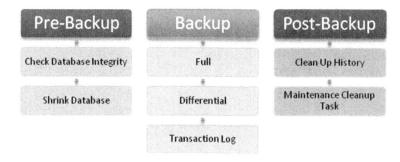

Figure 13-5. *Scenario 1 Structure*

That's a bit more streamlined, isn't it? Remember, we don't necessarily need to run all the tasks just because they're available to us. We can leave some of the internal processing alone that SQL Server does anyway, and just worry about the integrity of the data. I would call this the "bare-bones minimum, absolutely necessary tasks only" maintenance plan. I don't really think that this scenario would work for a whole lot of businesses out there, and if it does, it is probably because the DBA either doesn't understand maintenance plans or doesn't care to take the time to learn. Good thing you aren't that DBA; you are taking positive steps to enhance your own knowledge just by reading this book. When put into practice, the tools you have picked up from this book with definitely help you in your quest to better data availability and integrity.

Like I said earlier, this is probably the best scenario for a home database, or one that is not critically important. If you have a dependency on the data to operate your business, then I don't think that this is going to be the scenario you are going to want to go with.

Instead, you are going to want something *much* more robust; one that will perform the tasks that SQL Server does automatically, but when done as part of a maintenance plan, they are done completely and not just as a passing thought. Remember how SQL Server performs index restructuring and updates the database statistics after most queries; this factors in here because we are manually telling SQL Server to go ahead and make sure that those are ready to go for the next batch of data interactions after the maintenance plan has run successfully.

Scenario 2

This one is a bit more complex, but it's closer to what I am used to. For this scenario, you are going to want to remember that we are not going to go for the quick and dirty path like in Scenario 1. This process is actually much closer to the complete maintenance plan that we will build shortly; it looks like Figure 13-6.

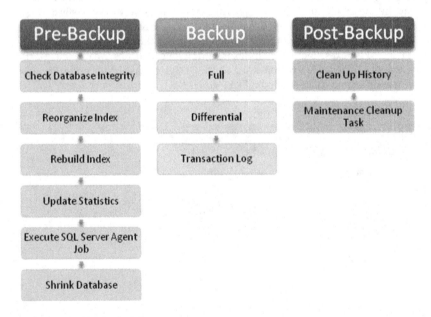

Figure 13-6. *Scenario 2 Structure*

Look familiar? It should. It's the same graphic as earlier. This clearly implies that we need to do all of these steps. Remember that, although we have *which* tasks defined that we want to run, we need to know *when* to run them.

Notice that, in both instances, I have left the complete backup schedule intact. This is because, even though you may have a smaller database, the data within the database is no less important to your business or your end users. Without that data, you would have no job. So the concept of database backups will remain in place, regardless of the size of the database.

The rule that I've always heard is that maintenance needs to be done when your customers are off the database. If you have a database that is in use 24/7, then you just have to determine when your database is used least, or set the schedule to fire when the CPU is idle. Remember that SQL Server gives you lots of options for scheduling, and there is going to be a solution to just about any scheduling issue you can think of. For this plan, we are going to fire this at midnight every night. We are going to have different tasks run at different intervals also, all of which I will demonstrate shortly.

Another important part to scheduling the maintenance plan is that you can always set precedence constraints on the tasks, which we will get into later. Those are lifesavers! What those do is say that, when you have a chain of tasks in a task, you want to do them in a certain order. You can also set what happens if the task fails, succeeds, or completes. You can imagine that we are going to be setting reporting and logging at these steps, so that we are aware of any issues that may potentially affect our end users.

Let's take a look at something interesting really quick. Double-click any of the jobs in SQL Server Agent. I chose bak Files, but you can choose whichever one you want. You should see Figure 13-7 now.

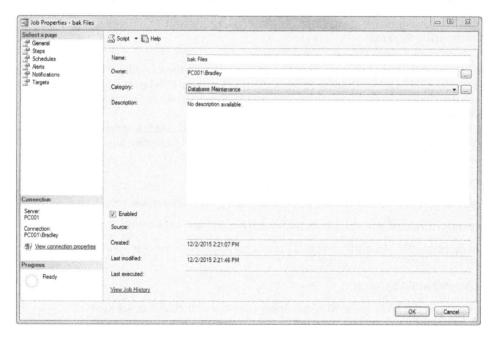

Figure 13-7. *Job Properties*

Same as before, what's the big deal? Click the Steps option on the left and expand the columns in the job step list field, as shown in Figure 13-8. Notice anything special here?

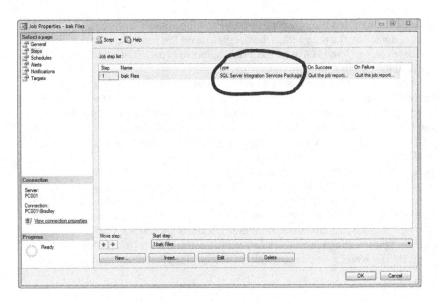

Figure 13-8. *Job Properties, Steps tab*

That's right; this is a SQL Server Integration Services package. I briefly mentioned this in the beginning chapter. That's how it was saved in the database and we didn't even know it. This opens up a whole new level of interaction with the database, because now that we have an SSIS package, we can put them all together to make one giant package.

Before we go on, I want to add the following caveat: you should have thorough and complete jobs at this point. What do I mean by *complete*? Double-check that all descriptions and names are filled in on all objects within the jobs, specifically:

- **General tab**: Description box.

- **Steps tab**, **General tab**: Name box (click Edit and change the "Step name" value).

- **Steps tab**, **Advanced tab**: "Include step output in history" should be selected.

- **Schedules tab**: We're going to remove these in a few minutes, so they can stay for now.

- **Alerts tab**: Should be blank.

- **Notifications tab**: Write to the Windows Application event log should be selected with "When the job completes" selected.

- **Targets tab**: Should be left blank.

Notifications should not be selected for individual tasks; instead, we are going to have the subplans take care of reporting and logging. E-mailing is a part of this function, which you will see shortly.

Guess what we're gonna do next?

Creating the Maintenance Plan

Finally! This is what we've been working towards for this entire book. We are going to create one package that will be the implementation of the maintenance plan that we will use to maintain the database from now on.

Show of hands for who thinks we are going to use Maintenance Plan Wizard to create this maintenance plan...? Guess what? We can't use the Maintenance Plan Wizard for this task, because the wizard is specifically for creating new tasks, not for combining them into a single package. We can make as many individual jobs as we want, but unless we put them all in one package together and run them on separate schedules, they will never work together. Also, leaving them to run individually, and not as part of an integrated solution, does not allow us to enforce the precedence constraints we looked at before; instead, we will simply run a task on a schedule, not knowing or caring if it actually worked or not.

Instead of that approach, we are going to work on the definition of *robust* maintenance plans; a one-stop-shop for all of our maintenance needs in one area. This is going to require a bit more tweaking of the individual plans, which we will look at now.

Editing the Jobs

The first thing that we need to do, in light of the knowledge that these are SSIS packages, is plan for the deployment of the packages. What does that mean? It means that each package is going to be run as a portion of a larger package, with precedence constraints and reporting/logging built in, and we need to make sure all of that is 100% set before unleashing it onto our development environment. We will do a lot of testing before we ever unleash anything to the production environment, right? Let's look at the individual jobs now, and tweak them to our needs.

Recall that our jobs list looks like what's shown in Figure 13-9.

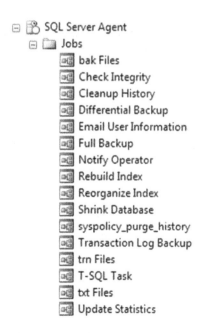

Figure 13-9. *SQL Server Agent Jobs*

Again, quite a few jobs! Each one of those jobs is going to be a part of the package later. For now, we are going to edit these, though; so start from the top and make the recommended changes.

Finalizing the Jobs

Double-click a job to show the General page. Then go through each of the steps described in the following sections, making sure that the changes are made as explained.

General Page Settings

The General page holds all of the "high level" settings of the job. What I mean by this is that the further abstractions of properties are further divided in subsequent pages, but the generic settings for the entire job are all here.

- Owner field should be set to the owner of the database.

- Category should be set to Database Maintenance.

- Enter a short description.

- Make sure that the Enabled check box is selected.

Steps Page Settings

Click the Edit button at the bottom of the screen and change the Step name on the General page to the task name (Cleanup History, Text Files, T-SQL Task—the job name, not the plan name). Notice that this screen is something new and different, since it pertains strictly to the settings used to run the SSIS package. There isn't a need to change anything in here yet, so leave this area alone.

Click Advanced on the left. This is where we defined the on success and on failure actions of the package. The individual package doesn't need an output file, since we will be doing that at the maintenance plan package level and not this level. Ensure that the "Include step output in history" check box is selected.

Click OK when you are ready to move on.

Schedules Page Settings

Remove the schedule by clicking the Remove button at the bottom of the screen.

You will see error shown in Figure 13-10 when doing this step.

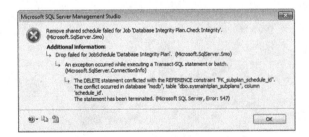

Figure 13-10. *Schedule error*

This is to be expected. Here's how we're going to take care of that for future schedule removals. Click OK on the error message and then click OK to close the job interface.

First of all, let's look at the available schedules by running the following query.

```
SELECT * FROM msdb.dbo.sysschedules;
```

The error in Figure 13-10 referenced the sysmaintplan_subplans.schedule_id column, so the short answer is to set these values to NULL using the following query.

```
UPDATE msdb.dbo.sysmaintplan_subplans SET schedule_id = NULL;
```

And that's about it for that. Now, when you go in to remove a schedule, you won't get an error because all of the schedules have been removed. They are still resident in the interface though. How annoying.

The sysjobschedules Table

The msdb database holds a lot of information about our jobs, including the schedules assigned to those jobs. In particular, the table we are going to reference is named sysjobschedules. We are going to write a query that will show us the information in this table, so we can see the schedules and how they work in the context of the jobs.

Here's the query we're going to use to see what's in that table; go ahead and run this in a new query window.

```
SELECT * FROM msdb.dbo.sysjobschedules ORDER BY schedule_id;
```

That query will return the information shown in Figure 13-11.

	schedule_id	job_id	next_run_date	next_run_time
1	7	827B7393-34F6-49D6-9D61-2EFE38C4FCD1	20151202	180000
2	8	F74BC679-83F7-4F20-B816-9E12A630EAF1	20151203	20000
3	9	417972BA-035D-449B-834B-279A277A4289	20151203	0
4	10	03231868-CD97-40D3-B8C7-145291A8C820	20151202	180000
5	11	6304C056-215F-4917-BF40-D5F94960B4EC	20151202	160000
6	12	9F20DD38-1D21-4D98-A63E-3EA0341AD95A	20151202	160000
7	13	A16D9958-8E27-49B1-96C7-FC9FFD0D7F5E	20151203	0
8	14	60791DF0-2CCF-41DC-ACB4-D87EA8873F04	20151203	0
9	15	DAF73C3A-047E-4D43-9942-F55DF367A1C2	20151203	0
10	16	07D82EA3-0681-49D0-A851-6AD4148BBAEC	20151203	0
11	17	49777CB7-A1BE-409B-809C-97FB1FDD3243	20151203	0
12	18	371F1954-C716-4F65-8312-F7D308D8FBCA	20151203	0
13	19	2CADBA7D-5763-4BFD-AFB2-4DBF0E356C24	20151203	0
14	20	D78C3C39-6CDE-4F74-AF90-DE49C11AD2B5	20151203	0
15	21	58C0D312-2DB3-4F14-AFE9-7B381EE68ADE	20151203	0
16	22	51C50E36-0876-43A1-9554-3B8C10707D14	20151203	0

Figure 13-11. *Query Results*

Let's put a little INNER JOIN magic on the sysjobschedules and sysjobs tables to show us what is going on. For clarification, sysjobschedules holds the scheduling information for the jobs referenced from the sysjobs table. What we want to do is show the job_id and name columns from the sysjobs table, and the schedule_id column from the sysjobschedules table. The following is the completed query.

```
SELECT msdb.dbo.sysjobs.job_id, msdb.dbo.sysjobs.name, sysjobschedules.schedule_id
FROM msdb.dbo.sysjobs
INNER JOIN msdb.dbo.sysjobschedules ON
sysjobschedules.job_id = msdb.dbo.sysjobs.job_id
ORDER BY msdb.dbo.sysjobs.name;
```

Run this query. You will see the results shown in Figure 13-12.

	job_id	name	schedule_id
1	60791DF0-2CCF-41DC-ACB4-D87EA8873F04	bak Files	14
2	9F20DD38-1D21-4D98-A63E-3EA0341AD95A	Check Integrity	12
3	A16D9958-8E27-49B1-96C7-FC9FFD0D7F5E	Cleanup History	13
4	03231868-CD97-40D3-B8C7-145291A8C820	Differential Backup	10
5	827B7393-34F6-49D6-9D61-2EFE38C4FCD1	Email User Information	7
6	417972BA-035D-449B-834B-279A277A4289	Full Backup	9
7	51C50E36-0876-43A1-9554-3B8C10707D14	Notify Operator	22
8	49777CB7-A1BE-409B-809C-97FB1FDD3243	Rebuild Index	17
9	371F1954-C716-4F65-8312-F7D308D8FBCA	Reorganize Index	18
10	2CADBA7D-5763-4BFD-AFB2-4DBF0E356C24	Shrink Database	19
11	F74BC679-83F7-4F20-B816-9E12A630EAF1	syspolicy_purge_history	8
12	6304C056-215F-4917-BF40-D5F94960B4EC	Transaction Log Backup	11
13	DAF73C3A-047E-4D43-9942-F55DF367A1C2	tm Files	15
14	58C0D312-2DB3-4F14-AFE9-7B381EE68ADE	T-SQL Task	21
15	07D82EA3-0681-49D0-A851-6AD4148BBAEC	txt Files	16
16	D78C3C39-6CDE-4F74-AF90-DE49C11AD2B5	Update Statistics	20

Figure 13-12. *Query Results*

That's better! That shows us the schedules left for us to delete. Let's go ahead and manually delete the schedule for the top one, bak Files, and then rerun the query. Figure 13-13 shows the result of this query.

	job_id	name	schedule_id
1	9F20DD38-1D21-4D98-A63E-3EA0341AD95A	Check Integrity	12
2	A16D9958-8E27-49B1-96C7-FC9FFD0D7F5E	Cleanup History	13
3	03231868-CD97-40D3-B8C7-145291A8C820	Differential Backup	10
4	827B7393-34F6-49D6-9D61-2EFE38C4FCD1	Email User Information	7
5	417972BA-035D-449B-834B-279A277A4289	Full Backup	9
6	51C50E36-0876-43A1-9554-3B8C10707D14	Notify Operator	22
7	49777CB7-A1BE-409B-809C-97FB1FDD3243	Rebuild Index	17
8	371F1954-C716-4F65-8312-F7D308D8FBCA	Reorganize Index	18
9	2CADBA7D-5763-4BFD-AFB2-4DBF0E356C24	Shrink Database	19
10	F74BC679-83F7-4F20-B816-9E12A630EAF1	syspolicy_purge_history	8
11	6304C056-215F-4917-BF40-D5F94960B4EC	Transaction Log Backup	11
12	DAF73C3A-047E-4D43-9942-F55DF367A1C2	tm Files	15
13	58C0D312-2DB3-4F14-AFE9-7B381EE68ADE	T-SQL Task	21
14	07D82EA3-0681-49D0-A851-6AD4148BBAEC	txt Files	16
15	D78C3C39-6CDE-4F74-AF90-DE49C11AD2B5	Update Statistics	20

Figure 13-13. *Query Results*

Just as we thought; it's gone! What does that tell us? It means that this table specifically stores the schedules for the jobs, hence the name sysjobschedules. It also tells us that we can now delete the contents of the sysjobschedules table, and that will remove all of our schedules.

Let's take a quick look at the structure of the sysjobschedules table in Figure 13-14 for a second though.

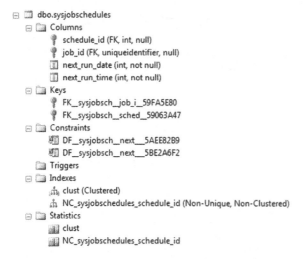

Figure 13-14. *sysjobsschedules Structure*

None of these columns are IDENTITY columns, but we can see those foreign constraints that stopped us from deleting the schedules earlier (the error generated by SSMS). Since there isn't an IDENTITY column to worry about, I'm going to recommend that we DELETE FROM this table.

This actually brings up a good point. What is the difference between TRUNCATE and DELETE FROM when clearing data from a table? Basically, when you TRUNCATE, the database engine doesn't bother with that whole transaction log thing, it just wipes the table and the pages. The TRUNCATE operation can be rolled back if it is part of a transaction. If it's not, you aren't getting that data back without restoring from a backup. TRUNCATE also locks the table, so don't use it on a table that is used a lot. DELETE FROM, on the other hand, simply deletes the specified information and logs it in the transaction log. DELETE FROM does not "restart" a table either; if you have a table with an IDENTITY column and delete everything in the table using the DELETE FROM command, the next IDENTITY value entered into the table is going to be the next value—even though there is no direct reference in the table. That means if you have 15 rows of data in a table; then run a DELETE FROM on that table; then insert a new row of data; the IDENTITY column value is going to be 16 and not 1. TRUNCATE "restarts" that table, so that when you have 15 rows of data and then TRUNCATE that table, the IDENTITY column starts back at 1 when inserting a new row of data. Big difference there!

That's not to say that you can't run a DELETE FROM command and not restart the numbering at 1 when the next row comes in. To do this, run the following query after running your DELETE FROM statement.

```
DBCC CHECKIDENT('[table_name].[column_name]', RESEED, 0);
```

This query forces the table to reseed the column with the value defined as the IDENTITY qualifier, which in this case is 0.

So, in both theory and in practice, you could run a DELETE FROM statement and then the preceding DBCC statement, and achieve the same results as a TRUNCATE statement (wipe the table and reset the numbering for the IDENTITY column in a table), except that we are able to have the DELETE FROM and DBCC statements as part of the transaction log.

Okay, let's go ahead and delete the contents of the sysjobschedules table, except for the syspolicy_purge_history record, by running the following query. Grab the job ID from the previous INNER JOIN query we ran before and insert that into the following query to run it.

```
DELETE FROM msdb.dbo.sysjobschedules WHERE job_id <> 'F74BC679-83F7-4F20-B816-9E12A630EAF1';
```

That's all you need to do. Remember, there is no IDENTITY column to worry about reseeding, so that command will do all we need for this table; clear out the schedules. If you open up the next job in the list, Cleanup History, notice the distinct lack of a schedule in the Schedules tab. Open any of them and check; they're all gone. Good job!

Alerts Page Settings

This page should be blank. That's okay, because we will be handling the logging and reporting from the package and not the individual tasks.

Notifications Page Settings

This is where we set the notifications earlier. This should be cleared out now though, much like the Schedules part above. We don't need to send an e-mail, but I recommend keeping the Write to the Windows Application event log option selected and with the "When the job completes" value. That way, whenever the job completes (either On Success or On Failure), it is entered into the event log.

Targets Page Settings

This page is blank by default. Leave it blank.

Saving the Changes

Click OK to save any changes you have made and you are done with finalizing the jobs. Repeat the process of finalizing for each job except for the one called E-mail User Information. Leave that job alone.

We aren't going to worry about the job titled E-mail User Information, since that one was specifically to show how the SQL Server Agent job task works. To keep this job from firing, just disable the task by right-clicking it and choosing Disable. You should see the interface shown in in Figure 13-15 when this happens.

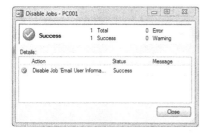

Figure 13-15. *Disable Jobs*

Also note that the job now has a little red down arrow in the Jobs folder, as shown in Figure 13-16.

Figure 13-16. *SQL Server Agent showing a disabled job*

This icon shows at a glance that the job is disabled.

Reviewing Your Schedule Needs

We have configured the tasks to add to the maintenance plan. Let's review what the schedule needs to look like for the maintenance plan (see Figure 13-17). Remember that we're following Scenario 2 also, where we will be using as many maintenance tasks as available for proper maintenance of our database.

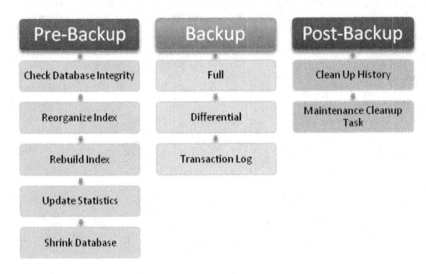

Figure 13-17. *Scenario 2 Structure*

I kept both of the Index tasks in there, as you can see. Remember how I said earlier that you didn't need both in one plan? I will be running those at different times; that's why they're both in there like that.

Adding the Tasks to the Plan

Are you ready to begin putting your plan together? Here we go!

Expand the Maintenance Plan folder and look for Backup Maintenance Plan. Double-click this and you should see the interface shown in Figure 13-18.

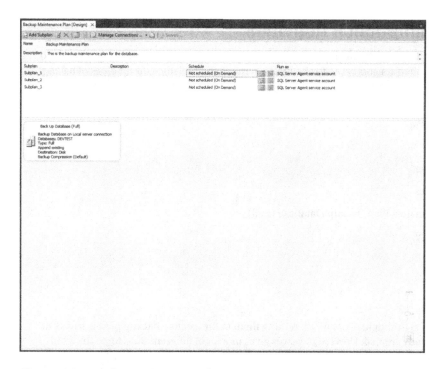

Figure 13-18. *Backup Maintenance Plan stage*

Unfortunately, the Subplan names don't carry over, and since we deleted our schedules, we need to update those really quick. Double-click the Subplan names to update the information, and notice how the stage changes when you click a different Subplan. This helps you to name them appropriately; Subplan_1 is Backup Database (Full), Subplan_2 is Backup Database (Differential), and Subplan_3 is Backup Database (Transaction Log). Update them using the interface and then enter the schedules.

Remember the schedule we wanted for the backups? Full backups are at midnight, differentials are every 6 hours, and transaction logs are every hour. Set your schedules for the three tasks to these values. You should end up with the interface shown in Figure 13-19.

Subplan	Description	Schedule			Run as
Backup Database (Full)	This plan will run the maintenance activities for the Full backup.	Occurs every day at 12:00:00 AM. ...			SQL Server Agent service account
Backup Database (Differential)	This plan will run the maintenance activities for the Differential backup.	Occurs every day every 6 hour(s) ...			SQL Server Agent service account
Backup Database (Transaction Log)	This plan will run the maintenance activities for the Transaction Log backup.	Occurs every day every 1 hour(s) ...			SQL Server Agent service account

Figure 13-19. *Backup Maintenance Plan Schedules*

Notice that the schedules are now set, the Subplan names are updated, and they are all set to run as SQL Server Agent service account.

What we want to do now is add the rest of the tasks to this maintenance plan. It's pretty safe to say that we are going to stick to the three backup plans shown in Figure 13-19 as our standard for backing up, and all of our maintenance activities are going to be done in those three windows. Not all of the maintenance tasks, but some at different times and for different reasons. Because of this, we are going to add the needed tasks to each of the three backup tasks, and enforce precedence constraints.

Also, when you save the Backup Maintenance Plan, the job names are updated. How very inconvenient! We can update these again later.

Full Backup Maintenance Activities

What tasks do we want to run along with the midnight full backups? Most of them, to be honest. For most installations, midnight is probably a good time to run maintenance activities since the chances of having users on is slim to none.

In particular, we want to run the following jobs, in this order:

- Check Integrity
- Rebuild Index
- Shrink Database
- Update Statistics
- Backup Maintenance Plan.Backup Database (Full)
- Cleanup History
- bak Files
- txt Files
- trn Files

These tasks will be run at midnight every night. Adding them to the existing backup plan is trivial, at this point, since they're already created. How? SQL Server gives us a lot of different ways to do things in different environments. In this case, we are going to add the jobs we already created to the existing Backup Maintenance Plan and go from there. This implies a couple of things, so let's go over that really quick before we push forward.

- Don't delete the "old" maintenance plans. The original jobs, which are going to be added to the Backup Maintenance Plan, are still linked to those original maintenance plans.
- Don't delete the jobs.

In other words, just because we are adding the jobs to the maintenance plan, you shouldn't assume that there isn't a reference remaining to the original plans. As long as it's structured how we have it, the reference will remain. Later, we will export the completed plans and review how to restore them. You will then see exactly how these references work together to create the maintenance plans as you now know them.

Adding the Check Integrity Task

Click the Backup Database (Full) subplan as shown in Figure 13-19. This will show the Back Up Database (Full) task on the stage, as also shown in Figure 13-18. Now, click and drag Execute SQL Server Agent job from the toolbar to the stage. You should see the interface shown in Figure 13-20 at this point.

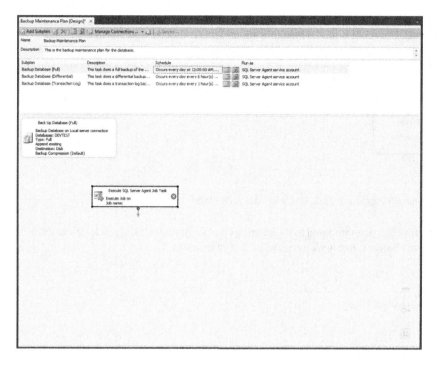

Figure 13-20. *Backup Maintenance Plan Stage*

All that says is that we have a generic SQL Server Agent job task there, but we haven't defined a task yet. To do this, double-click the task on the stage. Guess what shows up? Figure 13-21 is a big hint.

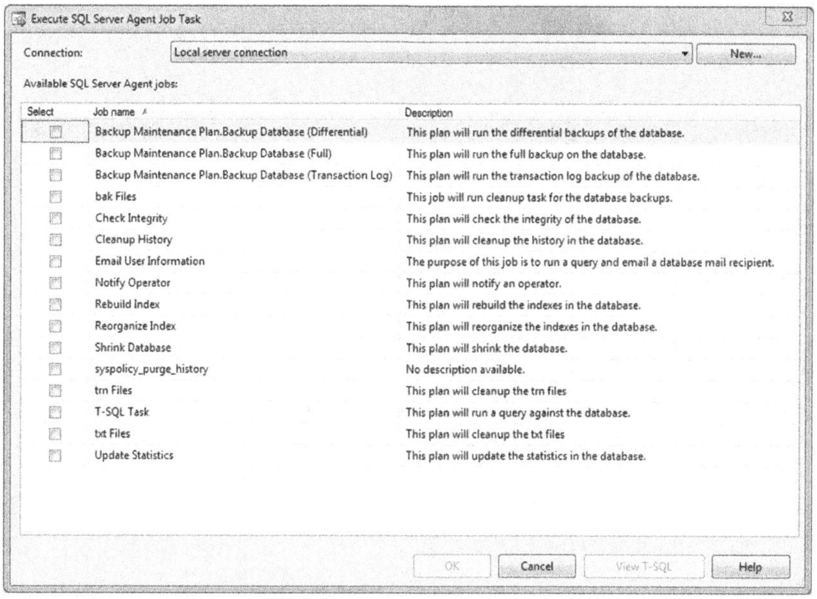

Figure 13-21. *Execute SQL Server Agent Job Task*

Look at that! All the jobs that we already created are lined up and looking nice and presentable (once I sorted the job name column). How cool is that? The implication of this is that we don't have to go back in and re-create what we have already done; we can just add them here and be done with it. Aren't you glad you put in all that work now? Since I already sorted the jobs, go ahead and click the check box next to Check Integrity, and click OK. You should now see what is shown in Figure 13-22.

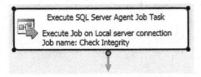

Figure 13-22. Execute SQL Server Agent Job Task on Design Surface Stage

That shows us that the task has been updated to the existing Check Integrity task. If you long-click the task name on the top, you can change it to Check Integrity, as shown in Figure 13-23.

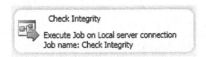

Figure 13-23. Execute SQL Server Agent Job Task on Design Surface Stage (updated)

Now I can easily see what this task is. At this point, you need to reorganize your stage a little bit. See how the backup task is way up on the top left? Just drag it more to the middle, and the drag the Check Integrity task above it. You should end up looking similar to Figure 13-24.

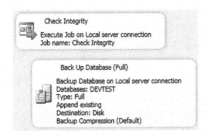

Figure 13-24. Execute SQL Server Agent Job Task on Design Surface Stage (completed)

Adding the Rebuild Index Task

Just like before, click and drag Execute SQL Server Agent job from the toolbar to the stage, but this time, place it in between the Check Integrity task and the backup task. You should end up looking similar to Figure 13-25.

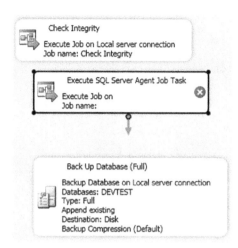

Figure 13-25. *Execute SQL Server Agent Job Task on Design Surface Stage*

Double-click the task that we just added, select the Rebuild Index task from the list, and click OK. Long-click and change the name of the task. You should see Figure 13-26 when you are done.

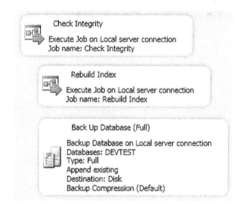

Figure 13-26. *Execute SQL Server Agent Job Task on Design Surface Stage (completed)*

Adding the Shrink Database Task

Click and drag Execute SQL Server Agent job from the toolbar to the stage, but this time, place it in between the Rebuild Index task and the backup task. You should end up looking similar to Figure 13-27.

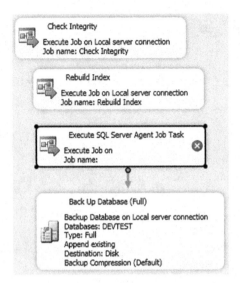

Figure 13-27. Execute SQL Server Agent Job Task on Design Surface Stage

Double-click the task that we just added, select the Shrink Database task from the list, and click OK. Update the name of the task by long-clicking and updating it. You should see Figure 13-28 when you are done.

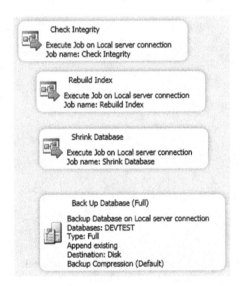

Figure 13-28. Execute SQL Server Agent Job Task on Design Surface Stage (completed)

Adding the Update Statistics Task

Click and drag Execute SQL Server Agent job from the toolbar to the stage, but this time, place it in between the Shrink Database task and the backup task. You should end up looking similar to Figure 13-29.

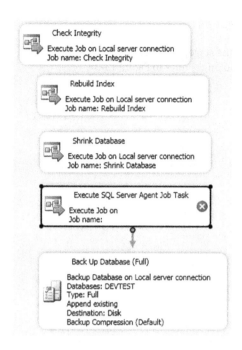

Figure 13-29. *Execute SQL Server Agent Job Task on Design Surface Stage*

Double-click the task that we just added, select the Update Statistics task from the list, and click OK. Update the name of the task by long-clicking and updating it. You should see Figure 13-30 when you are done.

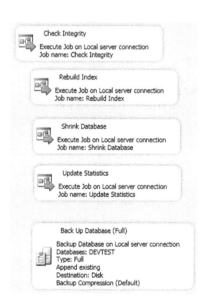

Figure 13-30. *Execute SQL Server Agent Job Task on Design Surface Stage (completed)*

Adding the Cleanup History Task

Click and drag Execute SQL Server Agent job from the toolbar to the stage, but this time, place it after the Back Up Database (Full) task at the bottom. You should end up looking similar to Figure 13-31.

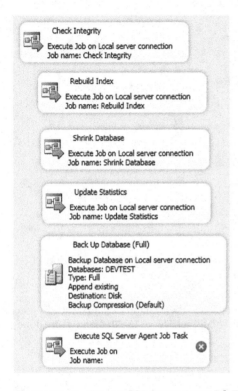

Figure 13-31. *Execute SQL Server Agent Job Task on Design Surface Stage*

Double-click the task that we just added, select the Cleanup History task from the list, and click OK. Update the name of the task by long-clicking and updating it. You should see Figure 13-32 when you are done.

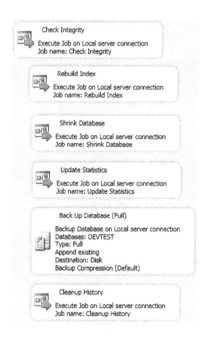

Figure 13-32. *Execute SQL Server Agent Job Task on Design Surface Stage (completed)*

Adding the bak Files Task

Click and drag Execute SQL Server Agent Job from the toolbar to the stage, but this time, place it at the bottom. You should end up looking similar to Figure 13-33.

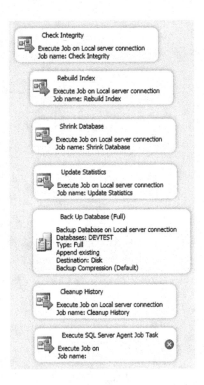

Figure 13-33. *Execute SQL Server Agent Job Task on Design Surface Stage*

Double-click the task that we just added, select the bak Files task from the list, and click OK. Update the name of the task by long-clicking and updating it. You should see Figure 13-34 when you are done.

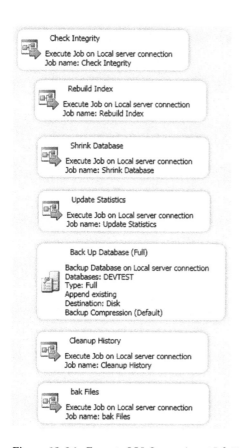

Figure 13-34. Execute SQL Server Agent Job Task on Design Surface Stage (completed)

Adding the txt Files Task

Click and drag Execute SQL Server Agent Job from the toolbar to the stage, but this time, place it at the bottom. You should end up looking similar to Figure 13-35.

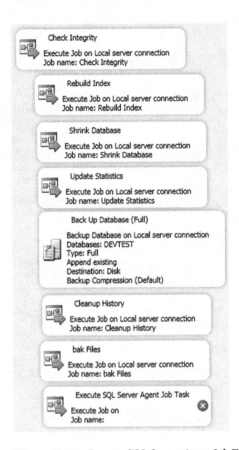

Figure 13-35. *Execute SQL Server Agent Job Task on Design Surface Stage*

Double-click the task that we just added, select the txt Files task from the list, and click OK. Update the name of the task by long-clicking and updating it. You should see Figure 13-36 when you are done.

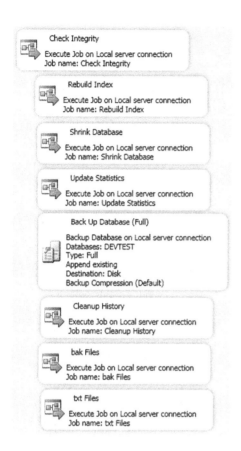

Figure 13-36. *Execute SQL Server Agent Job Task on Design Surface Stage (completed)*

Adding the trn Files Task

Click and drag Execute SQL Server Agent Job from the toolbar to the stage, but this time, place it at the bottom. You should end up looking similar to Figure 13-37.

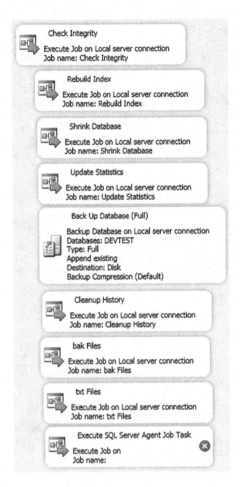

Figure 13-37. *Execute SQL Server Agent Job Task on Design Surface Stage*

Double-click the task that we just added, select the trn Files task from the list, and click OK. Update the name of the task by long-clicking and updating it. You should see Figure 13-38 when you are done.

Figure 13-38. *Execute SQL Server Agent Job Task on Design Surface Stage (completed)*

We will reorganize that shortly, don't worry.

Differential Backup Maintenance Activities

What tasks do we want to run along with the differential backups run every 6 hours? We want this to be sort of a refresh period; a quick water break, so to speak.

In particular, we want to run the following jobs, in this order:

- Check Integrity

- Reorganize Index

- Shrink Database

- Update Statistics

- Backup Maintenance Plan.Differential Backup

Wait. That's mostly the same list! Yes, because most of the same operations need to be performed whenever you back up the database. The main difference is that we are doing the Reorganize task instead of the Rebuild task, and we aren't cleaning the maintenance files or history. That is done only at midnight, so we are sure to stay in sync with the backup schedule. Remember the difference between reorganizing and rebuilding the indexes? Reorganize keeps the hotel built, and Rebuild tears it down and starts brand new. We don't need to take the time to rebuild when we can just run a quick reorganize task and continue on. This isn't sacrificing anything, since the nightly rebuild takes care of this extra step.

Adding these is going to be very similar to the previous part, so feel free to add them and skip ahead, if necessary.

Adding the Check Integrity Task

Click the Backup Database (Differential) subplan as shown in Figure 13-39. This will show the Back Up Database (Differential) task on the stage, as also shown in Figure 13-39.

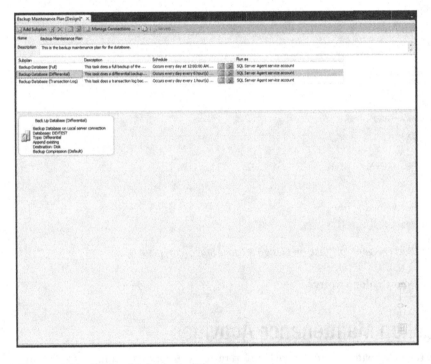

Figure 13-39. *Backup Maintenance Plan Stage*

Now, click and drag Execute SQL Server Agent Job from the toolbar to the stage. You should see Figure 13-40 at this point.

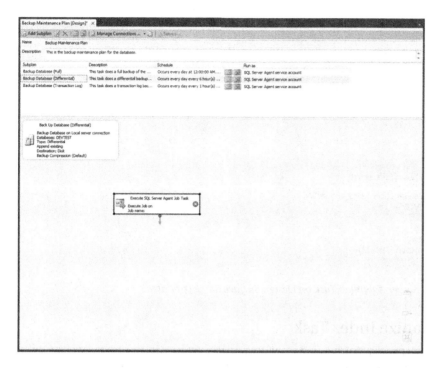

Figure 13-40. *Execute SQL Server Agent Job Task*

Double-click the task on the stage and click the check box next to Database Integrity Plan.Check Integrity, and click OK. Update the name by long-clicking the task. If you long-click the task name on the top, you can change it to Check Integrity, as shown in Figure 13-41.

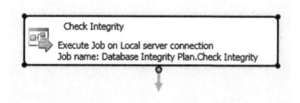

Figure 13-41. *Execute SQL Server Agent Job Task on Design Surface Stage*

At this point, you need to reorganize your stage a little bit. See how the backup task is way up on the top left? Just drag it more to the middle, and the drag the Check Integrity task above it. You should end up looking similar to Figure 13-42.

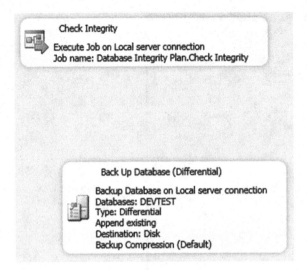

Figure 13-42. Execute SQL Server Agent Job Task on Design Surface Stage (updated)

Adding the Reorganize Index Task

Just like before, click and drag Execute SQL Server Agent Job from the toolbar to the stage, but this time, place it in between the Check Integrity task and the backup task. You should end up looking similar to Figure 13-43.

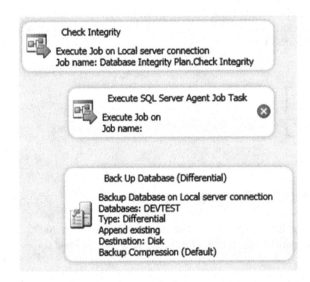

Figure 13-43. Execute SQL Server Agent Job Task on Design Surface Stage

Double-click the task that we just added, select the Reorganize Index task from the list, and click OK. Long-click and change the name of the task. You should see Figure 13-44 when you are done.

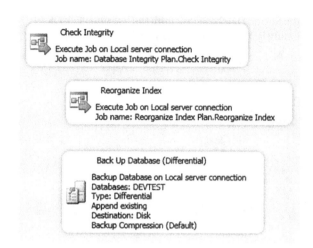

Figure 13-44. *Execute SQL Server Agent Job Task on Design Surface Stage (updated)*

Adding the Shrink Database Task

Click and drag Execute SQL Server Agent Job from the toolbar to the stage, but this time, place it in between the Rebuild Index task and the backup task. You should end up looking similar to what's shown in Figure 13-45.

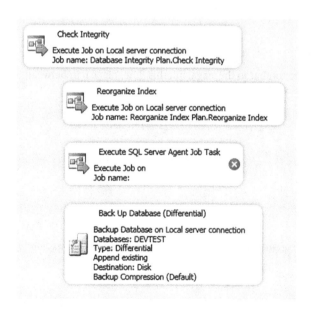

Figure 13-45. *Execute SQL Server Agent Job Task on Design Surface Stage*

Double-click the task that we just added, select the Shrink Database task from the list, and click OK. Update the name of the task by long-clicking and updating it. You should see Figure 13-46 when you are done.

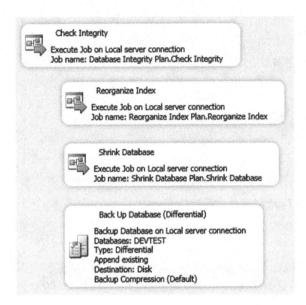

Figure 13-46. *Execute SQL Server Agent Job Task on Design Surface Stage (updated)*

Adding the Update Statistics Task

Click and drag Execute SQL Server Agent Job from the toolbar to the stage, but this time, place it in between the Shrink Database task and the backup task. You should end up looking similar to Figure 13-47.

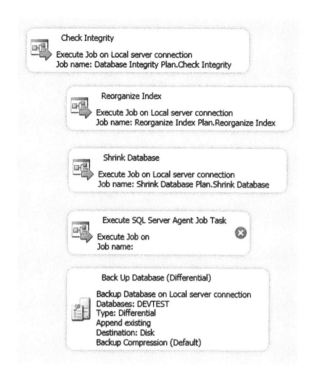

Figure 13-47. Execute SQL Server Agent Job Task on Design Surface Stage

Double-click the task that we just added, select the Update Statistics task from the list, and click OK. Update the name of the task by long-clicking and updating it. You should see Figure 13-48 when you are done.

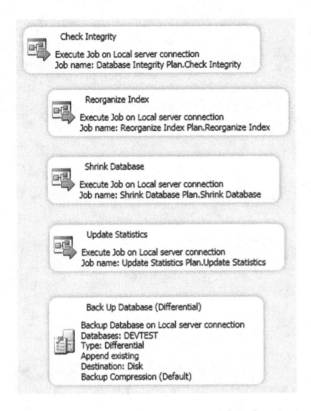

Figure 13-48. *Execute SQL Server Agent Job Task on Design Surface Stage (updated)*

Transaction Log Backup Maintenance Activities

What tasks do we want to run along with the transaction log backups run every hour? This is sort of the most difficult one, because we don't want to put too much burden on our server, but we want to be able to perform maintenance as necessary.

In particular, we want to run the following tasks, in this order:

- Database Integrity Plan.Check Integrity

- Reorganize Index Plan.Reorganize Index

- Shrink Database Plan.Shrink Database

- Update Statistics Plan.Update Statistics

- Backup Maintenance Plan.Transaction Log Backup

Adding these is going to be very similar to the previous part, so feel free to add them and skip ahead, if necessary.

Adding the Check Integrity Task

Click the Backup Database (Transaction Log) subplan as shown in Figure 13-49. This will show the Back Up Database (Transaction Log) task on the stage, as also shown in Figure 13-49.

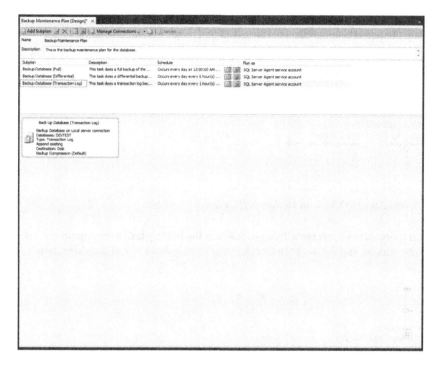

Figure 13-49. *Backup Maintenance Plan Stage*

Now, click and drag Execute SQL Server Agent Job from the toolbar to the stage. You should see Figure 13-50 at this point.

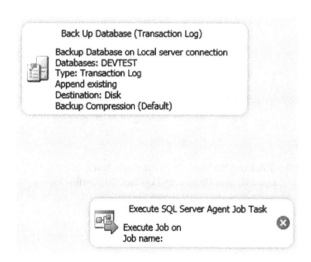

Figure 13-50. *Execute SQL Server Agent Job Task on Design Surface Stage*

Double-click the task on the stage and click the check box next to Database Integrity Plan.Check Integrity, and click OK. Update the name by long-clicking the task. If you long-click the task name on the top, you can change it to Check Integrity, as shown in Figure 13-51.

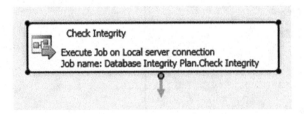

Figure 13-51. *Execute SQL Server Agent Job Task on Design Surface Stage (updated)*

At this point, you need to reorganize your stage a little bit. See how the backup task is way up on the top left? Just drag it more to the middle, and the drag the Check Integrity task above it. You should end up looking similar to Figure 13-52.

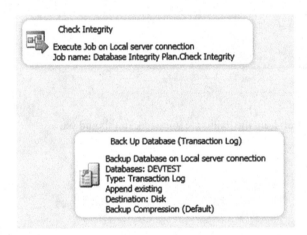

Figure 13-52. *Execute SQL Server Agent Job Task on Design Surface Stage (completed)*

Adding the Reorganize Index Task

Just like before, click and drag Execute SQL Server Agent Job from the toolbar to the stage, but this time, place it in between the Check Integrity task and the backup task. You should end up looking similar to Figure 13-53.

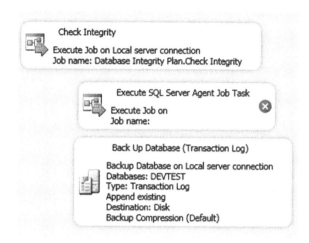

Figure 13-53. *Execute SQL Server Agent Job Task on Design Surface Stage*

Double-click the task that we just added, select the Reorganize Index task from the list, and click OK. Long-click and change the name of the task. You should see Figure 13-54 when you are done.

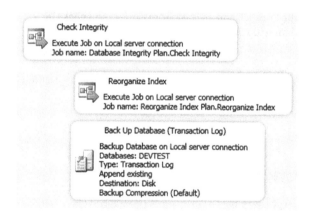

Figure 13-54. *Execute SQL Server Agent Job Task on Design Surface Stage (updated)*

Adding the Shrink Database Task

Click and drag Execute SQL Server Agent Job from the toolbar to the stage, but this time, place it in between the Rebuild Index task and the backup task. You should end up looking similar to Figure 13-55.

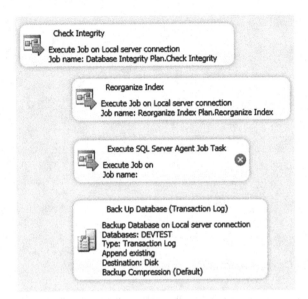

Figure 13-55. *Execute SQL Server Agent Job Task on Design Surface Stage*

Double-click the task that we just added, select the Shrink Database task from the list, and click OK. Update the name of the task by long-clicking and updating it. You should see Figure 13-56 when you are done.

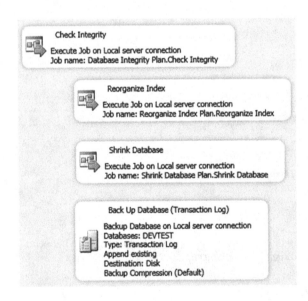

Figure 13-56. *Execute SQL Server Agent Job Task on Design Surface Stage (updated)*

Adding the Update Statistics Task

Click and drag Execute SQL Server Agent Job from the toolbar to the stage, but this time, place it in between the Shrink Database task and the backup task. You should end up looking similar to what's shown in Figure 13-57.

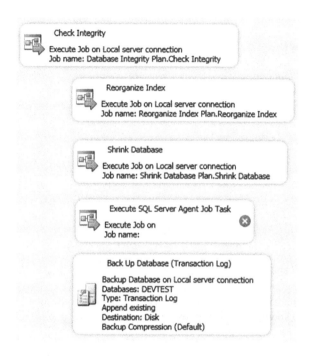

Figure 13-57. *Execute SQL Server Agent Job Task on Design Surface Stage*

Double-click the task that we just added, select the Update Statistics task from the list, and click OK. Update the name of the task by long-clicking and updating it. You should see what's shown in Figure 13-58 when you are done.

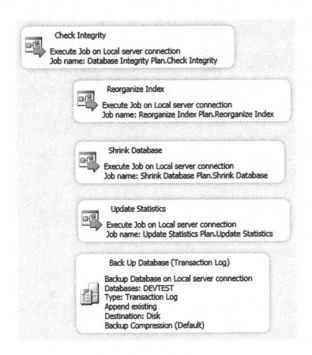

Figure 13-58. Execute SQL Server Agent Job Task on Design Surface Stage (updated)

So there are the three parts of the maintenance plan in place. But we don't have schedules for the jobs we just added. How is the maintenance plan going to know when to execute the packages?

By using the power of...

Precedence Constraints

What is a precedence constraint? Basically, a precedence constraint is what determines the path of execution for a task based on the outcome of an expression or constraint. Using precedence constraints allows us to assign pass, fail, or success values based on the state of execution of the task.

For example, let's assume that we have a Success constraint and a Failure constraint for a task. We could define a Notify Operator task as a result of the Failure constraint, and either define another task after the Success constraint, or let it cease execution normally. Enforcing precedence constraints in a maintenance plan workflow will greatly enhance the visibility into the tasks being run and the conditions they are executing under.

Let's start with the full backup tasks. First off, separate your tasks a little bit, as shown in Figure 13-59. Give yourself some room to work. There are nine tasks in here, so it's going to take up a fair bit of room. Note the yellow highlighter to show you how to structure these tasks.

Figure 13-59. *Full Backups Precedence Constraints Map*

Click Check Integrity and a little green arrow will appear on the bottom of the task. Click that arrow and drag it to the Rebuild Index task on the stage. You should see what's shown in Figure 13-60 when you are done.

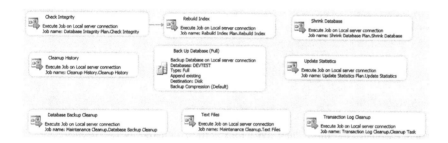

Figure 13-60. *Full Backups Precedence Constraints (updated)*

It kind of snaps to the task when it connects, doesn't it? That's good though, so you know where it is heading.

Now, if you double-click that green line, you see Figure 13-61.

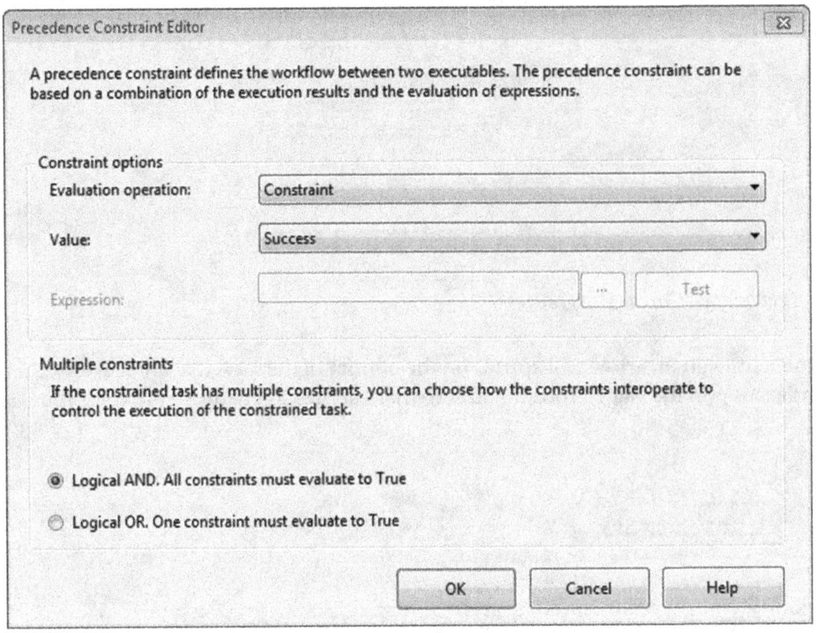

Figure 13-61. *Precedence Constraint Editor*

This is called the Precedence Constraint Editor. Let's take a look at these constraints for a minute.

Constraint Options

Constraint options allow us to define what operation to evaluate, and what action to take when an evaluated constraint is discovered. We need to choose a constraint and/or an expression to evaluate, and then define the return value based on the value of the constraint or expression so we can catch the condition and plan accordingly. The following list explains this in a bit more detail.

- Evaluation Operation
  - Constraint
  - Expression
  - Constraint and Expression
  - Constraint or Expression
- Value
  - Success: the job executes successfully, without error
  - Failure: the job fails and causes an error
  - Completion: the job completes, whether success or failure

Multiple Constraints

Yes, there can be multiple constraints on the task. This gives us greater flexibility in the interpretation of the task, as shown in the following list.

- **Logical AND**: All statements must evaluate to TRUE

- **Logical OR**: One constraint must evaluate to TRUE

LOGICAL AND means that we can define a lot of constraints in our task, and ALL of these constraints must evaluate to TRUE.

LOGICAL OR means that we can define a lot of constraints in our task, and ANY ONE constraint must evaluate to TRUE. This means that, in an n-based list of constraints, 1-to-n constraints must be TRUE, but always at least one, or the task fails.

Honestly, most of this can stay right where it is. We want a Success constraint, and the default is exactly that. That's not to say that you can't update this area to do what you want, but for this purpose, we don't need to update anything, so click OK.

It looks like you can add multiple constraints as well. Click the Check Integrity task, and another little green arrow appears. Drag it to the Rebuild Index task. You should see what is shown in Figure 13-62.

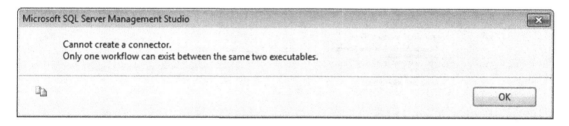

Figure 13-62. *Precedence Constraints error*

Okay, looks like a no. Which kind of presents a question as to why SSMS gave us the option in the first place, but that's a different subject. That's okay though, because we've got our constraint set up.

Now, do this for each of the tasks in the full backup plan as shown in Figure 13-63. Remember, the only constraints you want are Success constraints.

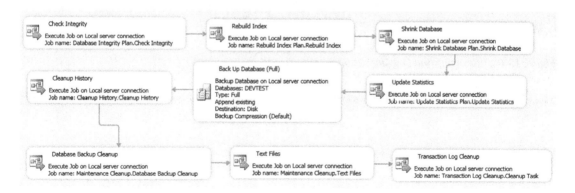

Figure 13-63. *Full Backups Precedence Constraints*

Figure 13-64 shows what your differential backups plan should look like.

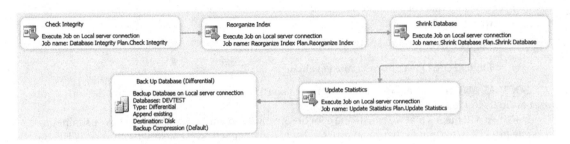

Figure 13-64. *Differential Backups Precedence Constraints*

And Figure 13-65 shows what your transaction log backup plan should look like.

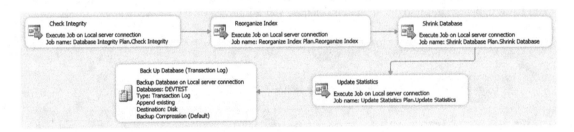

Figure 13-65. *Transaction Log Backups Precedence Constraints*

We can see that each of the tasks now have a literal workflow. Each task leads to the next task, and if it fails, it is logged.

Speaking of logging, what options do we have for reporting and logging of this maintenance plan? I'm glad you asked! Click the Reporting and Logging button in the taskbar, as shown in Figure 13-66.

Figure 13-66. *Reporting and Logging button*

Clicking that opens the interface shown in Figure 13-67.

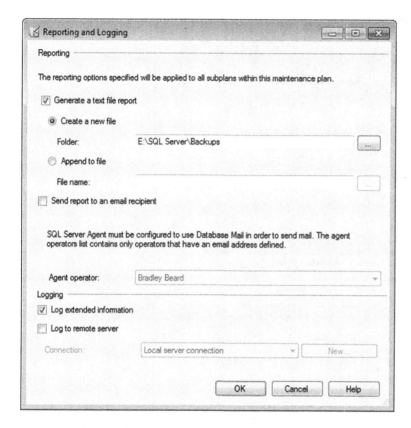

Figure 13-67. Reporting and Logging

This is the default screen. Look at that; we can generate a new text file report of the maintenance plan operations when they are run, AND we can send an e-mail to an operator, as shown in Figure 13-68.

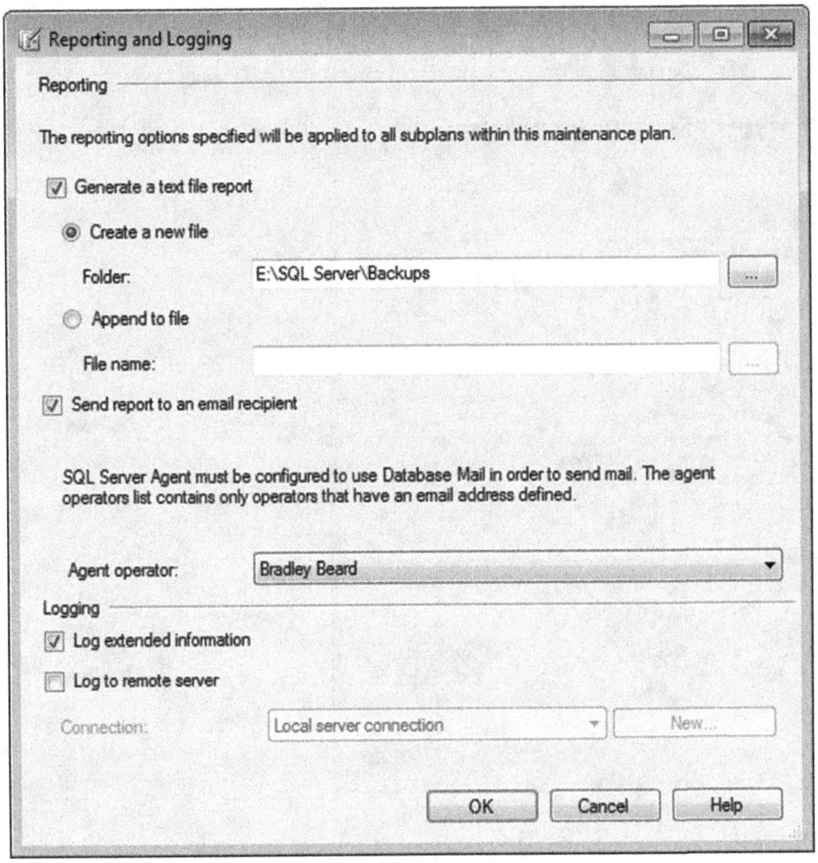

Figure 13-68. *Reporting and Logging (updated)*

That's very convenient! Once your interface is updated, click OK to continue. Save your work now, and bask in the glory of your nearly completed maintenance plan.

Note that, since we have set this, these reporting and logging settings are enforced for *all* of the subplans in the Backup Maintenance Plan. This is a good thing, so we don't have to keep setting them. Alternately, this also implies that if you need reporting or logging outside of these restrictions, you must create a new maintenance plan with different reporting and logging settings.

Let's review what we've done really quickly.

- We added the relevant tasks to the existing Backup Maintenance Plan.

- We added precedence constraints on the tasks, in the order we decided earlier.

- We added reporting and logging to the maintenance plan.

What this simply means is that the subplans of the Backup Maintenance Plan run at their scheduled time, starting with the first task and ending with the last task. When it is complete, an e-mail is sent with the maintenance text report attached. The SQL Server Agent keeps a record of this in its History logs as well. Whether it fails or succeeds, the operator is alerted.

Testing the Maintenance Plan

Now that it's all set up, let's run some tests on it. We set our operator to be informed, so we should just be able to run the maintenance plans, and then wait for notification.

Keep in mind that this will run everything, all of the tasks, in the order they are in. We want to start with full and then run the differential, and finally run the transaction log. You can't just right-click the Maintenance Plan though, because there are the three subplans in there. Instead, right-click the Backup Maintenance Plan.Backup Database (Full) job in the Jobs folder in SQL Server Agent, choose Start Job at Step... and observe what is shown in Figure 13-69.

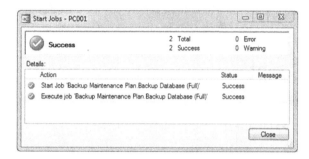

Figure 13-69. *Start Jobs*

Looks good so far.

Take it back a step and run the differential job now, and see what is shown in Figure 13-70.

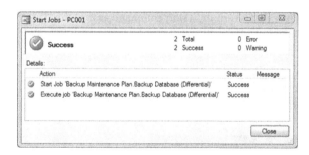

Figure 13-70. *Start Jobs*

Let's run the transaction log job to see what is shown in Figure 13-71.

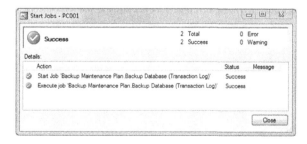

Figure 13-71. *Start Jobs*

Nicely done. If you've followed along, then you have probably received quite a few e-mails detailing the maintenance activities. Take a few minutes to familiarize yourself with these e-mails, and know what you're looking for. That way, in the future, you could conceivably scan an e-mail quickly for the information you need. You can also decide whether to leverage the usefulness of having e-mails sent when the maintenance activities complete, or to bypass this notification all together. Ultimately, it is your choice as the database administrator. Luckily, you've just learned how to adjust the settings of the maintenance plan to include or remove steps and notifications very quickly!

This proves that we have now accomplished our goal of creating a complete maintenance plan in our database that will take care of almost all of our day-to-day maintenance activities. Keep in mind that these jobs can be run at any time by running them from SQL Server Agent. Alternatively, you can also run a job with a script, which might be more up your alley. To do this, let's first look at the script and then understand what it does.

Starting a Job from a T-SQL Script

The script to start a job is sort of simple, and looks like this.

```
EXEC msdb.dbo.sp_start_job @job_name=N'Backup Maintenance Plan.Backup Database
(Transaction Log)';
```

In this case, I wanted to start the transaction log job. Entering this query into a New Query window and pressing F5 to execute it will show you the following status.

```
Job 'Backup Maintenance Plan.Backup Database (Transaction Log)' started successfully.
```

A little note about this script; it is a stored procedure that is running a start command against the sysjobs table in msdb. To take a look at this table, just enter the following query in a New Query window and press F5.

```
SELECT * FROM msdb.dbo.sysjobs;
```

Figure 13-72 shows what is returned from that query.

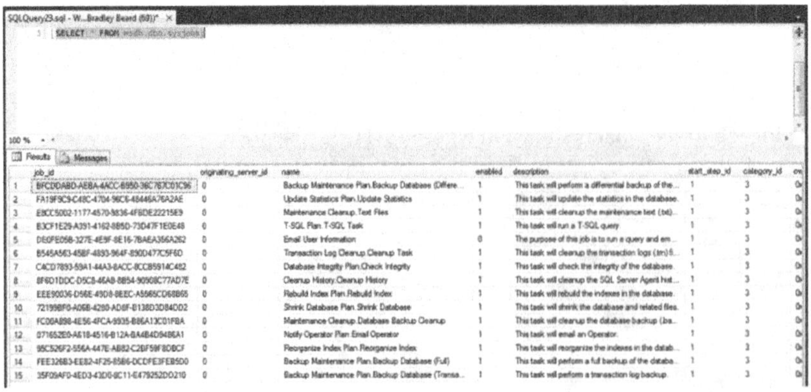

Figure 13-72. Query Results

256

Look familiar? That's all of the jobs we created, and some detail information too. Pretty cool!

Now, open up the Job Activity Monitor inside of SQL Server Agent. Figure 13-73 shows you what you should see at this point.

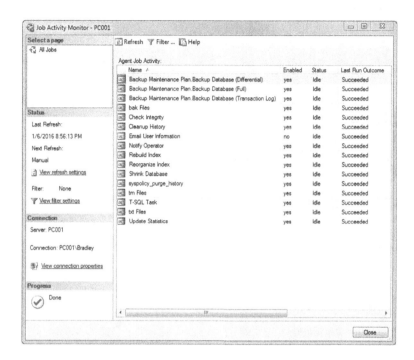

Figure 13-73. *Job Activity Monitor*

Well, there are all of our jobs, lined up for us and telling us all sorts of useless stuff. You can see that they all are enabled, except for E-mail User Information. They are all Idle, meaning they aren't currently running. They have all succeeded when they last ran. If you scroll to the right, you will see the columns Last Run and Next Run. Guess what those tell you? This is a great way to get a glimpse of whether or not your jobs are running correctly. It is right here if they aren't. You can right-click any of the jobs here and do some damage, so be aware of what you're doing.

■ **Tip** Is it important to note that you should *not* delete the extra maintenance plans. They are tied to the jobs they contain, and if you delete the maintenance plan, you will delete the job. Guess what happens at that point? Dunce cap. You guessed it.

One more thing before we close this out. In SSMS Object Explorer, click Connect and connect to Integration Services. If you can't connect to Integration Services, then just start SSMS as an Administrator and you should be good to go.

Expand the Stored Packages folder, followed by MSDB, and then Maintenance Plans. You should see what's shown in Figure 13-74 at this point.

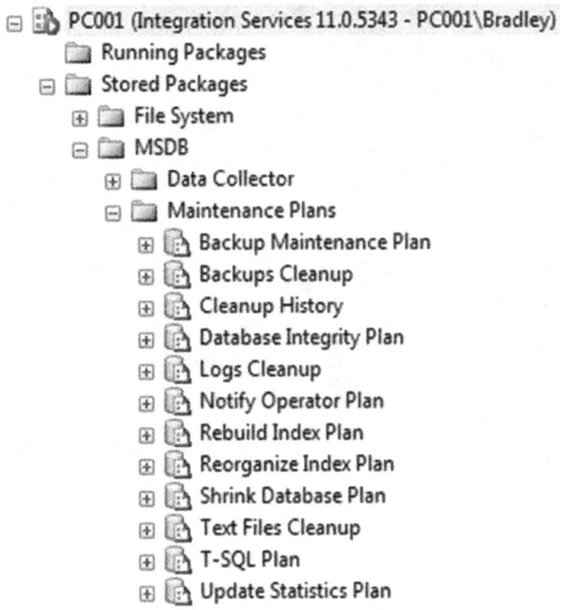
PC001 (Integration Services 11.0.5343 - PC001\Bradley)
Running Packages
Stored Packages
File System
MSDB
Data Collector
Maintenance Plans
Backup Maintenance Plan
Backups Cleanup
Cleanup History
Database Integrity Plan
Logs Cleanup
Notify Operator Plan
Rebuild Index Plan
Reorganize Index Plan
Shrink Database Plan
Text Files Cleanup
T-SQL Plan
Update Statistics Plan

Figure 13-74. *Integration Services Maintenance Plans*

Right-click our Backup Maintenance Plan and select Export Package... Figure 13-75 will then appear.

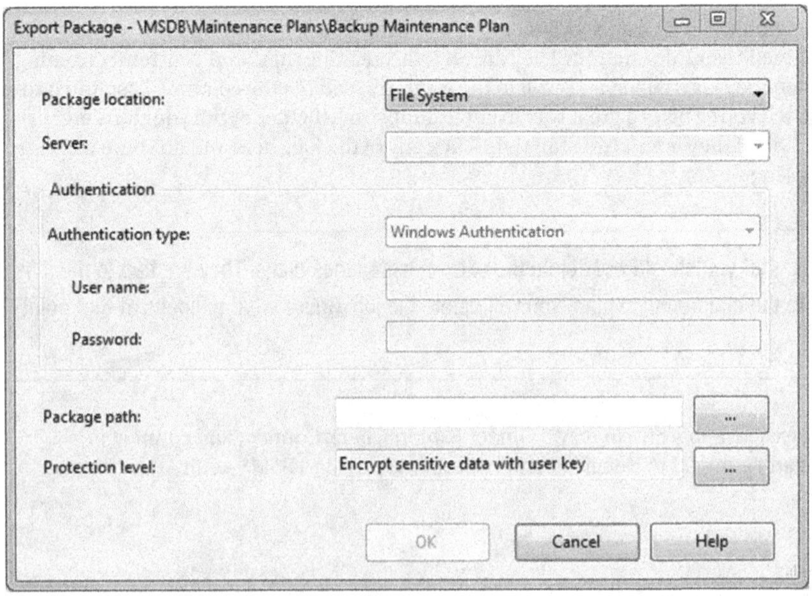
Export Package - \MSDB\Maintenance Plans\Backup Maintenance Plan
Package location:
File System
Server:
Authentication
Authentication type:
Windows Authentication
User name:
Password:
Package path:
Protection level:
Encrypt sensitive data with user key
OK
Cancel
Help

Figure 13-75. *Export Package*

We want to change the package path to a new folder in E:\SQL Server, so let's call it DTSX. That means our maintenance plan backup location is going to be E:\SQL Server\DTSX\Backup Maintenance Plan.dtsx, so enter that and then click OK. It's okay to leave all the other settings alone. If you check that directory, you will see that file now in there. You can even double-click these .dtsx files to execute them.

Do this for all the other maintenance plans, just in case. Now, we have a backup of all of the work that we've done, just in case something happens to our original files.

Let's test it! Oh, look, a nefarious individual has broken into the database and deleted the Update Statistics Plan maintenance plan. Look at Figure 13-76—it's disappeared!

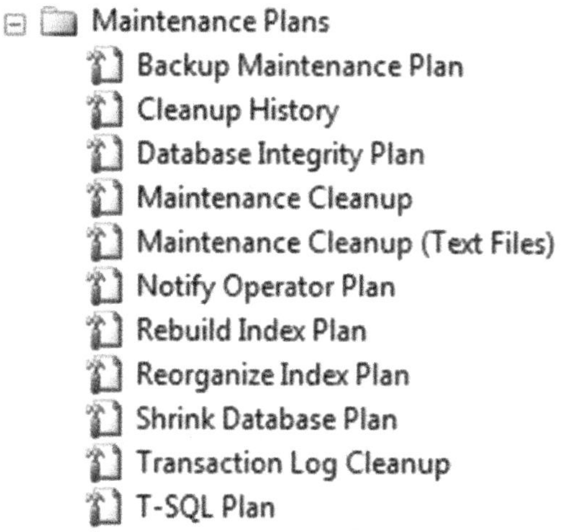

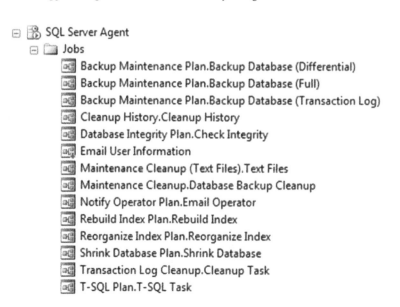

Figure 13-76. *Maintenance Plans*

Doggonit, Figure 13-77 shows that the job is gone too!

Figure 13-77. *SQL Server Agent Jobs*

Whatever shall we do? Oh yeah, we took a backup. Can we add that back easily? Yep.

Connect to Integration Services and check the Maintenance Plans folder. It's gone also. No worries though; just right-click this folder and choose Import Package... to show Figure 13-78.

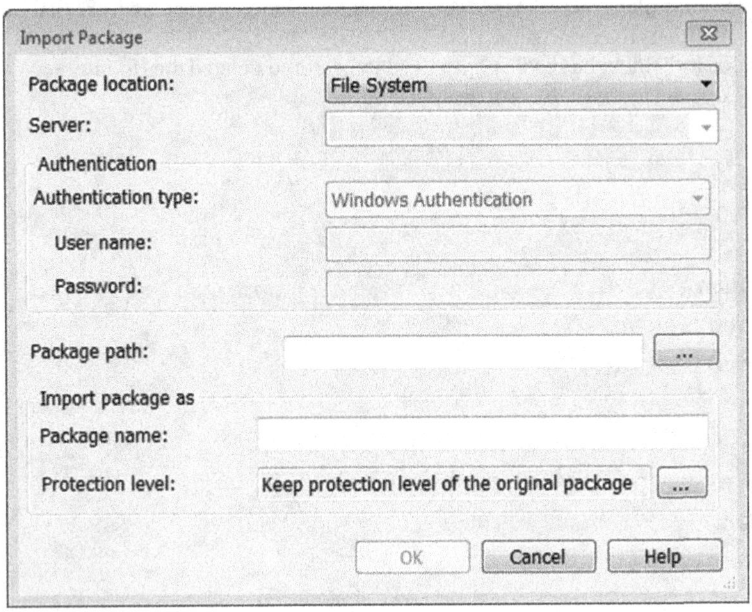

Figure 13-78. Import Package

Click the ellipse next to "Package path" and navigate to our DTSX folder location, E:\SQL Server\DTSX. Select Update Statistics Plan.dtsx to continue. Your interface should now look like Figure 13-79.

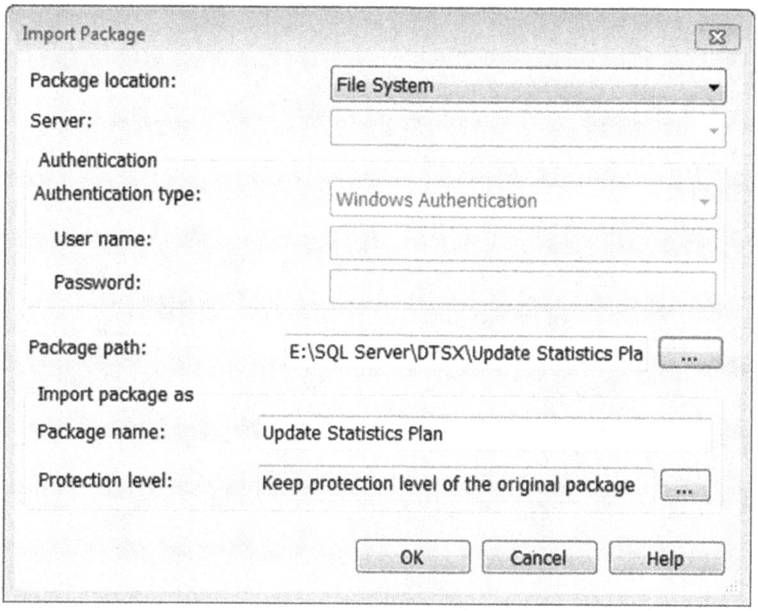

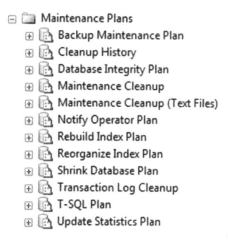

Figure 13-79. *Import Package (updated)*

Click OK and refresh this folder, and there is our plan again, as shown in Figure 13-80.

- Maintenance Plans
  - Backup Maintenance Plan
  - Cleanup History
  - Database Integrity Plan
  - Maintenance Cleanup
  - Maintenance Cleanup (Text Files)
  - Notify Operator Plan
  - Rebuild Index Plan
  - Reorganize Index Plan
  - Shrink Database Plan
  - Transaction Log Cleanup
  - T-SQL Plan
  - Update Statistics Plan

Figure 13-80. *Integration Services Maintenance Plans*

Go look at your Maintenance Plans and Jobs folders in the database engine. See anything interesting in Figure 13-81 or Figure 13-82?

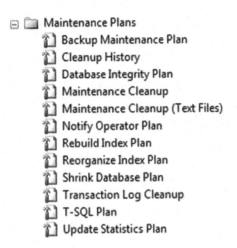

Maintenance Plans
- Backup Maintenance Plan
- Cleanup History
- Database Integrity Plan
- Maintenance Cleanup
- Maintenance Cleanup (Text Files)
- Notify Operator Plan
- Rebuild Index Plan
- Reorganize Index Plan
- Shrink Database Plan
- Transaction Log Cleanup
- T-SQL Plan
- Update Statistics Plan

Figure 13-81. *Maintenance Plans*

SQL Server Agent
- Jobs
  - Backup Maintenance Plan.Backup Database (Differential)
  - Backup Maintenance Plan.Backup Database (Full)
  - Backup Maintenance Plan.Backup Database (Transaction Log)
  - Cleanup History.Cleanup History
  - Database Integrity Plan.Check Integrity
  - Email User Information
  - Maintenance Cleanup (Text Files).Text Files
  - Maintenance Cleanup.Database Backup Cleanup
  - Notify Operator Plan.Email Operator
  - Rebuild Index Plan.Rebuild Index
  - Reorganize Index Plan.Reorganize Index
  - Shrink Database Plan.Shrink Database
  - Transaction Log Cleanup.Cleanup Task
  - T-SQL Plan.T-SQL Task

Figure 13-82. *SQL Server Agent Jobs*

So it added the Maintenance Plan, but not the job? Yes. But we're not done yet.

Go back to the Integration Services part again, and right-click the Update Statistics Plan and choose Export Package..., which brings up the interface shown in Figure 13-83.

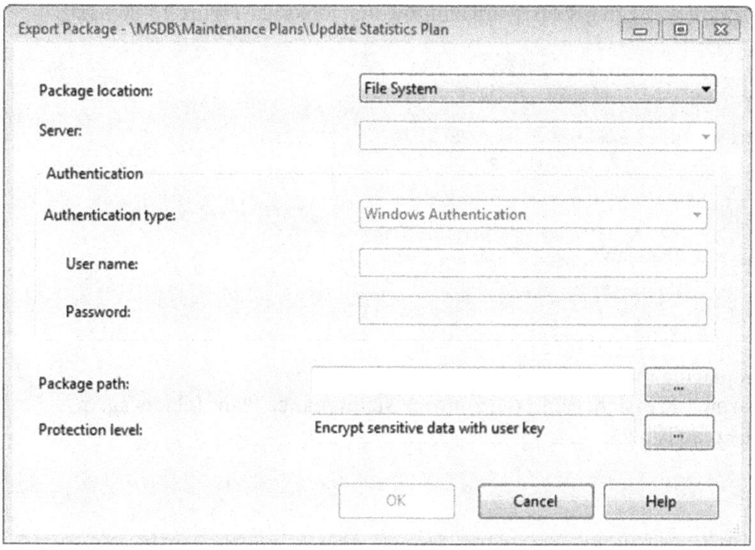

Figure 13-83. *Export Package*

We aren't going to export it to the file system; that wouldn't make any sense for what we're trying to accomplish. Instead, update your interface to show the values shown in Figure 13-84. For the Package path value, click the ellipse and expand MSDB, click Maintenance Plans, and then click OK.

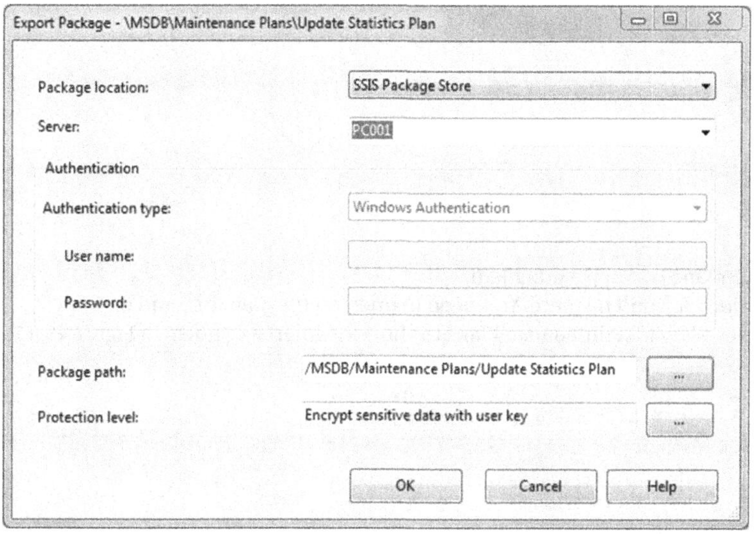

Figure 13-84. *Export Package (updated)*

Click OK when you're done. You're going to get a pop-up window that looks like Figure 13-85 next.

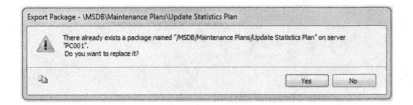

Figure 13-85. *Export Package alert*

Click Yes here, so that we're replacing the current package.

Skip back over to the database engine instance and refresh your Maintenance Plans folders again. You can see in Figure 13-86 that the plan is back.

- Maintenance Plans
    - Backup Maintenance Plan
    - Cleanup History
    - Database Integrity Plan
    - Maintenance Cleanup
    - Maintenance Cleanup (Text Files)
    - Notify Operator Plan
    - Rebuild Index Plan
    - Reorganize Index Plan
    - Shrink Database Plan
    - Transaction Log Cleanup
    - T-SQL Plan
    - Update Statistics Plan

Figure 13-86. *Maintenance Plans*

Still no job though. Weird, huh? One last step, young Jedi.

Even if you refresh the Jobs folder, it won't be there. You need to open up the plan first, and go from there. Double-click Update Statistics Plan in Maintenance Plans to show the interface shown in Figure 13-87.

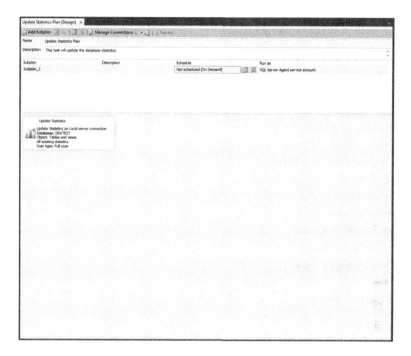

Figure 13-87. *Update Statistics Plan*

Double-click the Subplan name and update it to show what is in Figure 13-88.

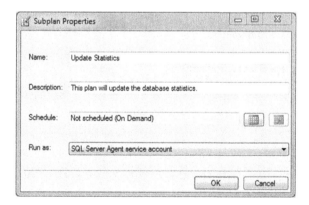

Figure 13-88. *Subplan Properties*

Save the plan now, and go back to look at your Jobs folder again, as shown in Figure 13-89.

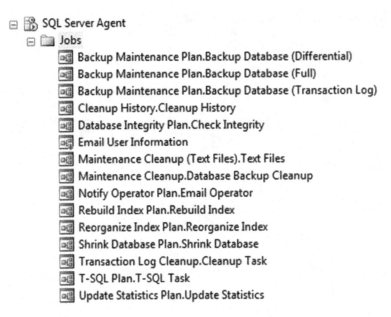

Figure 13-89. *SQL Server Agent Jobs*

There it is! You're going to need to change the name from Update Statistics Plan.Update Statistics to just Update Statistics though. After that's done, you should see the updated interface shown in Figure 13-90.

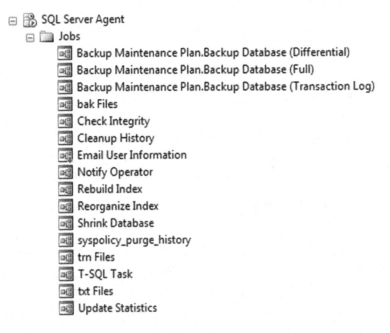

Figure 13-90. *SQL Server Agent Jobs, updated*

Let's verify that we have it back to how it was before though.

Double-click Backup Maintenance Plan and then double-click the Update Statistics task in the stage. You should then see the interface shown in Figure 13-91.

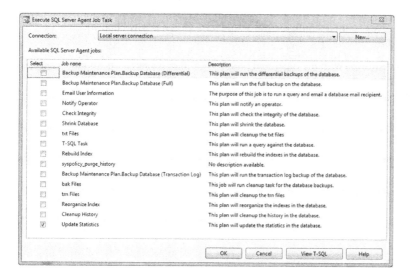

Figure 13-91. *Execute SQL Server Agent Job Task*

Right down at the bottom there… excellent! We have successfully restored our saved package.

Summary

Wow! We took all that we learned in the course of this book and put it all together into one cohesive plan. Let's take a quick look at exactly what this chapter showed us.

- We created individual maintenance plans for each time slice on the backup schedule, with each schedule having different tasks running at different times.

- We enforced precedence constraints on the tasks within each maintenance plan.

- We set reporting and logging on the tasks, with e-mails on completion of each task.

- We learned how to start a job with a script.

- We learned briefly about the Job Activity Monitor and its importance.

Let's examine a couple of things before we close:

- We could have done the exercises in this whole book without setting the Schedule in the individual chapters, but that wouldn't have led you to the knowledge of how the schedules work together with the queries in this chapter. I wanted you, the reader, to understand that those schedules aren't just arbitrary values, but are part of the overall maintenance strategy and should be treated as such.

- We also could have done the large majority of this book working with just the Backup Maintenance Plan in the Design Surface, but again, this wouldn't have given you the knowledge you now have on the why and not just the how. You can certainly do that if you would like—go back and do it from the Design Surface instead—as that would be a good exercise in your spare time. But eventually, you need to get back into the jobs portion of SQL Server Agent to configure the actual jobs, which is why I had you go through it like we did.

Congratulations! You are now finished with the meat and potatoes (tofu and kale) of this book. I hope that you have a fully functional maintenance plan now in place and that you are already dreaming of ways to expand upon this newfound knowledge.

Index

A, B

Backup Cleanup task, 108
   delete backup file, 113
     based on extension, 113
     specific file, 113
   maintenance tasks, 110
   plan properties, 109
Backup Database task, 3–4
B-Tree structures, 136
Bulk Logged Recovery model, 9

C

Check Database Integrity task, 3–4

D

Database administrator (DBA), 1
Database backup
   backup types, 7, 9
     absolutely ideal, 11
     differential, 10
     full, 10
     ideal setting, 11
     vs. recovery models, 10
     transaction log, 10
   maintenance plan, 12
     differential backup configuration, 18
     full backup configuration, 12
     job properties, 25
     transaction log backup
      configuration, 21
   recovery model, 7–8
     vs. backup types, 10
     bulk logged, 9
     full, 9
     simple, 9
   recovery models, 7
Database Consistency
     History report, 34

Database integrity
   database consistency report, 34
   definition, 33
   maintenance plan, 36
     check integrity task, 40
     job schedule, 36
     maintenance tasks, 38
     plan properties, 37
     report options, 41
     SQL Server Agent, 42
     wizard, 42
   structural integrity, 33
Database maturity, 207
DEVTEST, 15
Differential backups, 10
Distribution statistics
   description, 165
   maintenance task
     plan properties, 166
     report options, 170
     scan type, 169
     SQL Server Agent job, 172
     task order, 167
     update statistics task, 168
     update type, 169
     wizard progress, 171

E

Execute SQL Server Agent Job task, 3–4
Execute T-SQL task, 4

F, G

Full backups, 10
Full Recovery model, 9

H

Heap table, 131
History Cleanup task, 3–4, 107

© Bradley Beard 2016
B. Beard, *Practical Maintenance Plans in SQL Server*, DOI 10.1007/978-1-4842-1895-2

I, J, K

Index, 131–132
    B-Tree structures, 136
    categories, 132
    clustered indexes, 136
    definition, 131
    delete object, 133
    maintenance plans, 137
    new index, 133
    nonclustered indexes, 136
    primary key index, 132
    properties, 132
    rebuilding *vs.* reorganising, 137
    storage option, 135
Interface, 131

L

Logs Cleanup task, 117
    maintenance task, 117
    plan properties, 117
    report options, 121
    SQL server agent jobs, 123
    wizard progress, 123

M, N

Maintenance Cleanup task, 3–4, 107
    backups cleanup task, 108
    vs. history cleanup tasks, 107
    logs cleanup task, 117
    maintenance plans, 108
    text files cleanup task, 124
Maintenance plan, 206
    Backup phase, 207
    complexity, 207
    creation, 213
    database backup
        differential backup configuration, 18
        full backup configuration, 12
        job properties, 25
        transaction log backup
            configuration, 21
    database integrity, 36
        check integrity task, 40
        job schedule, 36
        maintenance tasks, 38
        plan properties, 37
        report options, 41
        SQL Server Agent, 42
        wizard, 42
    database maturity, 207
    DBAs, 1
    description, 2

    design surface, 3
        task options, 4
        vs. wizard interface, 5
    DML statements, 209
    indexes, 137
    planning, 209
    Post-Backup phase, 207
    Pre-Backup phase, 207
    precedence constraints, 211, 248
        constraint options, 250
        editor, 250
        full backups, 249
        multiple constraints, 251
    principles, 1
    reorganising indexes, 148
    set up, 2
    SQL Server Agent jobs, 213
    SQL Server Integration
        Services package, 212
    structure, 206
    testing, 255
    T-SQL Script, 256
        export package, 259
        import package, 260
        Integration Services
            Maintenance plan, 258
        Job Activity Monitor, 257
        query results, 257
        SQL Server Agent jobs, 262
        subplan properties, 265
        update statistics plan, 264
    wizard interface tasks, 3

O

Notifying database operators
    maintenance plan, 189
        Local server connection, 191
        Net Send operator, 191
        Notify Operator task, 190, 193, 195
        Pager operator, 192, 194
        SQL Server Agent job, 197
        subplan properties, 189
    operator profile, 199
        configuration task, 199
        maintenance plans, 202
        profile security, 200
        SQL Server Agent jobs, 202
Notify Operator task, 5, 195

P, Q

Pager Operator, 194
Precedence constraint, 248
Primary key index, 132

■ R

Rebuild Index task, 3, 5, 137
Rebuilding indexes, 131
Reorganize Index task, 3, 5, 137
Reorganizing indexes
    maintenance plans, 148–149
        plan properties, 148
        report options, 151
        SQL server agent jobs, 153
        task order, 150
        wizard progress, 152
    vs. rebuilding, 147

■ S

Shrink Database task, 3, 5
    disk space considerations, 156
    disk usage report, 155
    Maintenance plans, 157
        plan properties, 158
        report options, 161
        SQL Server Agent jobs, 163
        task order, 159
        wizard progress, 163
    transaction log, 157
Simple recovery model, 9
SQL Server Agent jobs, 45, 59, 205
    advanced option, 65
    alerts option, 62
        SQL Server event alert, 63
        SQL Server performance
          condition alert, 63
        WMI event alert, 63
    Alerts page settings, 218
    Alerts tab, 70
        General, 70
        Options, 74
        Response, 71
    Backup Maintenance Plan, 220
    differential backups, 235
        check integrity task, 236
        reorganize index task, 238
        shrink database task, 239
        update statistics task, 240
    disable jobs, 219
    distribution statistics, 172
    editing, 213
    e-mail, 45
        account settings, 50–51
        configuration task, 48
        configuration wizard, 47
        enable mail profile, 57
        interface options, 54
        new profile, 49

        profile security, 52
        Send Test e-mail, 56
        SMTP accounts, 51
        in SSMS, 46
        system parameters, 53
    full backups, 222
        bak files task, 229
        check integrity task, 222
        cleanup history task, 228
        rebuild index task, 224
        shrink database task, 225
        trn files task, 233
        txt files task, 231
        update statistics task, 226
    general option, 62–63
    General page settings, 214
    Gmail's SMTP, 80
        account setting, 81
        configuration wizard, 86
        database mail account, 82
        forwarding and POP/IMAP, 90
        manage profile security, 84
        profile setting, 80
        server access, 89
        system parameters configuration, 85
        testing, 88
    job creation, 61
    notifications, 63, 76
    Notifications page settings, 218
    Notifying database operators, 197
    query, 60
    schedule needs, 220
    Schedule page settings, 214
    schedules option, 62, 68
    shrink database, 163
    steps option, 62
    Steps page settings, 214
    sysjobschedules, 215
    table creation, 60
    targets, 63, 79
    Targets page settings, 218
    transaction log backups, 242
        check integrity task, 242
        shrink database task, 245
        update statistics task, 247
    transaction log backupsreorganize
        index task, 244
    TRUNCATE and DELETE FROM, 218
    T-SQL Statement execution, 180
SQL Server Agent logs, cleanup, 93
    history cleanup tasks, 100
    maintenance plan, 93
        job schedule, 95
        plan properties, 94
        wizard progress, 102

SQL Server Agent logs, cleanup (*cont.*)
  report options, 102
  tasks
    maintenance task order, 97
    maintenance tasks, 96

■ T

Text Files Cleanup operation, 124
  maintenance tasks, 125
  plan properties, 124
  report options, 127
  SQL server agent jobs, 129
  wizard progress, 129
Transaction log, 157
Transaction log backups, 10
T-SQL Statement execution
  click and drag technique, 178
  maintenance plan, 175
    Alerts tab, 182
    design surface, 176–177

job properties, 180
Log File Viewer, 184
Notifications tab, 182
Schedules tab, 182
source types, 179
SQL Server Agent jobs, 180
SqlStatementSourceType, 179
Start jobs, 183
Steps tab, 181
subplan properties, 176
Targets tab, 183
toolbox, 177
T-SQL plan, 184

■ U, V

Update Statistics task, 3, 5

■ W, X, Y, Z

Windows Management Instrumentation (WMI), 63

Get the eBook for only $5!

Why limit yourself?

Now you can take the weightless companion with you wherever you go and access your content on your PC, phone, tablet, or reader.

Since you've purchased this print book, we're happy to offer you the eBook in all 3 formats for just $5.

Convenient and fully searchable, the PDF version enables you to easily find and copy code—or perform examples by quickly toggling between instructions and applications. The MOBI format is ideal for your Kindle, while the ePUB can be utilized on a variety of mobile devices.

To learn more, go to www.apress.com/companion or contact support@apress.com.

Printed in the United States
By Bookmasters